The
Shining
Ones

by
Philip Gardiner

The Shining Ones

A journey through time with the world's most secret and powerful society.

By
Philip Gardiner
Edited by
Suzanne J Barbieri
Pictures by
John Gardiner
Artwork by
Philip Gardiner

Radikal Phase Publishing House
Willow Court
Cordy Lane
Underwood
Nottinghamshire
NG16 5FD
England

A catalogue record for this book is available from the British Library. ISBN 1 904126 00 6

Printed and bound in England by the
Phase Group, Willow Court, Cordy Lane, Underwood, Nottinghamshire NG16 5FD.

Contents

Foreword

This is not a story that wants to be told, but one that must be.

Everything you previously held to be true will be challenged here. As a magician hides the mechanics of his tricks from the audience by means of smoke and mirrors, so the secret priesthood of the Shining Ones hides our true history behind a tightly woven tapestry of symbols and lies.

Much of the symbolism in the world has been created by various cults and societies, and these symbols can be interpreted on many levels. If we believe their religious element then that is all we see. If we choose to reject that, we begin to see that the analogies within the symbolism are the same and this leads us to the secrets of these societies.

During my research on another book, I began to stumble across some peculiar similarities, and came to realise that there was a major long-term plot in existence. Its perpetrators even gave us their name: the Shining Ones. From then on, the more I found, the more amazed I became. It was as if a veil had lifted: once I knew how to look, I really began to see. I found that the truth has actually been in front of our eyes the whole time. When old texts are re-read in the light of the new perspectives this book will offer, we suddenly start to see the real story, which has been there all along.

While investigating this book, I met a direct descendant of Muhammad who said that Islam has had the truth since it began. Muhammad tried to show the truth, but history and its authors have created the myth that Islam is now. So many people seem to know that there is more to history and religion than meets the eye, but few of them have the whole story.

Not everyone was quite so helpful. In the beginning, everybody I questioned was obstructive. I spoke to a Pastor about the contents of the book. He stood up without a word and walked out on me. I later found out that he had his congregation pray for the demonically possessed researcher. Another Christian author in Scotland told me that the devil had taken my soul and that he had seen this devil one night when he was walking to his outside toilet!

Many of the larger cults I spoke to were very forthcoming. They gave me every piece of information their massive publicity machines could generate. They are used to people digging around and have an army of PR people ready and willing to take them on. The smaller cults were obstructive to the point of paranoia and wanted my name, address, educational history, publisher's details, names of everybody working on the project with me, and so on.

I went to Rosslyn, in Scotland to investigate the famous Chapel. While I was clearing some moss from a stone to read inscription a man turned up and asked me what I was doing. I told him I was researching a book on secret societies and he paid me my money back and told me to leave before he called the police. When I later asked the people from whom I bought the entrance ticket who this man was, they did not have a clue and said they had never seen anybody fitting the description I gave them.

Throughout the research of this book I have been pushed, verbally abused and threatened, all of which goes some way towards convincing me that there is something we are not supposed to know. The truth is there, waiting to be uncovered, but we have to clear away a lot of rubble.

With the passing of the Millennium, interest in the spiritual aspect of life has risen, while at the same time, church attendance is at an all time low. Instead, ancient Earth-aligned beliefs, in the guise of the New Age movement, are enjoying a rise in popularity. That there should be a return to 'old ways' is not surprising when we discover that these beliefs are not so

outdated after all, that the practises denounced as pagan actually form the basis of 'orthodox' religions such as Christianity.

Mankind is more in-tune with the Universe than we realise, and the cyclical nature of the Earth tells us that we are on the threshold of a new beginning.

The world is waiting for a new Messiah to show us the way. Whether he or she comes from the religious arena, or the world of politics, one thing is sure: like the countless others who came before, this Messiah will have been nurtured, shaped and placed here by the Shining Ones.

Nothing we can do will stop the new 'Messiah' coming. The world is a very large place and the society of the Shining Ones now has many Messiahs. When we start to make people see the truth, we must watch very closely for the reaction of the hidden leaders of the current elect. It must not be forgotten that these people are very powerful. If they want a project stopped, then that is what they will do.

There was an old man, now deceased, who said to me, 'You will never get this book published. The inheritors of the Shining legacy control the media and everything in it. Keep them out of the tale and you have a fighting chance, but what you say will not be the truth.'

I cannot do this. Truth is all. Without it, we have nothing.
Philip Gardiner

Introduction
A Secret Language

History is a lie. History is, as Justice Holmes said, 'what the people who won say it is.' It has been warped over vast periods of time to fit with each generation's idea of what is fact and what is truth. Without the existence of the Shining Ones, our history would have been totally different. This book is an attempt to draw back the veil of lies and altered realities to map our true history and discover where our future lies.

History is like a vast jigsaw puzzle. Only when all the pieces are laid down in the correct sequence can we see the bigger picture. The result is quite startling. We will see how mysteries of the ancient and not so ancient world can now be solved, from megalithic standing stones, the Holy Grail and alchemy to the truth behind religion and our present political systems. The story of The Shining Ones is the real history of mankind. Every twist and turn on the pathway of human evolution was put there deliberately by this group for a mysterious and extremely long-term goal.

In much the same way that modern day genetic research is showing how recently inter-linked we are, the research and subsequent conclusions set out in this book will show how our own political and religious belief systems are from the same source.1 There is nothing new under the sun. New religious systems are just renewed older religions with different names and different settings.

We can learn from this history and understand the cyclic patterns of human behaviour, which will help us to predict the future more easily. We will look at the existence of life and

Hermes

consciousness; trace where it came from and where it is going. We will move over millennia of mysteries to reason an actual history based upon fact and evidence. We will see whether there actually is a world-wide conspiracy, and if so where it is leading us. We shall establish motives, seek out new data, view existing documents in a new light to gain an overview of vast periods of time and civilisations and finally get to grips with the mysteries of faith. There are many new and revealing pieces of evidence within this book which are only sometimes hinted at within the documents or items used to support them.

One of the most disturbing aspects of 'The Shining Ones' come from the clear understanding that we have been lied to for centuries by one historian after another. Yet we must not lose sight of the fact that these professionals are responsible for piecing together huge amounts of information and giving supposedly factual accounts based on their own belief systems, which are in turn influenced by the time and location in which they lived or are living. Without the hard work of these historians, a book like this would have been impossible to write, even though its conclusions are in stark contrast to the accepted view.

We must also understand that many historians, artists, builders, politicians, religious and lay persons wanted to pass the truth on but could not. So they devised ciphers, codes and symbolism for the their own and future generations to decipher. Symbols are hidden all around us like a trail of clues leading towards treasure. We come into contact with them everywhere we go; from the symbolic architecture and stained glass windows of medieval churches, to,

Symbol of Phase transition

for example, the logo on a company van. My own company logo is symbolic of Phase Transition, the changing of one substance into another. For a marketing company, this was ideal. Only people who know about such things would be able to see this, however. Others would just see an arrow with a wavy line.

Mankind has used this subtle language for thousands of years. Through each generation, this alternative form of communication has developed and grown increasingly complex, making it more difficult to decipher. The only way to discover the secrets of symbolism is to break down each and every painting, building or text into every possible meaning, and consider both the people who created these artefacts and the time in which they lived. These finds must then be weighed

against known historical data, such as archaeological information.

One of the greatest works of symbolism on every level is the Bible. To the scholar who knows the alternative meanings of some of the apocalyptic texts it has been obvious for a long time that there is truth hidden away. But there are so many hidden layers that any number of meanings are possible and we must remember that lies are also hidden in code.

We must be careful not to read too much into texts as we could be in danger of perceiving them in the light of our own modern society. There have been many recent examples of books where ancient structures and texts are being taken as evidence of extraterrestrial visitations. Regardless of any other more earthly interpretation and a huge lack of understanding of the religious and cultural traditions of the time, this 'evidence' is abused for a pre-determined idea or theory.

Another example of this is how modern day evangelists use the Biblical book of Revelation as 'proof' of the Lord's imminent return. They point to hidden meanings regarding nuclear war and Middle Eastern dictators as if they had some kind of divine revelation themselves. The truth is, as any historian will tell you, that every generation since the writing of Revelation has claimed the end is very close. That is partly the point of the Gospel, misinterpreted completely, as usual. All of these false interpretations make it more difficult to break the code down into facts.

We shall begin by taking a look at our origins. The origin of life has always been a fundamental part of religion. The age of enlightenment of Darwin and his contemporaries drastically altered the religious outlook of the world. If we look at the truth behind the origin of mankind, we will see that Darwin was only 'discovering' what was already known, that this age of enlightenment was planned, it had to happen for the required changes to occur. We will see how ancient man and his religious beliefs were perfectly parallel to our current scientific beliefs, the difference being only in the terms used. Take the following pattern, which is common to the majority of the world's religions:

1) Only the God exists. He is supreme and is alone.
2) The heavens and earth are formless. Everything is darkness and/or covered by primeval waters.
3) Then there is light.
4) Heaven and earth are split apart.
5) The land is separated from the waters. Day and night are created with the new sun.
6) The land brings forth vegetation and eventually creatures.
7) Birds and animals are created
8) Man appears.2

As you will note, this pattern is also common to the current theories regarding the origin of species. It is completely in line with the big bang theory and yet seems to have emerged thousands of years ago. These patterns were especially notable in ancient Egypt, one of the mysterious forerunners of the world's faiths.

Previously, religion was responsible for informing us of our origins. Now scientists tell us to look for facts about our origins rather than philosophise about them, while at the same time they create new theories which are sometimes prejudiced and do not take into account all of our knowledge. The problem is that all the facts are not yet known, and scientists tend to not share ideas and theories with other scientists from different fields.

New facts come to light with every passing day. New ideas

regarding mathematical equations of the information of the laws of physics are proving some theories to be fact. We need to understand these facts and theories and must not be afraid to alter our own personal viewpoint once these new facts emerge. Our own personal truths must change or we shall risk becoming stale, inert religious fanatics. It is unfortunate that religious fervour in all disciplines (including science) can stop us seeing these marvellous breakthroughs, prevent us from moving on and evolving.

So many facts are hidden from us because of generations of prejudice and intolerance that some of them will be startling. No one will remain unaffected by the evidence presented here. Everyone who reads this book will have their own belief system or personal prejudice challenged and will not want to accept everything as fact. Much of the evidence here can be taken in a number of ways and, where this is known, each alternative viewpoint has been given. Where other views are required, these have been sought from original sources. I include in this all religious factions, whether classed as cult, occult or mainstream.

In our search for the truth, we will examine everything that is possible to fit into one book. We will start from before the big bang and examine whether any of what we are told is true, from Adam and Eve to modern science. We will then go on to see how our belief systems began and where some of the more paranormal explanations originated. There will be factual evidence of how our belief systems have been used, abused and manipulated by a secret and deadly group of individuals who have a history going back thousands of years. They have a name, they have a power base and they have a secret, locked away within their initiated few, which has major implications for the future of mankind. We will discover the

secret and reveal it.

There are thousands of best-selling books out there, which support mysteries that simply do not exist. This book will dispel those mysteries and put us back on the straight path. Why, in this supposedly enlightened age do we still believe and feed off the controlling lies of those in positions of authority? The answer is simple. Knowledge is power, therefore if you keep the knowledge for yourself, you keep the power.

When we come to leave old religions behind we are simply given a new one, more relevant to our age and to the political aims of the power brokers. Do we need the opium of religion or can we survive without it? Do we need the repackaged 'New Age' religions, or the pseudo-scientific cults that look towards UFO's for the meaning of life? This book will show how even the new belief systems are based upon the same old lies and the secret knowledge that we are supposedly too simple to understand.

The Shining Ones have manipulated us by many means, including psychology. Utilising the story of our origins, they played on our desire to know who we are and where we came from, and controlled our belief system from the start. They also understood some of the very basic and fundamental ways in which our brains work and are influenced. They discovered that we were influenced not only by people, but also by the world around us in more ways than we today can even comprehend.

If you are ready for the truth; if you can honestly say you have an open mind and are prepared to let go of misconceptions, then read on. Forget the false interpretations of myth and religion you have heard so many times, and know them for what they really are: the secret language of the Shining Ones.

Notes

Introduction

1   'In the Blood' by Steve Jones (Harper Collins) 1996
2   'The Copper Scroll Decoded' by Robert Feather. (Thorsons) 1999

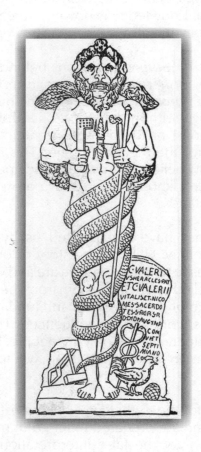

Chapter One

The Science of God

We have developed over millions of years to arrive where we are today, and even now we are not yet at the pinnacle of evolution, if indeed, there is such a thing. We are evolving daily. Maybe not enough for us to see in our short lives and maybe not physically changing with each generation, but we are evolving ideas and technical abilities: new and truly wonderful tools which help us, force us even, to change and adapt in a pseudo evolutionary way.

Regardless of whether or not there is a God, simple human knowledge of self, rationality and emotions all contribute to our present revolutionary pace. And yet, we still need to answer the most fundamental question of where we come from with the idea of God. Perhaps we should try to look at the whole thing in a different way.

To understand the beginning of space and time, our perception of beginnings, ends, and what came before must be challenged. There are many theories within this arena, some more acceptable than others. For thousands of years our views of where we came from were basically religious. From the Middle Eastern 'Word of God' creation to the myriad Hindu beliefs which claim that existence is but a dream in the mind of the creator, all of them have certain common themes but with local ethnic differences. The teachings of the hermetic sects claim the creation to be God's artistic side coming out, although He gets so involved, He can no longer separate Himself from His creation. As we will see, it is quite within the Laws of Quantum Physics for thought to have created the

Universe. With quantum theory, it is possible for anything to occur, even for a universe to come into existence on its own. This is something the New Age and religious exponents forget to say.

On the face of it, there does not seem to have been much of a challenge to these faith-oriented beliefs until the enlightened age of philosophy. This appears to be the time when man challenged all ideas, even his own. The early philosophers required their students to assume what they were being taught was wrong and to come up with their own ideas. Although man was challenging the assumptions of life long before the existence of the classical philosophers. There is evidence laid out in this book which goes a long way towards proving this. We can get an idea of how developed our ancestors were and how deep their understanding of the Universe, when we discover why and when they built and utilised the star oriented temples and megalithic structures. Apart from what can be learned from their buildings, new understanding can come from the early writings in which secrets have been locked away for thousands of years, only to be understood by those with the eyes to see.

We can see from these writings and structures that man has understood, or found the need for, a clear beginning and end. A cycle of life emerged and with it came a religious copy of this cycle, more complex and intuitive than we could ever imagine. Recently emerging data has put the beginning of civilisation further back in time, and has proved that there was greater knowledge among early peoples. With every passing day we find new evidence for the purpose of megalithic structures. The secret resonance, the effects of radiation causing lights in the sky, the planetary alignments, Earth energies and pathways, the symbolism of life and death; all these things are coming under closer scrutiny and many are being proven.

The fact that our ancestors knew so much about the cycles of life is partly the cause of the problem of understanding our beginning. These ideas and beliefs in life cycles over many thousands of years and our own in-built cyclical nature will not allow us to comprehend anything without a start and finish.

Accepting that we do not understand is a good beginning. We, by the very definition of being alive, with life and death, cyclic patterns, simply cannot understand the beginning, if indeed there was one.

Our whole lives are based around cycles. The element of time causes cycles to come into existence. Without time there are no cycles, without cycles there is no time.

On a simple level, cycles are about birth and death, sunrise and sunset, the waxing and waning of the moon, the changing of the seasons, the tides of the sea, the reproductive cycle of females. All these are inexorably linked with the entire universe. The difference between our ancient ancestors and us is that we have forgotten about these links while their whole lives revolved around this understanding. Our ancestors understood that the universe and everything within it revolved around a massive repetition of cycles.

We are only beginning to understand the harmony in which we have lived and the disharmony we are causing with our constant damage of the finely balanced environment, which has taken the last 15 billion years to achieve.

The earth has subtle energy waves which some call Ley Lines and which the Chinese call Feng Shui or Dragon Paths. These forces are scientifically proven to exist, although much that is blatantly unscientific is claimed for them by certain New Age sects. When we alter the environment, we alter the balance of these paths, and in turn, the subtle balance between the earth and the universe. We are also beginning to understand the effects we are having, not only on the environment but also on our own psyches. It is emerging that the energy of our surroundings does have an effect upon our minds. For example, some people suffer from Seasonal Affective Disorder (SAD) as a result of the lack of sunlight. This recently discovered cyclic problem affects us all to some extent, although some medical professionals in the sunnier parts of the world deny its existence. This shows that if we can suffer from problems because of a loss of sunlight (which is on the electromagnetic spectrum) then we could, in theory, suffer other problems caused by imbalances in electromagnetic radiation.

Our ancestors have shown that they understood these subtleties. They placed clues for us to find. All of their rituals, their religions, cults, gods, demigods, all of their lives, were linked to the cycles of the universe. We will see in later chapters how this developed into religion, how certain elements of mankind took this special knowledge and kept it for themselves.

Without cycles, there would be no life. The entire universe would be one great chaotic soup. And according to scientists, this is how it all began. Over the course of billions of years it settled down into regular patterns. Thermodynamics shows us that when two systems come together, for example hot and cold, an equilibrium is naturally achieved, albeit dependent upon many factors such as environment, velocity, mass and much more. This follows through from the universal scale right down to our own bodies and lives, which find equilibrium with the rest of the universe. Taking into account all the factors that affect us: the solar wind and flares, electromagnetism, gravity, heat, radiation, we still manage to come into balance with these things.

It is our understanding of this fact which has altered. We have come through thousands of years of beliefs, through a hundred years of rationalism and this perception has been lost, only now to have been found again through modern science.

Our magnetic world

The Thermodynamic Cycle shows how nature, in relation to heat and cold, constantly repeats itself. We can see this in the broader aspect of the Earth's seasons. The perfect man-made engine would reveal the Thermodynamic Cycle where all heat would be converted to energy without loss. Although in the 19th Century, Sadi Carnot showed how this would be impossible, as all engines must lose some heat. The same applies to the planet Earth, where we know it has only a certain life span. If the Earth kept all of its energy it would be perpetual and would cycle forever. As it is, the energy will be converted into something else the universe needs. On a smaller scale, this cycle also applies to us. At death we will convert to some other form of energy, after having lost energy all through our lives.

Electromagnetism also has a striking and profound effect upon us.

Electromagnetic Radiation waves are produced by the acceleration, or oscillation, of an electric charge. These waves are both electric and magnetic. The frequency of the waves can range from high to low. Visible light is a small part of the electromagnetic spectrum, as are X-rays, gamma rays, ultraviolet radiation, infrared radiation and micro and radio waves.

Electromagnetic waves need no medium for transmission. Therefore they can travel through almost anything, including space. Virtually everything gives off electromagnetic radiation, including the sun, the moon, stars and the Earth.

To call electromagnetic radiation 'waves', however, did not account for all the properties discovered. Max Planck showed that radiation occurred in finite quanta of energy and was, therefore, also particles. We now understand radiation in two ways, particle and wave, although they react together. The quantum theory can now be brought into line with electromagnetic radiation. A wave/particle is daily bombarding us and we have almost no idea what it is doing nor the effect it has on us.

In Geophysics, we study the phenomena of the Earth's magnetic field, the heat flow, seismic waves and the force of gravity. We also look into the outer-space activity that can affect us, such as solar winds and manifestations of cosmic radiation which affect the Earth's own radiation.

In Terrestrial magnetism (Magnetohydrodynamics or hydromagnetics) we have found that the magnetic field is related to the motion of fluid, which conducts electricity within the Earth. The rotation of the Earth within the gravitational pull of the moon and sun periodically imposes gravitational effects upon the earth, the changing tides and solid Earth tides, which in turn alter the electromagnetism of the earth. All these things happen cyclically and all these things affect us.

Every time a volcano erupts, the Earth's magnetic field alters orientation and strength. The depth of the mantle increases or decreases the conductivity of the electromagnetic wave. When the solar wind approaches, the Earth forms a magnetic sheath, called the magnetosphere, which acts like a giant natural dynamo more than 60,000 miles across. When the high-energy particles of solar radiation penetrate this sheath and enter the radiation belts we see the beautiful phenomenon called the aurora.

The electromagnetic wave possesses energy according to its wavelength and frequency. This energy is imparted into matter when the radiation is absorbed. Michael Faraday said that the electromagnetic field was the lowest form of physical reality. [1] The resonance caused by the various frequencies of the particle waves affects the molecules within our bodies. Every molecule in our bodies is held in place by various methods. When we are bombarded daily with fluctuating and cyclic electromagnetic radiation these molecules are moved, including those in our brains, which scientists admit we know relatively little about (see chapter 2). We have lived with this bombardment since the dawn of life. It must have affected our evolution, and we must retain some natural and deep link with this phenomenon.

A better understanding of these effects could be gained by research into such phenomena as Kirlian Photography.

This was discovered by Semyan Kirlian in 1939 when either he or another (it is disputed) received an electric shock whilst undergoing electrotherapy. The shock caused a spark and Kirlian wanted to see what would happen if he put light-sensitive material in the path of the spark. After much experimentation Kirlian managed to photograph an aura around his hand. Dr Victor Inyushin of the Kirov State University in Russia, a biophysicist, concluded that the photograph showed the existence of what he called biological plasma. This concept relates to healing powers, where better photographs have been achieved using the hands of healers. 2 Plasma, in this context, is the name given to the collection of positive and negative ions and is neither molecular, solid, liquid nor gas. It has no charge due to there being equal amounts of positive and negative ions, they are in equilibrium. Also discovered was the fact that Kirlian auras increased at the same time as the cyclic solar flares.

The Foundation for the Study of Cycles found that sunspot activity is intimately related to mass reactions within both the human and animal populations of the world. Research that stretches right back to 500 BC has shown that every 11.1 years, major upheavals and unrest in wars has risen. It brings a whole new meaning to the various religious beliefs about the controlling God of our lives that manifests as the Light.

So what effect is all this radiation having upon us? Will Kirlian Photography ever raise its head above the paranormal shelves in the book shops? What effect have the radiation and cyclic patterns had upon our evolution? The complexities of the formulae and ingredients are immense and too much for any computer model to predict the effects.

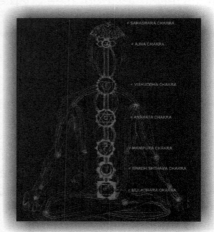

Chakra's, so called energy centres

Computers are already finding it very difficult to predict the next day's weather. The chaos theory with the butterfly, which flaps its wings in the

Amazon and affects the weather patterns of the entire world, is very real and is unpredictable at present. We would, therefore, find it almost impossible to predict the outcome and effects of so much data from the electromagnetic/cyclic scenario. We would have to take into account the weather (which we already know is unpredictable), the gravitational pull of our cosmic neighbours, the Earth's magnetic core movements, the temperature, our own daily effect upon the globe, manufacturing output, war, in fact you name it and it probably has an effect upon the planet's electromagnetic fields. And yet our ancient ancestors could predict with alarming accuracy the precise cyclic effects upon the globe.

They knew when a volcano was going to erupt and they fled. They predicted from the stars the subtle gravitational forces, and understood the physical and mental effects that would have upon us. They created vast amounts of information regarding astrology and the understanding of the patterns. Is there some clue here that shows us the secrets of the ancients? We are constantly amazed at just how much our ancestors knew without modern science. Are we yet to be even more astounded? We may find there is much we can learn from them.

From the earliest times mankind has worshipped the Tree. It is the symbol of immortality. Now we find that the genetic code found in humans, which limits our lifespan is not found in trees. The bristlecone pine of America is the oldest living thing on Earth (between 3,000 and 5,000 years old). It has no genetic code to limit its lifespan and is therefore immortal. What secrets did our ancient friends, The Shining Ones, hold?

In the next chapter we will look at the brain and its evolution. We will see what subtle effects the life of the universe can have upon us as far as science and parascience is concerned.

Notes
Chapter One
1   Quantum Theory. Encarta Ency.1997.
2   The Paranormal. Stuart Gordon. Headline.1992.

Chapter 2
Subtle Bodies

The Shining Ones exercised control by seeming to know exactly what we were thinking, what worried us, what pleased us and, most importantly, how the environment affected us. To manipulate mankind in this way they had to understand how the brain works. Our understanding and perception of ourselves and the world around us stems from this unique and complex organ. This understanding needed to be deeper than just the standard couch psychologist.

The brain reacts strongly, though elusively, to cyclic patterns in the environment, although we are yet to fully understand this. Functions such as sleep, consciousness, memory, imagination and our creative ability are all extremely complex and poorly understood. They too are affected by our reaction to cyclic patterns and electromagnetic radiation.

In all cultures, approximately 90 per cent of people use the right hand for manual actions such as writing. This has been linked to the brain's processing of language. In right-handed people, language tends to be mediated by the left hemisphere of the brain, the side which controls the right side of the body.

The cerebrum is symmetrical in structure. The two lobes are attached to the brain stem. The dominant hemisphere is occupied with language and the operations of logic, while the opposite hemisphere controls emotion, spirituality and artistic flair. The left hemisphere is usually dominant and is, in the majority of cases, the logical side. As the centuries pass, this is more likely to become the case.

The grave in Swaziland of a small Neanderthal child laid to rest over 80,000 years ago provides evidence of early religious burial, 1 which shows that Neanderthal man was connected with his more spiritual or artistic side. The Neanderthal man had a large cerebellum or old brain. This has been shown by the British psychologist Stan Gooch to be the more creative and instinctive element of the brain. Gooch argues that evolution came about through the battles in our own brain between the cerebellum and the cerebrum. Any added input from cycles and electromagnetic effects upon the brain could produce subtle changes to our evolutionary path. This is all circumspect, however, and without hard evidence as yet, as was Swedenborg's hypothesis that the cerebrum equated with intelligence and the cerebellum with wisdom.

The arguments for this assumption are good and should not be dismissed by scientists simply because of the link with the paranormal. In fact, to the credit of scientists, there are ongoing trials at various universities across the globe looking into paranormal activities and related scientific phenomena.

The evidence shows that women, who are by most accounts more in tune with nature and more intuitive than men, have larger cerebella. Historically, many of the great mysteries of the religious world come from the east and it would, therefore, be no surprise to find Asiatics, Jews and Aboriginals possessing larger cerebella than Europeans.

It is believed that the cerebella is more in use during hypnosis, which is the state associated with imagination and removal of responsibility. The ancient word for hypnosis is 'mekhenesis', which means to 'remove responsibility'. Tapping into the brain like this has been used and abused over the centuries to great effect. The speeches of Adolf Hitler, for example, produced mass hypnosis on a grand scale.

If the ancient priesthood of the Shining Ones had the skill to tap into this part of the brain, if they knew all the secrets of cycles, magnetism, and brain control to use for their own ends, perhaps this was this how large buildings such as the pyramids were constructed and tens of thousands of people were controlled and fooled into believing that the Pharaoh was a god. Perhaps this was how mighty nations fell without ever a battle.

Now we will look at how magnetism affects the brain.

Man has always revered birds. From the Shaman, flying in a trance state, across the land, to the artist's depiction of winged angels, something has always attracted us to these creatures. Maybe it is the way they can just take flight and disappear. Maybe it is a shared understanding of travel and migration, which speaks to our nomad hearts.

The bird is basically reptilian and therefore lacks a mammalian cortex and mid-brain. Their migratory instinct comes from the cerebellum or old brain, the same part of the human brain which governs our instinctive and spiritual element.

Many birds navigate using the sun and moon, others the north star. Research has shown that birds are also sensitive to the Earth's magnetic field. A homing pigeon that was blinded by frosted glass contact lenses and taken 1,000 kilometres away from home made the return journey without error. The reason for this is that between its eyes there is an area of tissue with over a million bar-shaped pieces of magnetite or lodestone. 2

Magnetite, a magnetised mineral of iron oxide, was used by

the ancients as a compass because it naturally swings northward. The Chinese knew of its properties and thought it magical. They used an implement containing magnetite in the shape of the Big Dipper constellation on divining boards. Although we have not yet discovered exactly how the bird uses the magnetite, we have seen that amazing feats of navigation are possible. In theory, the magnetite picks up the Earth's magnetic currents and triggers directional messages to the bird's brain.

The Royal Society for the Prevention of Cruelty to Animals have authenticated incidents of psi trailing, the ability of animals to find their way home even when lost. There have even been cases of lost or abandoned animals tracking down owners who have moved to new homes without them. It is also possible that this homing instinct exists within us.

Harmonia Macrocosmica, 1660
The idea of harmony in the universe

In 1970, Dr Robin Baker of Manchester University, England, experimented on humans to discover whether this was the case. Blindfolded volunteers were taken from their homes, disorientated, and then asked to point the way home. A majority, above the accepted mathematical probability, pointed correctly. When, in later tests, bars of magnets and brass were attached to the volunteers' heads, only the ones wearing brass could point their way home. The magnet had affected their ability to 'see' the way.

A Czech physicist called Zaboj V. Harvalik found that a percentage of the people tested could actually detect changes in the magnetic field as small as 1/1,000,000,000 of a gauss. A typical child's magnet is 1,000 gauss. If, in our ancient past, we actually did have this directional compass within us, would it be possible to get it back?

Maybe we have tried to retrieve the ideal. In alchemy, the idea of the spirit of the world or Anima Mundi claims there is a world wide spirit which gives us information, including our whereabouts and way home.

Many para-scientists have discovered electromagnetic effects emanating from ancient standing stones. The Dragon Project, specifically set up to monitor energies from such structures, states that all stone circles in England and Wales occur within a mile of surface faults which are known to cause certain electromagnetic effects. When these energy lines cross Ley lines and other ancient energy centres, many strange phenomena occur. A large cross-section of scientists and para-scientists have reported that peculiar effects upon humans can occur due to the radiation produced. These effects include dreams and psychic abilities, lights and noises. All of these occur more frequently at times of greater importance such as the Solstice.

Our connection with the Earth's electromagnetism can be seen in the ancient practice of dowsing. Today we use dowsing to discover underground fissures, water, artefacts and minerals. The dowser uses rods or a weighted pendulum and walks across an area. The rod or pendulum then moves accordingly at the precise spot. Dowsers say that the instruments are incidental and react only to the vibrations, waves or electrical magnetism which is being picked up by their bodies.

Scientists have shown that some people are sensitive to 1/1,000,000,000 of a gauss of magnetism, therefore there is a strong possibility that dowsing is a practical and measurable skill. This would explain how the ancients could plot Ley Lines and understand Dragon Paths or Feng Shui.

When working in conjunction with a German dowser, the Czech physicist Zaboj V Harvalik suggested that the adrenal gland was the organ used to detect the magnetism. He reached this conclusion because positive results increased when the dowser drank more water. This theory seems unlikely now unless it is in some way linked with the pineal organ. In later experiments, aluminium foil was wound around the head of the dowser and this blocked the signal. Strangely, so did a block of foil placed on the dowser's forehead in the area of the pineal gland. This is the same location as a pigeon's magnetite.

The pineal organ is one of the outgrowths of the pineal apparatus. In aquatic and gill-breathing creatures, it can form a photosensitive eye-like structure which is involved in the diurnal rhythm of colour change. In ancient reptiles, and still in the Tuatura lizard of New Zealand, it formed a separate eye on top of the head. It persists in higher vertebrates and may function as an endocrine gland, internally secreting into the blood and affecting distant parts of the body. In humans, this organ is buried deep within the brain, located in the Limbic system, which helps us to learn and has emotional capabilities. The pineal gland exerts some chemical reactions, which are not fully understood. Autopsies on mediums and spiritually inclined people have revealed larger pineal glands that contain clear fluid, serotonin, which in turn makes melatonin.   Serotonin, when depleted by amphetamines, causes mild psychedelic effects, which is why the drug Ecstasy is so popular. The administration of melatonin can help prevent jet lag and SAD. Strangely, it is also thought to

Imagery of Kether – Pineal gland, the symbolism
of the forehead, the path to God or Godhead.
Including, Egyptian, Christian, Hindu, Hittite, Buddhist, Mayan, Muslim,
American Indian

influence our rhythms of activity. Some believe it is sensitive to the rhythms and cycles of nature and is responsible for transferring that information to us, although there is little evidence to support this. The pineal gland is associated with colour recognition, and reptiles can change the colour of this third eye. It is also associated with measuring the length of the day and keeping track of the seasons.

Hindu tradition claims this area to be the centre of the sixth 'Chakra' or 'Sahasrara', the centre of man's spirituality and psychic abilities. This is the reason why people of many faiths wear a red dot on the forehead. Chakra means 'wheel' and 'energy centres'. The initiated are trained to perceive chakra as whirls of altering colours. In ancient Cabalistic theology, the 'Kether', or crown, is over the head and therefore relates to the pineal gland. The Kether is the crown of pure brilliance or shining one. It is the point where all life's energies spring from the Godhead. In Deuteronomy 6:8, the priests of Israel wore a phylactery on their foreheads, and in ancient Egypt we find the royal Nemes head-cloth, a piece striped of cloth with the Uraeus insignia at the centre of the forehead. In many Christian Cathedrals, there are portraits of Christians with strange marks on their foreheads, or carved stone images with

a circle, diamonds and triangles on their crowns or hats. 4 There is no explanation for these images, no reason given for these marks, they are just there and in some very symbolic positions. At Lichfield Cathedral in England, the pictures of Bishops are enhanced with these marks and face a large mystical image of the Virgin Mary with the bright rays of the sun shining from behind her.

At this point we should be aware of how far from science we can stray. Map Dowsing, for instance, cannot be explained scientifically, and some scientists point to the nose as the organ responsible for our directional senses. Many animals have a variety of senses which we are yet to understand, such as the ability to emit small electrical discharges, underwater vibrations, infra-sound and ultrasound. Some birds can detect polarised light, which helps them to see the fingerprint of their prey as it leaves a pattern across the ground. Snakes can see and produce images in infra-red radiation. Can man use more senses than we know? Should we believe that the dowser's skill is simply that they are more acutely in touch with their senses?

The term to be 'mesmerised' comes from the Austrian physician Franz Anton Mesmer (1734-1815) who believed the human nervous system to be magnetised. He coined the phrase 'animal magnetism' and claimed that magnetism from the planets had actually caused healing at one church in Austria.2 He developed a therapeutic regime, which incorporated iron magnets, magnetite and the laying on of hands. Mesmer built up a large following, many of whom claimed to have been healed by his 'animal magnetism'. The modern day term for mesmerism is hypnotism. Although using magnets and the left side of the brain to achieve a therapeutic response is still a relatively untried method, there is some evidence that our ancestors may have dabbled in it. As the famous Methodist John Wesley said, 'consider how far bodily disorders are caused or influenced by the mind.' 2 If many illnesses are caused by the brain, or effects upon the brain from electromagnetic radiation or other such unrecognised methods, then perhaps the brain can help to cure itself or be helped by the same methods which actually caused the illness. Alchemists hinted at this kind of belief many centuries ago.

Another belief we will look into is the sacred role of trees. Many modern New Age mystics believe trees to have healing powers and to be sources of Earth energy. There is some truth here, in that energy is emitted from trees, and there are very strong reasons why the tree should be held to be sacred, as we shall see, but does this energy have an effect upon our brains or vice-versa?

There are many faith healers, new age mystics and holistic practitioners around the world who claim to heal with the aid of the spirits, ancestors, Gaia, God, God's or Goddesses, animals and electromagnetism. It is time for a serious, scientific and historical study of the effects of these beliefs to see once and for all who are the frauds and fanatics and who are the real healers, if indeed any of them are.

New and modern techniques are emerging which might offer hints as to how our ancestors used their healing powers and allusions to the prayer life and meditative practices of the more spiritual ancients.

With Biofeedback, individuals mechanically monitor their own states of mind and body to gain self-control. This is similar to the Buddhist and Hindu methods of self-control via meditation, where not only do they control worldly desires but also bodily functions, such as appetite and body temperature. You will note that Hinduism and Buddhism stem from some of the oldest roots of mankind's religious mythology. The modern day counterparts use scientific tools to the same ends. They control heart rate, blood pressure, stress levels, halt the attacks of headaches and even monitor and alter their own brainwave patterns.

Medical specialists the world over are interested in this supposedly 'new' technique for cures of cancer and other life threatening diseases. Brain power used can release endorphins into the body which have pain relieving and mood elevating effects.

With Biofeedback, and an understanding of our environment and biorhythms in conjunction with the cosmic cyclic patterns, we may re-discover what we have lost. Biorhythms were discovered by Dr Hermann Swoboda and Dr Wilhelm Fleiss, who found that the human body is subject to a twenty-three and twenty-eight day cycle. Added to this was the thirty-three day cycle discovered by Dr Alfred Teltcher who observed the fluctuations in the intellectual performances of his students. These cycles lead us through peaks and troughs, mood swings and various other activity patterns. In later chapters, we will note the twenty-eight day cycle of the moon and the other related astrological and earthly cycles which have effects on us.

Japanese employers who lay off staff in regular cycles because of low mood swings have achieved greater efficiency. There are now small computer devices available which can monitor menstrual cycles as a method of birth control.

In 1981, the biologist Rupert Sheldrake put forward the hypothesis for what he called 'morphogenetic fields' (Greek 'morphe' for 'form' and 'genesis' for 'coming into being'). Sheldrake claimed that these fields, unrecognised by modern science, were as real as magnetic or gravitational fields. He claimed that by morphic resonance, forms and behaviour patterns are transmitted across space and time, and that growing embryos of the same species could tune into the morphic resonance and learn from the past, to give evolution that helping hand. If we consider that we have problems with the huge gaps in evolution, and the fact that many evolutionary scientists are looking at the 'big leaps' theory as being more acceptable, it may be that by learning from the past and adapting our genes while still an embryo, we could make these leaps.

Sheldrake supposed that this morphic resonance came from the memory bank of the past species. So when a species has learnt a new behaviour pattern it is passed down and effects a change in the future. This falls in line with Lamarck's evolutionary hypothesis of acquired characteristics. Let us look at evidence for such an idea.

The phenomenon called 'The Hundredth Monkey' has been put forward by adherents to Sheldrake's idea as being evidence for such a brain/mind transmitter/receiver. On an individual level we obtain new knowledge, which then erupts suddenly throughout the species. This comes from the explanatory folk tale of how a monkey in a cage is joined by an ever increasing numbers of monkeys. When the hundredth one arrives, the cage bursts and all the monkeys escape.

Modern research, especially that undertaken by the anthropologist and biologist Dr Lyall Watson, has shown a remarkable similarity in effect by observation. In 1952, the Macaca Fuscata monkeys of Koshima Island, Japan, were under close observation by primatologists.

To get the monkeys to come closer to the researchers, sweet potatoes were placed before them. The potatoes proved

unpalatable until a female monkey named Imo learned how to wash them. The young monkey taught the skill to her mother and other female monkeys, and by 1958 all the young monkeys were doing this. They also found that washing the potatoes in salt water had added more flavour.

The primatologists then noticed that the practice, once restricted primarily to the under fives, had now become common knowledge amongst the monkeys, virtually overnight. The phenomena did not stop there. The practice also erupted on completely isolated neighbouring islands.

This was not an isolated observable incident. In Britain, in the same year as the primate study began, our dairies first began to deliver milk in bottles topped with foil, through which birds can peck and drink the milk. Blue tits were first to learn how to do so. The initial spread of this practice was normal and comparable to previous observable examples and nothing was out of the ordinary. That was until 1955 when suddenly, and again virtually overnight, all blue tits and most of the great tits of mainland Europe were practising this. Could Rupert Sheldrake's theory of morphogenetic resonance be true? Is this a hypothesis that science should take seriously when considering new ways to explain our evolution?

Early on in his career, the psychologist Carl Jung described a manifestation he called potent primordial images. He believed that there is a vast, universal store of memory and images locked away deep within our unconscious. Sigmund Freud, however, considered them to be archaic residues, something we no longer need. This was in disagreement with Jung who saw them as vital to our psychic life, a collective unconsciousness, which we all shared, added to and took from. The idea was that many religious and primordial beliefs in spirits, souls, gods and demigods, ancestor worship and heaven were gleaned from our unconscious mind tapping into the collective unconsciousness. This may explain some of the shared images that Shamans and magicians experience when under the influence of psychoactive drugs, or the worldwide common images of near death experiences and even alien visitation.

Scientists are now pointing to the passing on of residual memory within our genes, and this may explain some of the strange effects, although we should consider that there could be truth in both ideas: genetic modification from memory and modification from a handed-down shared consciousness.

Science is looking into some of the more common paranormal experiences in relation to the brain. Extra Sensory Perception, or ESP, is one such area. This is the phenomenon where information is supposedly transmitted or received from one brain to another. Scientists have, as yet, been unable to prove the existence of true ESP, although they have had some unusual and unexplainable results. For instance, in 1966, Cleve Backster, an ex CIA employee who was an expert in using polygraphs, decided to connect one to a house plant (Draecaena) to measure the amount of water taken up from the soil. The idea was that as the polygraph measures blood pressure, muscular activity and electrical conductivity, it might also be able to measure the pressure induced within a plant when drinking.

The experiment showed that when he watered the plant, the conductivity dropped, just as it would for a human undergoing a pleasant experience. When Backster decided to burn the plant the polygraph needle jumped with increased conductivity; not when he actually burned the plant, however, but when he thought about burning it. When the experiments were increased in complexity, it was found that the plant did indeed react to what he called primary perception.[3] The experiments were also demonstrated by others, namely V.N. Pushkin and A.P. Dubrov, who showed that no mechanisms were used, just pure human emotion, with the same effects. And this is not something we have only just discovered.

A hundred years previously, the Indian physicist and botanist Jagadis Chandra Bose explained that by experimentation he had proven what he called 'pervading unity' in plants. By a series of blows he showed that the plants reacted and were irritated. In 1927, botanist Joseph Sinel was almost ridiculed when he claimed plants had a clairvoyant aspect to them. Plotinus (204-269AD) the Egyptian philosopher believed that plants aspired to contemplation. Plotinus was a neoplatonist with much admiration for his profoundly mystical works. His ideas were not ridiculed, it is only in our modern age that such thoughts are considered ludicrous.

We should also remember that plants are cyclically orientated. They can be sown only at certain times of the year, they open and close with the sun, they flower annually, they shed leaves by the seasons. They are almost perfect measures of the seasons and it is surprising that instead of the stars, we did not make more use of plants. There is much evidence of this kind of plant use and it may have been because of the margin for error and uncertainty of the seasons that plants were not as specific as the stars, but one would have expected to find more relevant mythology from ancient man than actually exists; although obvious pointers from Plotinus suggest a deeper knowledge of plants.

It is apparent that more research is required, but not in isolation from other paranormal phenomena, or some of the wider implications this may hold. We should remember the plant consciousness phenomena when we consider the human adoration of the sacred tree in a later chapter.

In the next few chapters we will look at our ancient ancestors and search for clues as to whether they understood more than we give them credit for. By understanding the nature of our existence, in a paranormal, scientific and spiritual way, we will find the reasoning behind early religious beliefs.

There would be little point in looking to the future or at modern rationalism for answers. The beliefs of ancient man came about through his understanding of the world around him. There was no science book to learn from and understand what the stars really were. He simply had to work it out for himself and attribute his own interpretation to the natural phenomena around him. How ancient man passed on these newly created beliefs and what he did with them is the subject of the next chapter.

Agni, god of fire

Chapter 2
Notes

1   Lifetide. Lyall Watson. Coronet Books. 1980
2   The Paranormal. Stuart Gordon. Headline. 1992
3   The Secret Life of Plants. Peter Tompkins and
        Christopher Bird. Harper and Row. 1973
4.   Lichfield Cathedral, Staffs, England. Remarkable
        imagery, Geofrey de Bouillon statue, numerology,
        symbolism, cross, trees, mountains, Marian cults,
        Illuminati, and much more. I have spent days at this
        Cathedral and have still not collated all the relevant
        symbolism contained within, well worth a visit.

Chapter 3
Heavenly Bodies

The Bible says that 'Christ is all and in all'. Did the early Christians and Gnostics understand man's relationship with the hidden forces of the larger universe?

The questions of whether early man understood and utilised the effects of cyclic patterns, electromagnetic forces and the closeness of his nature with plants and animals may be answered in the signs of the reverence he paid to these elements; his worship and ritualistic behaviour surrounding some of these basic and fundamental parts of the 'supernature'.

Cyclic patterns and rhythms dominate our lives, from the day to night patterns to the seasonal changes and their effects upon us. If we look at a few of the cycles which have become important to man we can see how we are affected by them.

Day/night cycles are different in other parts of the world. Some have longer nights and shorter days, for example, and their nature has adapted accordingly. Seasonal Affective Disorder is purely the result of long nights and weeks. On the equator, where the sun is stronger and is out for longer periods, SAD does not exist and is indeed refuted.

In certain parts of the world we have four seasons. Elsewhere, the seasons are different. Tropical regions have two seasons: wet and dry. Monsoon areas have three: cold, hot and rainy. In Polar Regions, the temperature change from summer to winter is abrupt.

Man, animal and plant life have adapted remarkably well to the different seasons they experience. We have seen previously how the pineal gland actually measures the seasons and length of day. This is how we adapt to the various seasons around the globe. Many species, including some types of bird, can accurately predict the weather to help them plan migratory patterns. The Orange Ladybird insect in the UK has never been wrong in its long-term winter predictions.

The moon plays an important part in all the religions of the world. Lunar cycles and human experience are intrinsically linked. The tidal flow of the world's oceans corresponds to the waxing and waning of the moon, as does the menstrual cycle, which has had a profound effect upon our early and later religious beliefs.

Menstruation occurs only during the fertile years and had symbolic meaning amongst early cultures. The menstrual blood of women is considered with awe and fear and may have much to do with the use of Red Ochre by ancient man. This blood is also derided and called unclean (even today, the women of Judaism go through a purification bath seven days after the end of the menstruation), a poisoning of woman for her sins by the great gods, although this appeared to be a much later addition as a result of the subtle battle of the religious sexes.

Menstruating women were often kept away from the other members of their tribe or village. This may be why the witches' Sabbat took place specifically on the day when the moon took rest, and was associated with evil. Ishtar, one of the Moon-Goddess's titles, was said to be menstruating on this day. The menstruating woman is also seen as a symbol of fertility, and in

some African cultures she is led around the home of one who wishes to become pregnant and asked to touch everything. The onset of menstruation marks the move from child to woman and was celebrated with Earth Goddess or Mother Goddess rituals and, much later, within the taking of blood in the Eucharist.

The Sabbat (Heart-rest of the moon), the moon's day of rest, the seventh day, was later taken over by the Jews who turned it into their day of rest and laid waste to the maternal, lunar religions, and inaugurated their paternal 'sun god'. Christians took this further, moving the day of rest to the Mithraic Sunday; the original moon day being Monday. [1]

The sidereal lunar month is 27.32 days and the synodic lunar month is 29.53 days. Both have different paths and different meanings dependent upon your culture. In the sidereal lunar year there are thirteen months per year. This is a matriarchal structure and is more than 3,000 years old. Originally, there were thirteen signs of the zodiac in this period, the thirteenth being Arachne, the spider.

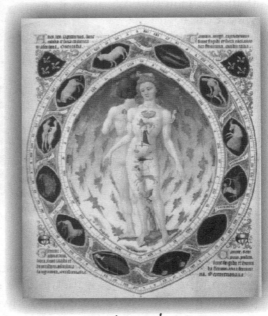

The instillation of a twelve-month period seems to have been an attempt by the patriarchal cultures to

Zodiacal Man

gain dominance, and thus we now have twelve months per year. It must be noted that twelve is a symbolically relevant number and should be watched for throughout this book. The elimination of the thirteen month period has come down to us today with the persecution of the witches coven, which has thirteen members, the number thirteen being considered unlucky, but more importantly the fact that Jesus had twelve disciples, therefore making up thirteen in total, the hidden number of Mother Earth.

The moon is tied up in many of our early cultures. The names of its associated deity vary due to locality, language and ethnic differences, but are all essentially of the same goddess. Aphrodite, Astarte, Badb, Brigit, Ch'ang O, Demeter, Hecate, Inanna, Isis, Ishtar, Maja Jotma, Tsuki-Yomi. Some of these names have been carried on, kept alive behind the scenes by the secret cults whilst they were subtly battling or even creating the front lines of the new or growing male-oriented popular gods such as Mithras and Yahweh.

Winged Inanna

The terms 'lunatic' ('moon-struck') and 'mental' are both taken from the moon, under the impression that such effects are brought on by the lunar periods, usually the full moon. It is not surprising that the moon was denounced as the 'mad' moon when we consider the patriarchal and matriarchal battles, which were being fought across the continents. The idea was put forward that the electrical energy of the body became drained at this time of the month, and caused the person to lose his or her faculties. Two hundred years ago, Lunacy was covered by English law. Kleptomania, arson and dangerous driving have been shown scientifically to increase at times of the full moon, so there may be some scientific reason for this matriarchal lost battle.

The Jewish Passover is celebrated on the lunar calendar; the Christian Easter ('Eoster' was the Anglo-Saxon goddess of spring) is calculated from the full moon after the vernal equinox. The full moon at the autumn equinox is celebrated as the harvest moon. The Jews had many moon festivals, such as New Moon and Full Moon (see Num. 28,11:14). The eclipse of the moon is considered by many cultures to be the union of the Sun God and Moon Goddess. This belief harks back to a time when the known world shared a common Priesthood, more of which later.

500,000 births were measured in New York in 1948/57. The results showed that more births occurred during a waning moon and the maximum after a full moon. In the North Sea coast of Germany, most births occur at high tides as the moon passes overhead. More children are born in the Northern Hemisphere in May and June than in November and December, and vice versa in the Southern Hemisphere. Size of offspring has also been mapped and shows a noticeable pattern dependent upon time of year. In the 1960's, Eugen Jonas understood the lunar aspect of ovulation and successfully increased the effectiveness of contraception to ninety-eight per cent. When he was presented with the birth charts of 250 newborn children he successfully identified the sex of eighty-seven per cent of the babies from planetary information alone.

Frank Brown of North-Western University, Illinois, found that oysters in his laboratory, a thousand miles from their Connecticut shore, opened at the same time as their home shores' high tide, which in turn is related to the moon's orbital pattern. Brown also proved that potatoes, rats and fiddler crabs are all governed by lunar periods. Within laboratories, the metabolisms of various creatures fluctuated in response to lunar patterns and geomagnetic factors. Now, years later, research is proving that all known sea creatures, when taken from their natural homes, still obey the same lunar cycles. At the time, many scientists thought Brown to be dealing with the paranormal sciences and ignored his research.

Amun Ra

The Sun - the Shining One, great light of the world - is venerated all over the globe as the light of life, the giver of heat and the most important cyclic symbol of all time. Our ancestors knew that it meant life or death. It was essential for the sun to return every day, for its strength to be renewed again each Easter. We say the sun is wise, and therefore in mystery plays around the world, light equates to wisdom. The strength of the sun gave rise to its being considered the most powerful of the deities. In the early developed civilisations the sun is always there. In Egyptian culture he is Ra, Re or Amun-Re. The scarab beetle is often used to portray the sun in some aspects, a symbol of self-regeneration and the early ideas of reincarnation. The sun is generally male and outwits the lunar female goddess as well as mating with her.

We sacrifice, dance (almost always, significantly, in circles), travel hundreds of miles and sing to the great light. We even give it human names such as Apollo, and include him in dramas. This, of course, hides a deeper and more symbolic understanding that the initiated, the ancient Shining Priesthood of the sun knew how to decipher. The cyclic pattern and life-giving nature of the sun is key to the secrets of the ancient Shining Ones.

The movements of the sun have inspired tales of where the sun god goes and why he comes back, of battles fought and death overcome. This last idea of overcoming death gives us the first hints at how man has used the sun god fables and mysteries to hide the secret ideas of how we ourselves could be reincarnated. Thousands of years of begging the sun to return each day and be reborn each spring led ancient man to develop his own re-birth rituals and ideas of how to accomplish it. Now, with thousands of years of additional mystery and symbolism, we find it almost impossible to decipher the magic secret.

Everyday we rise with the sun. Our bodies release hormones,

which waken, revive and regenerate us. In summer, our endocrine glands release more hormones that bring a sense of well-being. By late afternoon we feel more relaxed as the sun's strength wanes. The secret police of many countries often choose this time of day to arrest people, as they are more easily subdued. If we today understand how to utilise the power of the sun with the regenerative effects of holidays and by the dealings of the secret police, what did our ancient and less complicated ancestor do?

Sunspot activity affects our biorhythms directly in ways we do not understand. Evidence shows that it can be an irritant to our bodily functions and mental attitude. The Foundation for the Study of Cycles has produced some interesting results with their long-term research, including some of the following. There is a 3.86 year cycle in lemming suicides and North American lumber pine growth; an 11.1 year cycle of sun spot activity and serious upsurge in war and unrest. The Black Death and the Great Plague coincided with this solar turbulence. There is also an increase in traffic accidents every 11.1 years, a rise and fall in hemlines, and an increase of volcanic and earthquake activity.

The stars, the myriad shining ones, also have an effect on us. Michel Gauquelin, a French psychologist, placed the hypothesis that we are affected by the position of the planets at our time of birth firmly on the doorstep of science. He showed that the position of the stars had some indication as to what line of work one may enter later in life. This was not related to the practice of astrology or the horoscopes in the daily newspapers, but a serious, scientific data analysis. The psychologist, Hans Eysenck said, 'How ever much it may go against the grain, I think we must admit that there is something here that requires explanation'. His results, however, showed tendencies within the higher professionals and the same response was not achieved with unskilled workers.

The study of the stars goes back thousands of years. Some say 4,000 BC Sumeria was the first to do so. Others put this even earlier and say that ancient man was studying the stars 32,000 years ago. 2 Their evidence is an engraved antler from Abri Blanchard, France, with a strange pattern of notches or calendrical phases of the moon.

With all the evidence on patterns, rhythms and electromagnetism that affect our bodies, it is no wonder that modern science has taken another look at the ancient art of astrology, which has been neglected due to the widespread misuse of generic horoscopes.

Natal astrology deals with planetary positions at the time of our birth. Astrometerorology concerns the prediction of major earthquakes, climatic changes and volcanic eruptions. There is much evidence to suggest that certain animals, which can predict such occurrences, are born at a specific time of year that corresponds to certain astrological predictions. Cosmobiology is the study of the balance between cyclic behaviour, biological patterns, radiation and gravitational effects upon us.

Ancient peoples must have understood the precise mappings of these newly named sciences when they too predicted such things by the stars. It may be that ancient man was using both his 'hidden powers', and the tools of the earth around him. It may also be that the ideas and symbolism of Alchemy were just a few more steps along this path.

The Indian sage, Parasar, 'circa'. 3000 BC, used Natal Astrology in his work. Megalithic structures have many astrological and Earth alignments. The Pyramids map the stars, obeying the

Hermetic lore of 'as above so below'. Ziggurats, temples, floor paintings, carvings and forty-mile long lines etched into the ground all convey the ancient and global belief in astrological predictions.

The very earliest almanacs contained weather forecasts based upon astrological predictions. In the countries of Arabia, the position of the stars was consistent with the weather. The ancient priesthood would have appeared to be in the know all the time, and therefore would appear holy and godlike; it was little wonder that they became incorporated into the symbolic format and titles of the stars.

The term 'zodiac' has a meaning pertaining to animals, possibly 'animal map' or 'circle of animals'. This is seen more precisely in the ancient Chinese chart where every star sign has an animal name. The zodiac is belt of the gods, which lies nine degrees either side of the ecliptic plane, and contains the orbits of the moon and the major planets. The sun originally traversed these minor gods on a regular path and the various signs of the zodiac were blessed with his arrival. That the word 'zodiac' pertains to animals explains why it contains animal symbols, such as the ram and fish. These ancient anthropomorphic beliefs were included into the sky, in the same way that pagan gods were taken on as saints by the Christian church. Later on, the saints received their own stars and were painted with them in ecclesiastical fervour. In some of the world's zodiacs, such as the Chinese version, there is a tree at the centre.

The Babylonians, and especially people in the Middle East, studied the stars mathematically and attempted, even as long as 5,000 years ago, to scientifically log the reactions and effects of the stars. They produced a calendar and perfect measures of time, essential for a people without clocks. Carl

Jung suggested that the zodiac was an archetypal component of the psyche of mankind and he linked it with the theory of the collective unconscious.

The patterns and rhythms of the stars, with their gravitational and radiation activity have enormous effects upon our universe. But could they also affect us individually and collectively? The cosmic radiation hitting and passing through our planet is millions of years old. It comes in cycles, as does the solar wind. The cycles increase and decrease, but nevertheless there is a pattern. Our species has been on this planet, and life has been part of the vast universe long enough for there to be some marked and observable effect.

There are a vast number of other cycles in which we are involved, such as urinary cycles, sexual cycles, stock market crashes, epidemics and a host of other minor cycles. A study of history will show how generations experience the same mistakes, and successes, all in a cyclic pattern.

The Buddhist Wheel of Life reflects the understanding the ancients had of this cyclic life of ours. It depicts, amongst others, creatures of passion, stupidity and hatred, and shows how we endlessly repeat the same things. The Wheel culminates

Hindu mandala
The idea of cycles

in the twelve links in the chain of causation on the search for truth.

We should be on the look out for common threads; links between civilisations and time. The web that man has spread across the many thousands of years is complex and cluttered. Historians would have us believe that various human achievements sprang up spontaneously and simultaneously across the continents. Mathematically, this is in error. There are too many coincidences, too many simultaneous eruptions of human culture and achievement, from the buildings that share a common purpose as solar and astral temples to the emergence of the ancient cross as a symbol.

As you read the following signs and histories in the next few chapters, remember that there is no easy way to show everything that is linked, there is simply too much information and much is hidden in secret societies. The reasons for the links, which are not separate accidents, will become clear later on.

In 1957, Tom Lethbridge wrote a book called 'Gogmagog'. He claimed that Druidism and Brahmanism were linked and shared a common origin. We will show just how close this was to the truth. Lethbridge believed that their ancient religion was somehow related to and existed for the Earth Goddess, also associated with the Moon Goddess and often cross-linked. This is true in that She was one of the deities worshipped by the ancient priesthood, to whom the Brahmins and Druids were related. The Earth/Moon Goddess, or Mother, had many names, Gaia or Ge, Isis, Astarte and eventually culminating in the Virgin Mary (Mother of God), and leading to the cult of the Black Virgin, which itself seems to be related more to Mary Magdalene than the Mother of God.

Lethbridge was so upset by the reaction to his hypothesis that he 'retired' to Devon and took up dowsing, itself uniquely linked to the ancient Shining Ones' culture. Unfortunately, the effect of this was to fuel his adversaries' opinions of him, even though he discovered some remarkable facts, which to this day are highly regarded by dowsers. He showed that different substances or items produce different swing rates of the pendulum. The pendulum is well known for being the most accurate dowsing implement and in Lethbridge's case this proved to be true. He found that the age of items gave a different rate, as did the surrounding emotions. A pebble thrown violently reacted differently from one thrown in a less aggressive manner. Work carried out by other dowsers has shown that while the rates differ between dowsers, the principle remains the same. This difference may be due to the rate at which the dowser absorbs the emitted energy, but it is hard to understand why the rates are uniformly different. If there had been a pattern of irregular rates this would be sufficient evidence to ignore the practice; as it is, we have evidence enough to require further investigation.

Although some of the conclusions drawn by Lethbridge are open to debate, we are left wondering whether there is any evidence for humans being able to pick up energy. As we have seen, electromagnetism is in all things and we are open to its power, as are animals. The theory is that we transfer this energy to the implements used. This may explain why some dowsers have different rates, but still keep the same proportions as Lethbridge's work. In the Vietnam War and World War 1, dowsers were used to help the Army find unexploded shells and locate mines. Modern oil companies use the skills of the dowsers to locate oil.

There is much evidence to show that ancient man practised dowsing, or radiesthesia, in one form or another. In the Tassili-n-Ajjer caves in the Sahara of South-Eastern Algeria, there are ancient pictoglyphs, approximately 8,000 years old, which show what appears to be dowsing. Thoth, the Egyptian god of wisdom and writing, and the Greek Daedalus, both closely associated, are credited with its invention. The importance of Thoth will become apparent later, and we should keep in mind that he was involved in this originally priestly practice.

The Chinese, the masters of Feng Shui, have also been credited with the invention of dowsing from the 3rd millennium BC. In

Balance

the Bible we find that Moses (the patriarch who, according to Acts, had all the knowledge of Egypt) was adept at finding water with his rod. The writers of the Bible vehemently opposed the tradition of dowsing, mainly due to the fact that just about any lay-person can dowse, therefore could take the secret knowledge away from the priesthood and reduce their power.

Later, the Inquisition of the Catholic church found it necessary to stamp out dowsing once again, whilst many Abbots continued the practice in secret and even wrote extensively on the subject, albeit symbolically. What would be the reaction of the church if they were to find out that their own prophets, including the Saviour, practised divination? As we shall see later, they simply ignore the fact.

Among the other forms of divination to look out for is Bath-Kol: divination by means of the heavenly, divine voice. By interpreting this sound, the ancient Jewish prophets could announce the Will of God to the people. If ever there was a tool to keep the sacredness of God within the elite then this is it. This practice appears to be worldwide in all cultures but is carried out only by the initiated few.

Necromancy, the art of raising spirits from the dead to discover answers, is another form of divination that has strong links with the Bible. The Witch of Endor, in 1 Samuel 28, summoned the spirit of Samuel for Saul to question. Saul paid the price for this sin, but this demonstrates the existence of this ancient practice, which stretches back to beliefs in the underworld or place of the ancestors; a belief and a divination practised all over the globe. Was this a practice common to the ancient priesthood who may have travelled the world? The period fits well, as we will see.

Astrology is a form of divination relating to the stars. This too was practised globally at the same time as necromancy.

The interpretation of dreams, Oneiromancy, is a worldwide custom and one which also appears within the pages of the Bible, as well as many other holy books from just about every other religion and culture from our ancient past. Sometimes the dreamer would choose a specific location and take an hallucinogenic substance to bring on a dream, which only the priest could interpret. In the Bible, the one with the ability to interpret the dream was the chosen one of God - the Shining One, a special person or priest.

Scrying is the method of using a crystal or shining ball, mirror, or, more correctly and more ancient, a shining stone. Only a priest, or latterly clairvoyant, could read the message received. This art goes back to and even further than the Egyptians. Gypsies (the word is said by some to be derived from 'Egyptians') still use the crystal ball today. Hebrew tradition has it that Adam received wisdom from a shining stone, and Nostradamus used a bowl of water, as did Zeus.

Geomancy is the ancient from of reading messages from the earth. The word comes from the Greek word for Mother Earth, 'Ge' or 'Gaia', and 'mancy' or 'magos' meaning knowledge. Ancient Greek, Latin and Arab writers tell us about Geomancy. This divination technique is also global and is referred to in the Bible, in some remarkable places, as we will see in later chapters. That such a paternal religion should be involved in a maternal belief is startling. The timescale of the spread of Geomancy across the globe is much debated. There is, however, no doubt that it was universally used.

In Geomancy, the earth is drawn upon by hand or with sticks and a response read. Special codes or symbols are used, which are known only by the initiated. The symbols are usually lines, dots or stars. The final symbol is probably the one we should remember as this includes the symbol of the fish, although not in modern Geomancy techniques. The Arabs used random marks and read these. In other parts of the world, earth was thrown into the air and the shapes it formed as it fell on the ground were interpreted.

In China, the most complex form of Geomancy was Feng Shui (literally, 'wind and water'), the interpretation of the Earth energies and the use of this reading to discover where best to place tombs or temples. The Chinese use a similar technique on humans in acupuncture, a very popular and reportedly effective alternative medicine.

The Chinese called the powers of the Earth, 'Yin' (female, negative) and 'Yang' (male, positive). As we know, everything, including energy, matter, and magnetism, has a positive and a negative, so once again, our ancestors were there before us. Modern day dowsing has shown that sites such as Stonehenge, Glastonbury, Newgrange, the pyramids of Egypt and the ziggurats of South America are all situated on these so-called ancient energy lines. This is yet another example of the global aspect of these ancient beliefs, which spread through cultures without altering the ethnicity of the population, but fitting in with it. This ancient priesthood did not change or improve the lifestyles of the general population, which is why it has been so difficult for archaeologists to discover their existence, instead they simply passed on knowledge, shared the power amongst themselves and the few who wished to become Shining Ones.

There are subtle hints, missed by orthodox history, which are beginning to reveal the patterns of an antiquated hierarchy of special priests. Once we are alerted to their existence, it becomes obvious that they were there all along. If we read any part of the Bible again and replace the words 'Lord' or 'God' with 'The Shining Ones', it will become apparent how deeply rooted into our cultures and lives this priesthood really are.

There are many belief systems in the world, but they all come from one basic and undeniable core, invented and evolved separately by the Shining Ones. The next chapter will look at our origins and help us piece together the riddle of this elusive priesthood's existence.

Chapter 3
Notes

1   Woman's Mysteries. Esther Harding. Rider. 1971
2   Human Antiquity. Feder and Park. Mayfield Publishing.
      1993

Chapter 4
The Ancient Link

Ritual has always been an important part of man's worship and takes many forms ranging from ancient fertility rites to the communion of the Catholic Church. Whether in an attempt to reach up to god or connect to the Earth, the dramatisation in ritual of a desired outcome is believed by many to have a beneficial influence on the result. Many such ancient rites are still practised today. To try to understand some of what ancient man might have experienced, I contacted a modern pagan group and eventually received an invitation to an evening of ritual.

I drove to a bar and met up with thirteen very ordinary individuals from the County of Derbyshire. Their daytime roles ranged from graphic designer to solicitor. They were far removed from what I had been expecting. We had a drink and I asked the group a list of prepared questions. Why do you do it? Who do you worship? What is the experience like? Their response was 'wait and see'. We all walked back to our cars and drove to a private wood. The land was owned by one of the group and the spot in the wood used for the ritual a highly guarded secret.

It was a long walk from the car to the small clearing. The group told me to stand about six feet from the circle, which had been cleared of stones and undergrowth. I stood in the cold light of the moon and watched as they opened their bags and laid out long white robes of silk and cotton. They then stripped naked and ritualistically dressed each other in the robes, completing the transformation with items of jewellery the like of which I have seen only in a museum. One male and one female remained naked and took up positions opposite each other at the extreme of the circle which I now noticed contained the image of a pentacle. With caduceus-like staffs in hand, they were a raw and ancient sight to behold. A peculiar feeling enveloped the scene as the solemn silence was broken and very slowly each person began to hum. On its own, the sound was nothing spectacular but as each person joined in, the sound became awesome. I recalled how I had heard Buddhist monks produce a similar vibrating sound, an ancient and mysterious noise that simply must have existed in man's repertoire for thousands of years.

One by one they each lit a small candle and began to walk, slowly at first but increasing in speed as the humming grew louder. The sight was eerie. The man and woman began to follow each other around the circle, like the sun and moon in constant cycle. The others forced the two closer together until eventually, and in an almost electric and sexual spark, they embraced and fell to the floor amidst a frenzy of pagan noise and movement. Several of the group motioned me to join in with their worship, but

The pentagram
Now a symbol
of witchcraft

I was fixed to the spot in amazement that this sacred ritual was still alive and well just a few miles from my front door.

The scene mirrored their emotions and aided them in their obvious analogy of the ancient beliefs. It carried on for some time until it seemed the sun and moon were satisfied. We regrouped, all very orderly, and returned to our respective homes. I was probably the only one who came away from the night's exercise without a sense of satisfaction. Although I certainly gained a deeper understanding of the mind of ancient man.

For ancient man to live, prosper and procreate, he had to understand and use the world around him. He had to know what was edible, and when and where foodstuffs would be ready for him to eat. His knowledge of the seasons would tell him to prepare a store for the winter. But what happens when spring comes too late, the frost does not lift and the store has been raided? Or what about the summer when there is no rain and the crops fail? In moments of desperation, ancient man cried out to the gods. The basis of human belief in gods is need, and our ancestors had a structure of gods that reflected the science, as they knew it, of the world around them.

A few years ago I had a friend over from Africa, a Pastor in a Pentecostal movement. He told me how his fellow countrymen and women were so 'alive' to God. When we sat down to dinner, the Pastor ate like a starved man. I had never seen such enthusiasm. It made me think about how we can carelessly toss a half-eaten chicken to one side, without thinking of the people without food. We can always drive down to the supermarket and fill up the cupboards again. The people in his village have an eighteen-mile walk, in searing heat, just to fetch water. This is why they are 'alive' to God.

In his deepest need, man cries out to God and finds strength and comfort in his faith. It appears that no one is immune to this peculiar survival instinct. In times of dire need, even a confirmed atheist may find himself praying. We, in the capitalist world, with all our needs and wants satisfied, are walking away from the idea of God. We may replace Him with mathematical equations or New Age deities, but we are not looking solely to God to fulfil our every need any more. The people in the Pastor's village, on the other hand, need God to bring the water in the rainy season, they need the miraculous powers of His healing spirit when illness strikes and they need the unity that God can create amongst them.

Our ancestors had the same needs. Water could be scarce or, adversely, there could be flooding, although in the Egyptian delta this was considered to be the wondrous work of the gods and was prayed for each year. The gods were needed to bring the warmth and life-giving rays of the sun, the most important of all gods even today, as we shall see. The Earth was worshipped and was believed to mate with the rising sun of spring and summer and bring forth her fruits. These basic beliefs were humanised as all beliefs have been.

We emerged with a triad of colour, red, white and black, as the first symbols of our life's needs. Black was emblematic of death and darkness, white of new life (semen and milk) and red of the blood of fertility or war. [3]

Before we go any further, we should take a brief look at the origin of man. This will give an insight into a number of things. Firstly, not all the images we see regarding the origin of man are true. In our relatively recent history we have theorised about our origins from a purely rational and logical point of view. Previously, we believed in the religious ideals of God the Creator, whether this was from a Christian, Islamic or other

main religious viewpoint. Unfortunately, in our rationalist zeal we have thrown out a lot of good information, such as the anthropological theory that folktales should be seen as relics of ancient cultures, and actual occurrences and beliefs should be taken seriously.[4] Secondly, and most importantly, we shall see the vast periods of time over which man has evolved and this will help us to see how the unified theory of a single priesthood, who held the secrets of the gods, could have been there almost as long.

The Universe, as we know it is believed to have come into existence 15 billion years ago. The Cambrian explosion (the lowest division of the Palaeozoic era) happened approximately 530-590 million years ago. Then, somewhere in the mists of time, man evolved from something. This last sentence is about as accurate as we can be, based upon current data, although there are many books stating our evolutionary existence and progression as fact. Regardless of these new theories, anything other than to say 'we evolved in some way', is hypothesis. There are tools in existence which have been found to date from 25 million years ago,[1] and yet modern anthropologists inform us that man (in one form or another) came from Africa between 1.5 and 2 million years ago, although recent discoveries are even altering this idea. Our origin simply cannot be defined with any hard and finite accuracy.

Approximately 100,000 years ago, Homo Sapiens apparently split into Homo Sapiens Sapiens and Homo Sapiens Neanderthalanis in the Middle East. In Bilzingsleben, Germany, however, we have found three circular structures made from bone and stone, dating from 400,000 years ago. In Terra Amata in France there are post holes and stone circles dating from 300,000 years ago. From 2.5 million years to 125,000 years ago in Gona, Ethiopia and Europe we have vast amounts of tools and religious artefacts.1 Bones dusted with red ochre, which itself will become more important in religious circles, skulls packed with clay and held aloft on posts. We are supposed to forget all these things.5 We are told about the few discoveries that match the theories and the remainder become anomalies, whether or not there are more finds from before their theories. There has been a recent upsurge of anthropologists looking more deeply into the dating of our origins and we should see some improvement in this area soon.

Africa is generally believed to be the cradle of mankind. Recent testing on the genes of archaeological discoveries has shown the possibility that this is true. The theory (albeit from very few discoveries) goes like this: 5 million years ago a type of hominid, which resembles modern day man, inhabited the south and east of Africa. Over 1.4 million years ago, the tool-making hominid evolved into Homo Erectus and Homo Habilis. The earliest supposed find of Homo Sapiens, who came together to form nomadic groups and set off to discover the world, dates back to about 200,000 years ago.

Migratory patterns have been mapped and show that these early Khoisan speaking peoples spread all over Africa. Their descendants were pushed out by incoming Bantu speaking peoples who had mastered domestication and agriculture.

The missing element is the tremendous number of finds that date from before this 'standard history'; evidence which has, for nearly a century, been brushed under the carpet. For instance, in 1872, at the Anthropological Institute in London, a presentation of a remarkable find from the now famous Red Crag formation in Suffolk was given. The collection of sharks' teeth from an ancient sea which existed some 2.5 million years ago were shown to have a small hole drilled through the

centre of each. Each hole had sediment from the Red Crag formation still in place, thus proving their origin. The peculiar and strangely fascinating 'error' was that the holes had been drilled prior to them having been dropped into the ancient sea, 20 to 25 million years ago. This is just one example of evidence which has been 'ignored' because of the problem it raises.

It is highly possible that modern man may have developed alongside the other so-called species of early man. Whether or not he evolved from them, he may have lived and hunted alongside them. The early religious ideas of these mixed species were similar and widespread. The clay of the earth, or red ochre, had huge importance for early man, especially if we consider the earliest forms of the colour red as the symbol of Earth's and woman's fertility.

Early man developed his belief systems over a vast period of time, and the spread of these ideas began. But this did not happen in isolation, as standard science would have us believe. This spread of ideas evolved in earnest and built up into a vast power base, which differed from the normal political or royal powers, in that it was to become a spiritual power-base much like the original Catholic Church: the church that can be found in most, if not all, of the countries of the world. As the cultures, politics and historical backgrounds of every country differ vastly, the church base simply takes on some of the local characteristics and blends in; so much so that in future historical writings we may never know that they were there. And yet the religious power of this church has stamped its authority on the various locales of the world, sometimes to their benefit, but not always in the best of ways.

The church influences the minds of the people, changing the history of the country without being held responsible for it.

This is real power: to hold it without being accountable, to have the knowledge for yourself and to use that knowledge for whatever means you wish, regardless of the longer term goals; to have as members royalty, politicians, philosophers, warriors or the military and the masses. Exactly how many church leaders become politicians, kings and queens or great warriors is debatable, but it is not as many as those already in power who become members of the church and can become influenced by their spiritual leaders.

In 46,000 BC, a Neanderthal man was buried in the south of what is now France. His remains were found in a cave and his body had been packed with red ochre clay. This substance has become known as the 'blood of the earth', and it is believed that this style of burial was a symbolic returning of the body to the earth from where it came; a re-entering of the blood red womb of Mother Earth. Here we have a very different picture from the perceived view of Neanderthals.

This highly sophisticated ritual shows a remarkable understanding of the cycles of life and death: to rise up from the earth and return once again. If we take one of the future meanings of red ochre into account and work backwards to this find, we can say that it is symbolic of what the gods used to make man and therefore by stuffing the corpse in such a way it is symbolic of giving new life to the body and therefore a type of reincarnation or rebirth in the afterlife or ancestor home.

In 6,400 BC, a young Indian child was buried at the settlement known as Koster in southern Illinois, America. The body had been dusted with red ochre. Asking the gods to give the prematurely dead child another chance and dusting him/her with the symbol of rebirth could have helped the mind of the gods in their decision to offer the child new life in the 'land of the ancestors' or paradise.

This extrapolation is not implausible, as it is borne out by similar finds. In Swaziland, the buried skeleton of a child was discovered, which had been returned to the earth and dusted with ashes and red ochre. Later beliefs from this and nearby areas held to the idea of rebirth and reincarnation, so there is no reason to assume this belief was not held earlier.

Years later, Neolithic man was painting himself with red ochre as a symbolic gesture of his rebirth and initiation into the new life of the gods. In the outback of Australia, the anthropomorphic figures of the Wondjina, which date back to 10,000 BC, show a distinct red band around the heads of the priesthood. Evidence from Australia shows that they were magically adept at utilising and chemically altering the earth around them to produce the red ochre needed for their rites. The colour red was merging with the form of the life-giving sun: fertility and life coupling symbolically. The origin is not certain but it seems likely that the sun, with its spring morning red rays of life, representing the fertility of woman, was imitated on the human body and indeed in Neolithic wall paintings.

By 7,500 - 6,000 BC in the so-called cradle of civilisation, the Middle East, there were, cults of female, bull, sun and skull worship. The skull cult packed the skulls of the dead with red ochre clay and placed shells (symbolic of the sun's shining rays of light) on the eye sockets. In this area, the bull was often taken to represent the sun, the skull was symbolic of the human, and the female was the fertile mother earth/moon goddess, thus a trinity of beliefs developed.

In Catal Huyuk in Turkey, the trading route of the known world, sculptures of bull's heads as the sun god have been discovered. Here, the Mother Goddess was worshipped as a

three-in-one deity who was also to become greatly important. Red ochre, rebirth and reincarnation go hand in hand here. The archaeologist James Mellaart claimed that the cult of the Mother Goddess from Catal Huyuk was the basis of our own civilisation. There is no explanation of how Catal Huyuk built up its technical abilities so quickly. Could there have been influence from some outside source? Possibly a sacred priesthood, skilled in the art of knowledge and able to pass on a world's supply of such knowledge? Were they originators of such stories as Atlantis and Lemuria? The religion here was well developed and elaborate from day one. [1]

Some of the skills expressed in Catal Huyuk were known in other parts of the world, but there is no evidence of migrating peoples. This has always been the problem when we have nations rising from nowhere and we do not have peoples disappearing elsewhere or any genetic evidence of inwardly migrating Atlanteans. (In fact, the Atlanteans were supposed to have sacrificed to the Bull cult of Poseidon in a ritual of cyclic nature, as did the people of Catal Huyuk).

At a site dating back to 60,000 BC in Molodova, Russia we have portable tents and windbreaks made from mammoth bones. Other sites, equally as old, reveal similar tales. Is there any reason why nomadic peoples, such as these (some say the Kurgans), could not have populated these places and been given knowledge by the ancient priests or druids?

For a long time, these early rituals and beliefs spread over vast distances. Local minor ethnic alterations will become more apparent as time passes and our priesthood will take on the various differences and merge them, almost cyclically, into first one front religion and then another. What will emerge first are the surface religions of the politicians and leaders, which were incorporated into the politics of the relevant race or culture, but below that, we will see the basic patterns of the ancient priesthood. These elements emerge directly from the reasons we hold our beliefs. The life giving light of the sun will merge into the god of the western world. The mother earth and moon goddess will merge with various identities at face value, but will always be there below the surface. The worship of a female deity is worldwide and where Christianity has taken root, the Virgin Mary has been substituted. Where Islam is dominant, Fatima, the daughter of Muhammad and mother of three, is venerated. The stars in the sky will become minor deities and lead us through the seasons of life. Mountains, trees, animals, divination and symbols will all be seen to be below the surface of any country's main religion.

All the countries of the world share a common religious belief system. To have such a system spread over vast areas of the globe, especially when most of it is covered with water, would require an early understanding of the stars for navigation and a possible homing instinct with the use of lodestone, or magnetite. The technical ability to create ships must also have been available.

The evidence is beginning to prove that ancient travel was possible. In Southern Asia, there are engravings and cave paintings of deep-sea creatures which would have been impossible to know of without having gone out to sea.2 There are also paintings of dolphins and whales. Boats that are capable of such travel have been discovered from as long ago as 40,000 years. In the Middle East, canoes hollowed out from whole tree trunks have been found which date back to 7,500 BC. Plato claimed that in the time of Atlantis (9,000 BC or 900 BC depending on how it is taken) it was possible to travel from Atlantis to the further islands, possibly America. In Holland, there is evidence of boats capable of carrying large stones

possibly for early stone circles. The Biblical Noah myth, the Babylonian Gilgamesh Epic and China's Noah, Yu, who stopped the floods, shows that in pre-history there was a time of sea-faring beliefs.

In 4,500 BC, sailing boats were seen on the Euphrates in Mesopotamia using the stars to navigate. From archaeological data, it is possible to state that this basic belief system could have developed as far back as 100,000 years ago. This would explain why its tenets are basic to the core, and revolve around purely cyclic ideas which no longer seem to hold any meaning to us. So what beliefs are we looking for? How will we be able to recognise the ancient tracks of our universal priesthood?

Firstly, we are looking for ideas of the sun as the giver of life. This universal belief could have sprung up anywhere at anytime without outside influence, although when we see that so many other ideas also sprang up all over the globe the mathematical probability of this universal belief explosion is small.

Once we have found the Sky God or Sun God form, we need to establish whether there are any symbols or titles centred around this deity. 'Father' and 'light' are the two most basic, and many language different names stem from these titles.

The next deity to discover is the wife of the Sun God, the Mother of us all and many other minor deities. She is worshipped as the Earth Goddess who mates with the Sky God and maintains the cycle of life and death. She is also sometimes known as the Moon Goddess, mainly because the cycles of the moon coincide with those of women. The two great bodies in the sky mate at particular times of the year and fertilise the earth with new abundant life. Eclipses are particularly important for this mating procedure and many

ancient buildings and writings show that this was eagerly predicted, all over the world.

Stars are also important. The great shining ones of the heavens; minor deities of the Sun and Moon/Earth. They inform us of the times, seasons and longer-term cycles. They guide us around our world and we can predict so much from their movements. They are the many eyes of the unreachable gods looking down upon us.

Trees too are universally revered. They represent the Tree of all Knowledge, of Life, of Sorrow; the symbols of life and regeneration. We can use the tree for fire, to build shelter and transport, whether by land or sea. Ancient knowledge of how to gain medicine from certain trees is being rediscovered every year. Trees provide the world's breath with their oxygen output. Clothes are made from the bark and weapons produced from the branches and trunks. We can dye our clothes using the fruits and bark, we even eat their fruits. Mankind discovered that communication was possible via trees, whether by burning the wood or by producing paper. In a more metaphysical way, the tree shows us the order of the universe with its perfect geometric patterns in the circles of the trunk rings, the leaf patterns and the clever balancing act of the roots and branches. There is no wonder that it is called the tree of life: we live from it as virtual parasites.

The tree figures in folklore throughout the entire globe and is central to all world religions. The Norse 'Yggdrasil', the Shaman's World Tree, is an evergreen ash which supports the universe. It has three roots which extend into the underworld, 'Niflheim', the place of the giants 'Jotunheim' or 'Midgard', and the place of the gods, 'Asgard', the trinity of the Norse people. The tree is fed by sacred streams of living water from three sources. The highest branches of Yggdrasil shade the home of warriors, Valhalla, the Norse heaven. Odin, the 'Great Shaman', was sacrificed on Yggdrasil.

Desecrated Buddha

Vishnu was born beneath a Banyan tree and, like Buddha, was enlightened, or born again, under a Bo tree. The Biblical meaning of 'born again' is 'change of heart' or 'enlightened'.

Christianity has an intrinsic relationship with trees, from the Garden of Eden's Tree of Knowledge and Tree of Life, to the Germanic use of the hazel tree, with twigs formed into a cross shaped charm. In Celtic lore, the hazel tree was the Tree of Knowledge, the nuts from the hazel were believed to bestow wisdom when eaten. Teutonic belief has man created from the Oak tree.

The Maypole dance of 'Merrie England' is a relic of tree worship, and there is much folklore scattered across the world regarding surviving rituals from the tree worshipping past of mankind. Joseph of Arimithea brought a symbolic tree with him in the form of his staff and planted it in the Glastonbury Tor where today it is venerated by all who believe.

In China, the tree was trained into the now familiar bonsai. The practice, which dates back as far as 1,600 BC with the Shang dynasty, is an attempt to slow down the life of the

Shaman

tree and therefore render it a symbol of immortality. The Immortals of the Chinese were called the Hsien, or the Eight Immortals the part-Hsien. They were believed to live in the sacred mountains and hold the secrets of life. They looked into the nature of trees as being the elixir of life, a practice remarkably similar to the alchemists of Europe and the Middle East.

In Persia and Egypt, the trend caught on from the Chinese, showing that spiritual and philosophical ideas were widespread. The Chinese scholars and mandarins known as the 'Literati' were a sacred and secretive group. They travelled broadly and were the first to develop calligraphy in China.

Much like Thoth, the Egyptian god of writing.

Australian aborigines say that a tree once joined the Earth to Heaven. It is hardly surprising that nomadic aborigines should hold the tree to be incredibly important when we consider that it was, and still is, vital to their lifestyle.

Across the world, the tree has been employed in divination, whether by using the twigs or branches as tools for water divination or testing love by placing two acorns in a bowl of water and 'reading' the result. Not surprisingly, hazel rods are preferred for dowsing.

From Asia to Africa, the Mediterranean to Europe, the fig tree has been venerated as the tree of plenty. The Roman god Dionysus was attributed the fig tree. Muhammad swore on it and Buddha is said by some to have found enlightenment under the pipul or fig tree. Adam and Eve covered themselves with the leaves of the fig and some believe it to be the 'forbidden fruit'. Tradition has Judas Iscariot hanging from a fig tree, infesting it forever with evil spirits, although other traditions have Jesus sheltering from the rain under the leafy branches.[4]

Burnt ashes from trees are said to be sacred. The Aztecs of South America and the Brahmins of India rub ash into their skin when preparing for ceremonies. In Jewish and Christian folklore, sackcloth and ashes are a sign of humility. The Palm Sunday practice of burning palm leaves and scattering the ashes on the heads of the congregation or simply making the sign of the cross on the forehead is reminiscent of various cultures around the globe especially in Africa.

In the Gnostic Jewish cult of the Qabalah, the Tree of Life (taken originally from the Shaman's World Tree) is symbolic of

many things; the junction of the three worlds, water, earth and heaven, in exactly the same way as the Norse Yggdrasil. In Norse myth, the Serpent of Midgard wraps itself around the tree. The snake also appears in the Garden of Eden. In Sumerian myth the serpent represents the fertilisation of Mother Earth.

To some, the tree symbolises the 'Mother Earth' side of nature and the sheltering protection she offers. The Qabalistic Tree of Life is both the Tree of Life and Tree of Knowledge from Eden and is therefore symbolic of both the knowledge of good and evil and regeneration or rebirth. Trees are also believed to have developed eventually into the pillars of stone megaliths.

In ancient folklore, the dying god is almost always killed on a tree and so too is Christ. The biblical word for the Cross on which Christ was killed actually means tree. It was common practice for the Romans to crucify using trees. In fact, it was unusual to crucify using a cross beam. Jesus died fittingly on the symbol of re-birth and regeneration. He probably faced east, the direction of the rising sun, although as he died at sundown, he would have had his back to the dying sun, symbolically ignoring death but also facing it. Jesus therefore died, as above and so below, as the sun dies, it also rises again. We shall look into this aspect in more detail later on.

The fruit of the apple tree is said to confer immortality. Heracles went in search of the apples of Hesperides, the fruit of eternal life. The apple of Asgard guarantees perpetual youth. Some say that the apple was the forbidden fruit of Eden, although Genesis does not say what the fruit was, some say the fig, which is symbolic of sexuality; although it is as likely to have been an apple because of its inference of sexual and carnal knowledge links it with similar uses of apples in other mythologies: the golden apple of Aphrodite; the Hellenistic belief that the apple gives sexual prowess and knowledge. In Greece, the tossed apple was an invitation for sex. Three golden apples thrown were by Hippomenes at the feet of Atalanta, who wins the race. The Celtic 'Conle' is given the irresistible desire to enjoy the pleasures of the Celtic fairyland by an apple. The apple is globally used in sacred rites and religious practices from the Druids of Europe to the priests of Haiti, America, Scandinavia and Greece.

The crucifixion of Christ

The Yew tree has also crept into popular superstition. The ancient Britons planted Yew trees close to their Temples prior to the introduction of Christianity. The custom is not thought to have been Roman, as evidence shows that the Yew became the funeral tree of the Celts after it had already been used as a Temple tree.8

A Greek Orthodox legend tells of the importance and hints at the secret Masonic understanding of the cross of Christ. The legend goes that on his death bed Adam asked his son Seth to go and ask a cherub for some fruit from the Tree of Life. The cherub refused, but gave him a branch with three twigs instead. Seth planted this branch at the head of his father's grave. Years later Hiram, the master mason and architect of Solomon's Temple, had the now fully-grown tree cut down for use in building the Temple. Because the devil had persuaded Hiram to cut down the tree, when it actually arrived on site, the architect rejected it because of its inferior building qualities, and had the tree thrown east from Jerusalem where it later served as a foot bridge. Later tradition says that the Queen of Sheba refused to walk upon the sacred bridge because she knew of its origin. Solomon then had the trunk brought into the Temple where it remained until it was used to crucify Christ.[9]

The symbolism of this tale is rich. There is an underlying story which revolves around the tree. There were three twigs sent from the Tree of Life - the trinity. Planted at the head - pineal, Kether. The devil wanted the growing tree cut down, causing a sin to be used in the building of the Temple of Solomon. The architect was too clever - masons should, therefore, be as knowledgeable as Hiram to obtain True Life from the Tree of Life. The 'Son of the Tree of Life' was thrown east towards the rising sun and towards new life and rebirth. The Tree was then used during its next life as a foot bridge for the people of God, the most humble of services, and later as the Tree of both death and life in the crucifixion of Christ.

This example shows that we should always be aware that there is more than one meaning to most religious stories or fables. Myths hold deeper secrets of the beliefs of man and can highlight how old some beliefs are and how they are interlinked. This Greek Orthodox story, which includes Masonic beliefs, also has links with older Islamic beliefs.

There are more links between faiths, beliefs and religions than

their stories. One other sacred, and universal, aspect is the use of numbers. These hold secrets at deeper levels and often need a trained eye to reveal the true meanings.

There is not one faith on the planet which does not in some way respect, revere or attach mystical significance to numbers. In some cases, their symbolism is beyond the science of modern man, and in others the secrets are known but kept hidden from the populace. Some would have us believe that God's existence can be proven via mathematics, and maybe that is part of what the ancients were up to with their weaving of patterns and strange hidden passages in the pages of the Bible and elsewhere.[6,7]

Tales of Simon the Just from the Holy Land show how numbers are included in stories for the initiated. Simon's basic teaching was that 'there are three foundations of the universe: the Law, Worship and Almsgiving'. Simon was led by the initiated Shining Ones. We will come to understand who and what these people were as time goes by.

When entering the Holy of Holies, the most sacred place any priest could enter, Simon was always accompanied by an angel (which means 'messenger'). This angel took the form of an aged man, with a beard (symbolic of so many things), and was always dressed from head to foot in white, just as the Shining Ones always are. It may be that the story of the angel wearing black prior to his death was a sign of disapproval or respect, the meaning is unclear. Suffice to say that this image of Simon is a sacred and mystical one and anything attributed to him should be taken seriously. The fact that 'three' is paramount in Simon's most famous of sayings is important. We shall come to see just how widespread this idea of three is.

In Hinduism, Brahma is the absolute Godhead. With the

partners Vishnu and Siva (Shiva), they are called the Divine Triad, or Trinity, and have become a three-headed deity. The supposed origin of Hinduism is Jainism. In the Sacred Book of the Jainas we have an example of the threes. 'One should ever make his own self radiant by the light of the three jewels,' says the book with all the secret teachings for those with the eyes to see and minds open enough to understand. For us to truly understand, to see the light, to be 'enlightened', we must utilise the three jewels. They should be followed every moment, without ceasing. The three jewels in question are right belief, right knowledge and right conduct.

In Buddhism we have the Three Fires of greed, hatred and delusion. These are the key reasons why people are tied to the perpetual rebirth. Along with the Three Marks of impermanence, suffering and substance built into everything, making everything futile and pointless, we should, therefore, follow the Three Jewels and escape. In Buddhist belief the Three Jewels, similar to the Hindu, release us from the clutch of rebirth. The initiate would say, 'I go for refuge to the Buddha...to the dharma...and to the sangha.' They are the path to enlightenment: the father, son and spirit.

The ancient Druids, successors to and practitioners of the Shining Ones ways, held belief in a holy triad: the Infinite Light or Beli, the Illuminated Man and the Finite Intermediary

A modern image of a druid

or Taran. Again these are much the same as the Hindu and Jainist and Christian beliefs. The Shamans of Central Asia believed in the same triad or trinity and held a similar Druidic belief in the three worlds of heaven or underworld, earth and sky. This 'threefold world' belief is an indication of the origin of the Shining Ones, it is the historical beginning of the major beliefs and traces directly back to Bon-po in Central Asia.

It is no long stretch of the imagination to suggest that with the disciples of the Bible, known contacts with European and Asian countries and their vast learning, they did not at least hear of these Druidic and Shamanistic Triads, not to mention the Hindu and many other beliefs in trinities. Neither is it a long shot to suggest that the trinity of Christianity was probably instigated to include as many pagans or 'Gentiles' as possible. It may also be true that Christianity was being led by the Shining One priesthood and therefore included the trinity because that is what its beliefs were. The Druids took on Christian beliefs in a Gnostic way and symbolised the Christian trinity with Yesu (now of course 'Jesus') carved on the right branch of a tree, Beli (or shining one) on the left and Taran at the centre.

The Shamans of history often went into the Underworld via trances which lasted three days, symbolically escaping the cave like womb as in re-birth. The Shaman, incidentally, would rise to the Sky-World via a great notched tree ladder.

The Taoist tradition, in the forty second chapter of the Lao-tzu, gives the statement of Cosmic Gestation with the following words:-

'The Tao gave birth to the One
The One gave birth to the Two
The Two gave birth to the Three'
The Three gave birth to the myriad creatures.'

Even as far away as China we have the trinity needed to create life. The rites from this are called Feng-teng or 'Dividing the new fire or light', and are all tied up in cyclic and cosmic renewal patterns.

The T'ai-chi is represented by three candles, the immanent moving Tao of nature, yin and yang. They represent the Three Spirits of the Transcendent Tao working in that nature. The language differs from the more European Threes, but the basic elements are the same. There is also evidence of a cross cultural link in the duality/yin and yang essences in Genesis 8:22:

'While the earth lasts seedtime and harvest, cold and heat, summer and winter, day and night,
shall never cease.'
(The New English Bible)

Again, the language translates into Indo-European British in different ways, but the basic dualistic beliefs remain the same and similar Chinese poems can be found.

The gods of classical Greece ruled over a threefold world of heaven, sea and Earth with the trinity of gods, Zeus, Poseidon and Hades, which then became the Roman pagan trinity of Jupiter, Neptune and Pluto. In Norse myth, the place of Asgard had three high thrones waiting to be claimed. In most fairytales we have the threefold repetition of an action as this seems to be important. The fairytale of the three golden sons is global in various forms and is steeped in symbolism, which at childlike face value would not be seen. The myth includes astrologers being tossed into water in the form of children, the birds of truth, the water of life and a singing, knowledgeable tree.

Zeus

In the 1920's the French scholar Georges Dumezil argued that all religions are made up of pantheons of deities which always fall into three distinct groups: kingship or priest, which is known as first function; warriors ,or second functions; and supplier, giver or third function. His Indo-European links were strong and need not be repeated in full here. The idea of a trinity on a global scale, however, shows more than just a dissolution theory. It shows a well thought out plan actually happening. A plan which is subtle and almost hidden from us, but not from those with the eyes to see.

There are many other important numbers, such as twelve, which will become apparent in the next few chapters. Twelve includes the tribes of Israel, the months of the years, the collective gods of Scandinavia, the Aesir, the Greek Amphictyonic League of tribes and the Greek pantheon had twelve members, and there are many more examples, as we shall see.

Another element we should watch out for is that of animals. They were used widely in various images, from the Sun God Ra of the Egyptians as the Ram and Ass to the global Bull cults of the world which strongly indicate the existence of the Moon Goddess in this cult. Within these animal rituals there are beliefs and practices; strong ancient links which need to be drawn out.

Of course we must not forget mountains, burial practices, magic and the vast array of sacred symbolism, such as crosses, all of which make up a vast network of

Brahma, Vishnu and Siva – the trinity of the Hindu faith.

ancient links in the story of our unseen past.

The next chapter will show us how the various ancient cultures have shared, for a very long time, more beliefs than we would assume. These beliefs are shared for a reason: the ancient worldly priesthood of the Shining Ones; the manipulators of our past, present and future.

Notes
Chapter 4

1   Page 110. Ancient Traces. Michael Baigent. Viking. 1998.
2   Late Quarternary Sea-level Changes and Archaeology. Andel.
3   The Forest of Symbols (taken from the book Signs, Symbols and Ciphers - Decoding the Message) Victor Turner. New Horizons. 1998
4   Dictionary of World Folklore. Alison Jones. Larousse. 1995.
5   Red Ochre or Haematite/Hematite. Oxide of iron, crystallising in the trigonal system. Occurs in many forms rhombohedral crystals from Elba, bedded ores of sedimentary origin from pre-Cambrian world. Also as a cement and pigment from sandstone. (Dictionary of Science and Technology, Wordsworth). According to The Paranormal by Stuart Gordon the Aborigines of Australia knew how to smelt the yellow hydrated iron oxide to produce this red ochre which is a form of magnetite mentioned earlier in chapter 1 and 2. Is there some link here between the migratory ideas of early man and his knowledge in an almost alchemical way of red ochre?
6   Proof. Radikal Phase Publishing House Ltd, Underwood, Notts. P. Gardiner. 2002
7   God's Secret Formula. Peter Plichta. Element. 1997.
8   The Origins of Popular Superstitions and Customs. T. Sharper Knowlson. T. Werner Laurie Ltd. 1930.
9   Folklore of the Holy Land. J.E. Hanauer. The Sheldon Press. 1907. The tale is included in this book although the interpretation is only possible by having a knowledge of all the symbolism and myths, just as the story explains that the masons should seek knowledge as a way to obtain True Life.

Chapter 5
Light from Darkness

We can trace the development of the Shining Ones priesthood back to one specific place, via Christianity, Judaism, Jainism, Hinduism, Egyptology, Babylonian myths and even South American sky worship.

This new understanding throws light onto many areas, including the supposedly spontaneous eruption of similar beliefs and ideas around the globe, the fact that so many of our beliefs today are basically the same, and the extraordinary links between the various buildings and monuments of early man.

Through investigation into the spread of ancient belief, via the Shining Ones, we shall discover how and why man built these wonderful monuments and for what purpose they were used. We shall also see the process ancient man went through when using monoliths and megaliths.

But why did this belief system spread so easily? Why do the New Age mystics of the modern world have such an easy job convincing us of the ancient wisdom? The answers to these questions come from the realisation that humans are more in touch with the universe, the Earth and the hidden forces around us than we can comprehend. Our modern sensibilities and rationalism have taken us further away from this. It is no longer logical to believe in the sun as the god of life and light, and yet in some respects we must understand, even scientifically, that this is true. The sun is not a god, but it does

give us light and life and without it we would die. The word 'god' is simply a term used without the existence of rationalism and science.

Ancient man had no scientific understanding of the electromagnetic current around the globe. He understood it in his own way, just as he understood the cycles of life through his rituals and dramas. He began to take on the more mystical aspects of life, to organise them into specific groups and utilise 'special' people who were more 'in tune'. These special people were sometimes attributed powers of foresight, the ability to predict weather patterns - as do many birds - and to decipher foreign languages.

Weather predictions would have been essential to the agriculturally evolving hunter-gatherers and would have demanded a high price. This sometimes involved human or animal sacrifice, and there is much

Mithraic sun god

evidence to support this. The sacrifice of bulls and rams became widespread, especially within the cult of Mithra (the festival of Mithra takes place on December 25th), where bathing in the blood of the sacrifice was considered to have a redemptive effect. The saying from the Roman world was, 'by the bull-sacrifice and the ram-sacrifice, born again for eternity'. There is evidence that they believed the act of sacrifice would give new life; a perfect opportunity to continue the cycle of life, a cycle which was to be revisited in the Christian passion play.

The priesthood or Shamans (they had many names across the globe such as 'Ollave' in Ireland and the Celtic Bard or Druid) would have appeared awesome and godlike to the people of the tribes and it is no wonder that in later years many legendary figures were actually deified, adding to the growing pantheon. They were vessels of knowledge, living books of the past.

A kind of hybridisation took place from real priest/kings to gods or giants. In Genesis we have unique examples of this. 'The sons of God saw the daughters of men, that they were fair; and took them wives...and there were giants in the earth in those days', Gen. 6:1. Is this the idea that man has degenerated and actually reduced in stature since those ancient days?

Ogmios
Giant god

These were the 'men of renown', men from days long past, with mighty powers who still

held the people in awe. The Anakim were the race of giants in Joshua's day (Joshua 14:15) and the Antediluvian Nephilim in Gen. 6:4, Num. 13:32 and Deut 1:28. The King of Bashan (Josh 12:4) Og, was 'of the remnant of the Rephaim'.

Tradition has it that Og lived for 3,000 years and walked beside the Ark during the flood. Phonetically similar to Og is the Sumerian Ogma, who has been linked with the Cerne Abbas giant land picture in England. This in turn has been linked with Dyaeus, which means 'the Shining One' or Dyaus Pitar the 'Shining Father'. This is a Sanskrit term for 'father' and links remarkably to the Dyaus Pitar of the Indo-European Shaman origin where great sacrifices were made towards this great god or Shining Father.

According to Greek mythology, the giants were the 'sons of the earth' (Greek, 'Ge genis' = sons of earth) which would link with the Hebrew sons of God, the switch between matriarch and patriarch. The Greek giants, the sons of Uranus and Gaea, the Mother Goddess, fell to earth from the blood of Uranus in much the same manner as the angels of the Hebrews, who also were against the gods.

In Irish mythology, the giants were actual gods who had fallen from heaven, and in Nordic legend they fought against the gods. Most giants are said to live below the ground, which is symbolically a cave, the dwelling of the Shamans, and are said to possess the powers of the Earth Goddess. The modern image of the slow and stupid giant is at odds with ancient symbolism; it is very likely that this may have been an attempt by the Christian church to dispel the worship or reverence of the old ways.

The 'Cader Idris' or 'Seat of the Giants' in Gymedd, Wales is where Idris, the Welsh prince and astronomer, is said to have

sat in the distant past. This shows the belief that these ancient people of stature were once our leaders, had a deeper understanding of the stars than we do and came from the gods.

Most giants are said to be bearded. The reason for this becomes clear when we discover the significance of the beard. It is primarily the ancient symbol of manhood and power, which eventually became the symbol for wisdom, authority and even divinity.

We find in old literature that many insults against rivals were derived from the lack of a beard. This is why Egyptian rulers always wore beards, whether real or false. Queen Hatshepsut is known to have worn a false beard on Egyptian State occasions as symbol of her divinity and power. Pharaohs' tomb masks display long beards, which show their divinity after human death. Baal the Canaanite and pre-Judaic god was bearded and this may be one of the reasons  we today imagine our God to have a white beard. Another reason for this is that El (meaning 'Shining One' or more simply 'God'), the Canaanite high god or 'creator of created things' also wore a beard. El later became the Hebrew creator god (Elohim) and Yahweh. El was married to Asherah, as Jewish tradition has Yahweh married to the Mother Earth, and the symbol of El was a bull showing his power and might.

The significance of beards dates back much earlier than the Egyptians. The magic of the Shamans often used the beard, and most Shamans were seen with beards. This magic comes through in the Biblical story of Samson and Delilah, where Samson loses his strength when he loses his beard. All the prophets of God, including Jesus, wore beards. The Essenes especially wore beards. The Knights Templars and many more carried on this tradition.

Many of our traditions and images seem to have developed from Shamanism. The term 'Shaman' is said to come from the Sanskrit 'sramana' 'one who knows', or possibly a Slavonic term denoting the practice of the Samoyeds of Siberia and meaning 'to become excited'. The Shaman was able to deal with otherworldly powers and speak with the gods in much the same way as all the prophets of later religions. He or she was able to heal using ancient and secret techniques.

It has been said that Shamans were the first to interpret the 'secret currents' or 'ways' of life.2 These healing ways were sometimes effected by the use of herbs and other plants and sometimes from the 'secret ways' of the Shamans. The 'secret ways' used the knowledge of our bodies' electromagnetism, earth energies and possibly kinds of acupuncture. They would understand the cycles and the balances required, and apparently miraculously heal their patient. Today, Holistic practitioners use electromagnetic meters and electric impulses to monitor, measure and administer in similar ways.

Early explorers often called these Shaman 'medicine men'. When America was 'discovered', the Indian Shamans were called medicine men, highlighting the existence of the priest/king/doctor figure. Many of their ways were highly reminiscent of Alchemy. In Greece, 'circa.' the 6th century BC, the Shamans were called 'iatromantis' which means 'physician and soothsayer'.

Shamans were known as 'travellers of the air', an allusion to their flying abilities; 'purifiers', the obvious term for their baptismal skills; 'thamaturgus' (which means 'miracle worker' and was applied to the Christian Saints in later years); and

'Speaker of Oracles' for their prophetic show of knowledge. Like the Essenes of later years, they abstained from alcohol and sex, and lived an ascetic life. To control their hunger they ate a plant called 'alimos' (meaning 'not hungry'), which has been compared to the coca leaf of the Peruvians. Their beliefs were in the physical body and the spiritual soul, which travelled to the place of Apollo. They carried out their healing by entertaining the power of the spirit of Apollo to keep the body alive. Falling out of favour with Apollo would bring illness, and only the Shaman could restore this favour, as saviour and purifier.

'Medicine man' was just one aspect of the Shaman's role. It may have been that at some point in the past these roles were split between the priesthood as they were in the Hebrew history. According to some, with archaeological finds we have all mankind's ancient myths under one idea in the Shaman.10 The magic of the Shaman is the ability, or seeming ability, to manipulate nature to his or her own ends.

From the early days of Shamanism, high places, such as mountains and trees, were important, and linked to the idea of getting closer to the gods or ancestral spirits. North American Shamans are suspended by their wrists, hooked through the flesh in the style of crucifixion. The pain is believed, by many ancient cultures and Gnostics, to bring on the trance and move one closer to a knowledge of god. In Norse mythology, the god Odin gained knowledge with the same method of self-sacrifice as he hung from a spear impaled upon the World tree of Yggdrasil, the Tree of Life. He visited the Underworld for this knowledge, and gained powers of raising the dead, prophesy, shape shifting and flying.

The parallels are obvious. Christ was risen from the dead after his ordeal. He could foretell the future, and after he had been resurrected, he shape shifted, as he had previously been flogged to the point of being unrecognisable, and yet after his resurrection there is no mention of the awful state in which he would have been. He visited the Other-world in his symbolic death and following his 'otherworldly' ministry he 'flew' off to Heaven. This 'cross' ritual is highly reminiscent of Hindu temple rituals where arms are outstretched and the initiate receives salvation from the gods. Trance-like states are common to all faiths and can be traced back directly to the ancient Shaman or early magic man of our pre-historic relatives, to early 'grove rituals' and the secret mysteries of the druids.

Cave paintings, from as far back as 17,000 years ago, show the rituals and trance states of the Shaman. The tribe or group would go to a black cave, symbolic of the womb, and enter the ecstasy via dances. The hypnotic and evocative sounds of the leather drums, the eerie, flickering light from a single flame and the Shaman's mystical chanting would all add to the mystery. Often, these vision-inducing trances were brought on by fasting and here we must be reminded of the Biblical prophets who went away into the wilderness, sometimes into caves, and fasted for days on end. Later they would return with some great and mystifying word of god. Another aspect was that during a vision a Shaman can understand the words spoken by a foreigner. Trilles, an investigator into Shamanism noted:

'During one of our voyages with Le Roy, we arrived at a village one evening and met a witch doctor who described to us in detail the route we had taken, the stops we had made, various meetings, the food we ate and even the conversation we exchanged. Here is a typical example: On the way we came across a small tortoise and Le Roy said, "There's tonight's dinner", and because we were very hungry, I added, laughing:

"And if necessary we'll add the guide's head to it!" We were speaking French, so the witch doctor could not have understood a word, yet, without budging from his village, he had seen us in his magic mirror and repeated everything we said.'12

In the Bible we have the interpretation of languages in Acts, when the spirit came down upon the disciples. This shows how the prophets and apostles were inheritors of the Shaman knowledge. The people were in the service of the shaman and self-elected priest-king, and this may explain how such monuments as Stonehenge and the structures of Central and South America could have been built.

Quetzalcoatl

Quetzalcoatl, the pre-Columbian god of air and water, the creator god, is the essence of a Shaman. His magical and creative abilities, in the use of blood and sacrifice and in his clothing, all show his origins. He is the great white bearded god. He came to the shores long ago in pre-history and it is very likely (especially with the travels of Thor Heyerdahl) that he travelled from Europe with a retinue and brought the ancient tradition with him to South and Central America, long before Columbus.

Trilles also tells us about Shaman and how 'It is possible that tribal unity and awareness could be much stronger than we think, sustained by the activities of the priests, magicians and singers who go from tribe to tribe, rediscover them, visit them, as if called in some unaccountable way - through their mysterious sciences.' They travelled widely, were respected, maintained tribal unity and used the mysterious sciences. The

Shaman used words and names as if they were sent from God. Simply naming a man would have him dead and this idea of the 'word' being the power carried on explicitly in the Bible to the prophets and the fact that Jesus would cast out demons with just a word and, indeed, how Jesus eventually evolved into 'The Word' himself.

We also have the Biblical story of Shadrach, Mesach and Abednego, great magicians for the Lord, who were bound and tossed into the heated flames of a furnace (Book of Daniel) and emerged completely unharmed. Shamans are said to be able to control the laws of physics and simply cast off the pain of such a torment. On Fiji they eat a delicacy called the 'masawe' root. The cooking of this root is called the 'vilavilareivo' ceremony, which means 'he who enters the furnace'. Many other tribes actually do enter the flames in the practice known as fire walking. Initially, this was the role of the Shaman, who would amaze people with his powers over nature, as did the three magicians of Daniel.

The aim of the Shaman was to free his thoughts from his physical body. In the same way that Buddhists and Hindus try to achieve this result, the Shaman attempts to 'remove the obstacles'. To become what is known as an 'Angakok' (phonetically similar to Annakim and Anannage), he must call down the positive power of god. Just as the spirit touched the apostles and flames licked above their heads, so too this powerful spirit comes upon the Shaman and is called 'gaumanek' which means 'illuminated' or 'shining'. The Shaman literally becomes the Shining One on earth.

'....a mysterious light which the shaman suddenly feels in his body, inside his head, within his brain, an inexplicable searchlight, a luminous fire, which enables him to see in the dark, both literally and metaphorically speaking, for he can now, even with closed eyes, see through darkness and perceive things and coming events which are hidden from others.'13

There is nothing different here from the experiences of the Biblical prophets, the Egyptian priesthood and the Hindu and Buddhist monks. Enlightenment is experienced in much the same manner the world over.

The Shaman also regularly takes himself away from the tribe into solitude to contemplate nature and god. This is common to many of the faiths of the world. It is essential for these people to move away from their tribe or town for some time. This may have been a time when they met up with others of their kind who had also withdrawn to the wilderness. Even today, we have pastors and priests who take themselves away on retreats to be alone with God, and to exchange ideas with like-minded men of the cloth.

Many Shaman express moments of great spirituality. They experience times of joy and sadness, comparable to those experienced by Christians in the western world; the Toronto Blessing is a perfect example.14 In the midst of these experiences they gain their 'gaumaneg', their enlightenment or 'shining'. Whilst contemplating beneath a tree, Gautama became the Buddha, or enlightened one. Jesus took himself away on Gethsemane and was saddened by the thought of his death, but coming back he was enlightened and able to continue his work.

Like Moses, the Shaman was not just a prophet of the most high god, he was a magician and sorcerer with his Caduceus staff and divination skills. He was able to descend to the depths of hell, as was Jesus, and return once again. And, like many a prophet of other future faiths, he could ascend to whichever of the seven stages of Heaven he needed to go. Celtic representations of meditating man and other Druidic similarities show us that this Shamanistic belief spread throughout the known world, and this is basically why future additions to the tenets of the Shaman were readily accepted worldwide.

Shamanism is still alive today in comparative cultures such as that of the American and South American Indian, African, Central Asian and Siberian. Here, he performs his roles, and his soul ascends ritualistically to heaven during an ecstasy probably brought on by narcotics, meditation or sacred dancing. The belief takes the form of a duality of good and evil, light and dark. This carried on into the major religions, all of which have this dualistic belief at their core.

According to Ward Rutherford, there is evidence to suggest that the religion of the Shaman spread with the Bon-po religion of Tibet.[1] In this Bon religion, the Shaman controlled three worlds. A bull image represented Sky God, and presided over sacrifices for him. There was also an Earth Goddess and a smaller pantheon, along with early beliefs in reincarnation. They originated in what is now called Tibet, and this seems to have been the birthplace of the Shining Ones' belief system and probably even the original school of the priests.

From Tibet and Central Asia came Hinduism and eventually Buddhism with their many Devas, which, incidentally, is Sanskrit for 'Shining One'. In Hinduism, a Deva is a group of exalted beings. There are three kinds of Deva: enlightened mortals, spiritually superior mortals and Brahman (the first of the divine Triad of Vishnu, Shiva and Brahman). In Buddhism Devas are gods and reside in heaven. According to modern mystics, the Devas arrived on earth before humans and remained dormant until we reached the appropriate level of

evolution.

Deva

In the Hindu 'Mahabharat', the tale of ancient India, we find much in common with Egyptian and Sumerian cults and also a remarkable indication of the crossing of language between Hindu and Celtic. 'Mahab' is Hindu for tale or history and the Celtic 'Mab' is the same, such as the 'Mabinogion', which is the Celtic version of their history.

The Hindu scriptures were written by a priestly elite called Brahmans, who probably evolved from part of the Shining One culture. According to Simon Weightman in the Handbook of Living Religions, Brahmans were 'unrepresentative of the beliefs and practices of the great majority of Hindus at any given time'.3 Therefore the scriptures and teachings were not commonly practised, yet history would have us believe differently.

The Chandogya Upanishad Instruction Concerning Brahma tells us, 'That, indeed, is below. It is above....It indeed is the whole world.....The Soul, indeed, is below. The Soul is above.' This is the beginnings of the Hermetic, 'As above, so below'. In Hinduism, the first of the 'I am' god statements comes from the Upanishads. Upanishads means secret teachings, and was not meant to be shared. Later we find that the Song of Solomon, a collection of various canticles dating to about the 5th century is actually a virtual re-writing of earlier Hindu mystic poems.

There is new evidence emerging from Takla Makan in Central

Asia, of the use of similar types of woollen cloths between the Celts of Europe and the Chinese. Also, the mummies which have been found are physically the same as the standard red haired Celts of 3,000 years ago. The Celtic cross with the winding snake is extremely similar, if not identical, to Hindu Votive tablets and later Persian seals, and is reminiscent of the Caduceus, which is the title of a number of wands appearing in Mesopotamian cultures around 2,600 BC. It consists, as do the Hindu and Celtic images, of two serpents twisting around a rod or staff. In later Roman times it became the wand of Mercury who was associated with Hermes and Thoth, whose relevance shall become apparent. The two snakes represent two dualistic chakra energies from the Hindu beliefs, spiralling up the spine to the brain. In medieval times, we see this image repeated in the Cabalists' Tree of Life.

In northern Europe, similar fertility rituals to those found near Takla Makan have been discovered, which also show the local Tocharican language of Central Asia to be similar to European languages of the time. Not only that, but the mummified remains of the local elite were also bearded. This is strong evidence that long distance, cross-cultural travel and commerce were possible, and actually happened. This does not, however, only concern travel and commerce. The rituals and symbols are the same. Behind the front of trade and commerce, behind any politics, we have the similarity of ritual and symbolism and, therefore, religion or belief. The basic beliefs, even as recently as 3,000 years ago, are the same. This shows that same beliefs are being cultivated, across thousands of miles over long periods of time. The Bon-po religion and Shamanism date back to 50,000 BC.

Hinduism is probably the oldest religion on the planet. Within the Hindu tradition there are many beliefs, which stem from the many localities and probably the huge trade that has spread historically through the country. The basic elements of the Hindu faiths are not only fundamentally the same throughout, they are also the same as those in the rest of the world. With Hinduism, we see the evolution of the Shaman or Shining One idea being added to by various leaders, politicians (to help them become gods) and priests to control the masses and keep them happy.

The core elements of the Shining Ones' ways have always remained, and it is this hidden belief for which we are searching. In the Hindu tradition we find some of the old familiar beliefs, now so common to us from other religions and cults. Female goddess, Male god (here known as Shiva, one of the trinity), animals, trees, purification by water, fire sacrifice, Shamanistic trances induced by Soma (a plant believed to heighten spiritual awareness, also used later by Zoroastrians and called the plant of illumination), a trinity and marking the date of birth so that a horoscope may be drawn up. In the Bhagavad Gita (4:5-11) we have some striking similarities.

'I have been born many times, Arjuna, and many times hast thou been born. But I remember my past lives, and thou has forgotten thine.
'Although I am unborn, everlasting, and I am the Lord of all, I come to my realm of nature and through my wondrous power I am born.
'When righteousness is weak and faints and unrighteousness exults in pride, then my spirit arises on earth.
'For the salvation of those who are good, for the destruction of evil in man, for the fulfilment of the kingdom of righteousness, I come to this world in the ages that pass.'

These same beliefs are carried on in Buddhism. The Buddhist 'Bodhisattvas', regarded as enlightened or shining beings, actually refused to go to Heaven, and chose to help out

mankind or set things in order. They were actually thought of as 'Amida' or Saviours, and the process that they undertake guarantees the return of the future saviour, who is also expected by Christianity, Islam, Judaism and many more faiths.4 Virgil, writing 19 years before the birth of Christ, recorded the widespread belief in the expected individual Messiah who would rule a peaceful world. The only difference here is that we see the cyclical nature being taken into account more strongly, with repeated effects, although this too will end one day.

There is much to link Christ to the Buddha: purification by water, receiving enlightenment at the age of thirty, the Temples of Brahma (especially the 'Svarga' Brahma Temple, Alampur 7th century 5) in the same format as the Cross-shaped churches of Christianity, the cross itself as a symbol, the trinity and God as One (Bhagvan ek hai, same as Islam), the number twelve and much more.

Buddha said,
'Who sees dhamma sees me. Who sees me sees dhamma', Christ said, 'If you had known Me, you would have known My Father also; and from now on you know Him and have seen Him.'7

Buddha sent us on the path to the truth, the way to life with his eightfold path to righteousness. The way of the truth can only be through the Three Training's, morality, concentration and wisdom, all these focus the mind on to the path. To do this we must practice yoga or 'yoke' ourselves (Jesus said to take his yoke), and obtain the help of the 'Siddhis', or powers. These are what we now call the paranormal, telepathy, feats of memory and magical powers, all of which are related to and used in many, if not all, of the other faiths.

Traditionally, Buddha was said to have fought many magical battles, as did Moses and others in the Bible. Other more Shamanistic acts were carried out by the Buddha, such as shape shifting, which we can also find in other traditions around the globe, especially related to the other Shaman beliefs. The remarkable links with Christianity become more apparent when we remember that until approximately 500 AD the Christians also believed in reincarnation, and many strange traditions are attributed to the magic and Shamanistic acts of the Apostles. Later, Jesus and his 'advisors' came to be influenced by these earlier writings and used them in their own recruiting zeal.

This early belief system also had influences on other religions. The first of the dead, born from the Sun, the judge of men and king of the dead is called Yama. His kingdom is Paradise where those of his family and friends will be reunited one day. Anyone who is familiar with the Bible will see the similarities here. There is much evidence to suggest that the ascetics and early Gnostics, if not Jesus himself, actually visited Tibet and the surrounding area. In the Mandala, or Circle, we can see the symbol of the universal cycle that the beliefs shared. This is a Hindu and Buddhist image later shared with Chinese, Japanese and European Gnosticism and Alchemy.

In the 'Rig Veda' (rig = songs, veda = sacred or secret), we have the Hindu Agni as a sage, priest, king, protector and father. He is commissioned by men to convey our messages to god by going up to heaven. He is in essence a Shaman and Shining One. No surprise when we find out that Agni means 'The Shining One', so that 'he may illuminate the nights'. Agni inhabits the mist between human and god, he is the historical blurring of the point at which man ceases to be man and moves through the magical powers of the pen and the mind into that holy place of godhead. He is an example of how a

Shining One, an actual person, takes on the likeness of a god.

Some of the Upanishads writings make sense when placed against the future alchemy. We can see in them what the alchemists saw when they looked back at these 'secret teachings'. 'They will then be purified by the Light of the inner Reality, and that Light will be revealed.' This purification process took on many forms. Symbolically, it became gold in alchemy.

A few examples from the Hindu scriptures will help us see where some of the future faiths got their ideas.

'I have known beyond all darkness, that great Person of golden Shining. Only by knowing him does one conquer death'
'He is the great Light shining forever.'
'He is the Light that gives Light to all. He shining, everything shines'
'Light of all lights'
'He dwells within all'

The Chakra, a Sanskrit term meaning 'wheel', are thought of today as points of energy on the human body. They distribute the universal pranic energy around the body, in much the same way as the idea that the spirit of god enters our body and distributes itself, making all of our being pure and holy. This energy is seen in swirls of colour, which, when we take into account the colour aspect of the chakra on our forehead, the crown or pineal gland can be understood in a more scientific, if controversial, way. Those who aim to see this energy are trained over many years of meditation and hard strenuous labour. It is not something that can be tried in a laboratory, or tested by us at home. Drugs may be used to induce this sight, but only after much training. To see these energy points helps the healing process and measures our spiritual progression.

In China, acupuncture techniques may have something to do with being able to see these energies. The flames raising from the heads of the spiritually cleansed Apostles in Acts may be a symbolical sign of this effect. After all the head, being the crown, Kether, and considered in all cultures to be the vehicle for the soul, would be the place to symbolise this fire for god, the choosing of the shining ones.

In Buddhism, we eventually have the 'Enlightened One' with the small dot on the forehead and all the other commonly shared basic beliefs that Buddhism entails, with threes, twelves, Sun and Earth Gods. The idea that Buddha is not one man, but one of many, is an indication that there are or were many other Enlightened or Shining Ones, and, like Buddha said, there are more to come, perhaps set up by the same sacred and elite priesthood, which seems to have set up the others.

In Jainism, which probably dates from only 2,500 years ago, roughly the same time as Buddhism, and stems from the same area, we have an even more remarkable cross fertilisation of ideas which raises the question did any of these people actually exist or were they just one man?

The available Sanskrit sources show us the practice of life-cycle rituals as do all the other early traditions. They conceive time in vast cyclic terms as do the Hindu and Buddhist faiths. These particular traditions tell us that in each half-cycle there will appear twenty-four great teachers, 'Jinas' or 'Tirthankaras', much like Buddha or Amida. The word 'Jinas' is phonetically similar to the Assyro-Babylonian 'genius' or 'jinn'. These were superhuman guardians or saviours, which later became the jinn of the Islamic world, a class of spirits, formed by the fire and living on the sacred mountains (Heaven) of Kaf which encircle the world. Their forms are sometimes those of enormous men or giants, which leads to the idea that these ancient, probably real, people take on new and larger forms as time goes by, the giant imagery being the idea of a more ancient and superior, spiritual people.

The first known Jainist Jinas was probably the 9th century Parshva and was succeeded by Vardhamma Jnatrputra, the last in this cycle. This last Jinas was given the title 'Mahavira', which means Great Hero. At thirty (same age as Jesus and Buddha, although some say 35 or 29 for Buddha), he abandoned his life as a warrior and took up the role he was born to. He died at the equally significant Hebraic age of 72. As happened in Christianity and Islam, the leadership of Jainism was taken over by the disciples and spread throughout India, in collusion with the Buddhist and Hindu faiths, sharing monasteries and 'walking the road together'. The disciples wore simple white garments, when they wore anything at all, which we will see became incredibly important right down to the Knights Templars.

As with all other faiths, the Jains are in the search of absolute knowledge to release them from the cycle of rebirth.

Seek and ye shall find, anyone who wishes to enter

Knights Templar

the kingdom of Heaven must be born again. Another aspect is the renaming of the priesthood. Each new priest was given his official title, after which his old name was rarely used. This is also used in the Biblical context of Angels and Archangels, which are both official and spiritual titles.

The Jains also go through ritual deaths and rebirths via fasting, as did

Angel

the Jews of the same period. They were a nomadic priesthood, travelling and spreading the news, or so we are led to believe. It is probable that they simply travelled from one Shining Lodge or monastery to the next. In the same manner that our modern day preachers travel from one church to another, or how the travelling monks of western Europe moved between monasteries, sharing the latest philosophical thoughts and trends.

In the temple rituals, the 'Tirthankaras' image is shown (at Mathura) standing with arms and hands held out at the side in the symbol of the cross. This is strangely reminiscent of the cross of Christ.

The cross was deeply rooted in Jainist beliefs, especially the ancient cross of the Swastika. Opposite a small Benedictine

monastery in the Town of Lambach, Austria, lived a young man by the name of Adolf Hitler. He learned from the Benedictines, becoming 'intoxicated' with the 'solemn splendour' of it all.[6] During this time in his life he improved at school. The Benedictines taught him how to orate, to preach, and many finer mystical aspects of life. Above the doorway of the monastery is a stone arch, carved with the monastery's coat of arms. The most prominent feature of this coat of arms is the swastika. How did this ancient symbol come to be used by a murderous dictator (or pawn)?

A ninth cenury Buddha showing the swastika in the pineal position

From Bon-po and Tibet, to Siberia and the Steppes, the Shaman ideas cultivated the first civilisations of man. The Kurgan (meaning 'burial mound' in Russian) spread south and west, populating large areas of land and finding local Shaman who shared similar beliefs, which had possibly spread earlier with this ancient priesthood. The Kurgans, virtually founders of Sumeria the first so-called civilisation, were in the area around 4,500 BC and helped to spread the beliefs further.

In Sumerian creation myth, the Anannage (phonetically similar to the Hebrew Anakim or giant race, and Angakok, the

Shaman from Greenland to Alaska), or Great Sons of Anu, the shining one, were the founders of their culture. Anu or An was the chief Sky/Sun God of the time and means 'Shining'. The Anannage therefore means the 'Sons of the Shining One'. Part of their creation myth states, 'At Kharsag, where Heaven and Earth met, the Heavenly Assembly, the Great Sons of Anu (or Shining One) - the Many Wise Ones', which shows that the leaders, spiritual, priestly and godly, were related to the Shining One sect and even received their authority from the father of the Shining Ones. The part 'where Heaven and Earth met', is symbolic of the sacred mountains and this gives us the clue that this was somewhere with impressive Heaven-like mountains, such as Tibet. It continues, 'Mankind learned from the Shining Ones; they set things in order'.

Ninkharsag 'the Lady of Kharsag' was the wife of the leader, and in the myth she asks the Council of Seven to create her an Eden. This is the very same Eden or plain/plateau as in the Bible myth and the Council of Seven is the same as the Seven Archangels or Messengers of the Bible who came down from

Heaven/ the Mountain. The Trees of Life and Knowledge are the secrets of the Shining Ones, secrets which will stay with them for thousands of years, to be told only to the highest Shaman, Priest, Prophet or Shining One.

Angel, Anannage and Anakim have much in common. They are indicative of the ancient ancestors who brought the secrets to the rest of the world.

The building of
a Ziggurat

There are also other links between the cultures. The Biblical flood myth matches that of the Sumerians and ends with the Tower of Babel, in Babylon, which was part of the Sumerian empire. This shows that the secrets ended up, at that time, in Babylon. The Sumerians built their towers or Ziggurats with seven levels, as attempts to build closer to heaven, to be like the mountains, and link them with Earth as in the dream of Jacob's ladder. Was Jacob's ladder a mountain somewhere in the near East?

In their dreamlike trances, the Shaman saw seven levels to heaven, as did the Hebrews later on. Seven, as we know, has become a very important and 'lucky' number over the years and this may be due to the astrological links with the ancient knowledge of there being only seven planets. 11

From Central Asia, the near East and Middle East, we are led towards the Egyptian culture. The age of the Shining Ones took on glory in spectacular style with the blossoming of this fascinating culture.

Even today, the word 'Egypt' conjures up magical images of Pyramids and Pharaohs, dry desert mysteries and moonlit Nile scenes from long ago. Plato began the mystery with the words attributed to the priest of Sais, 'Oh Solon, Solon, you Greeks are all children... young in mind, you have no belief rooted in old tradition and no knowledge hoary with age'. Plato was of course insinuating that the additions of the Greek pantheon were taking the nation away from the truths of the ancient beliefs. Those with the eyes to see would know that they had to stay firm to the old ways, the secret ways, for the initiated few only. But Plato was also talking of the fantastic culture of the Egyptians and how the Greeks could be like them.

The pyramids will be discussed in a later chapter, but how did an ancient culture seemingly appear from nowhere and start building with such knowledge and enthusiasm?

Herodotus tells part of the tale when he said that Egypt was 'the gift of the Nile'. Without the Nile there would have been no Egypt as we now know it. Location is paramount in creating a civilisation, just as developing a business is reliant on the surrounding suppliers and customers, distribution accessibility and centrality.

Excavations at Hierakonpolis in 1983 show quite clearly the early farming development of the Egyptian culture.8 In 3,800 BC there was a habitation of approximately 100 acres known to pre-historical Egyptian tradition as Amratian period of the Neolithic. Here we find the first Egyptian tombs, although they are basic when compared to the later mountain style pyramids. They were covered with earth mounds, much akin to the Kurgan burial mounds and similar to the styles all over the globe at that time. For instance, at Mohenjo-dara in the Indus Valley, very similar buildings were being erected, there was also evidence of bull cults and sun worship.

At other Amratian sites along the Nile and at Hierakonpolis we can see the burials of the elite class; the imagery is consistent with the theory of the Shining Ones beliefs. Around 4,700 years ago, King Djoser constructed the first of the great Pyramids at a place called Saqqara. The kings had become priest/kings, sons of the great shining one in the sky and they began to build their own stairway to Heaven.

We need not seek out some ancient Atlantis as Egypt's precursor; it had been fermenting in the hills and mountains of Central Asia for centuries. The rituals of rebirth, the belief in sun gods and moon gods, the animals and cyclic patterns were all handed down from the Shamans of earlier times: the

ancient Devas, Anakim, Anannage, giants and men of renown. The title passed on to the Egyptian akhs, which means 'glorious, splendid' or 'Shining Ones'. The akhs are the gods of the past, ancients brought to life and worshipped by the masses under a new light, organised and put forward in their various symbolic forms by the elite priesthood. With influence from Sumer, North Africa and Mesopotamia, the Egyptian deities took shape, but behind them were the same beliefs of rebirth. There is one way in which Egyptian, Greek and Roman deities, and the Christian and European pagan deities, can be easily cross-referenced (i.e. Mercury, Thoth, Hermes), and that is that they are simply the local names given to various attributes of the ancient Shaman and priest of the darker history. They are the same, and are based upon real people from the past, just as Noah is probably based upon somebody. This same belief system passed on its incredible knowledge of the stars, astronomy and astrology. The Egyptians took this knowledge and turned it into an epic. The knowledge of the heavens is the knowledge of the gods and therefore eternal, ritualised life.

The Godhead of the Heavens was Ra or Re, the infinite god, the Sun. Horus and Osiris were the gods in men, incarnated as man only then to be reunited with god after death. This is basically the Christian myth. In Egyptian mythology and Christian lore, the bee is said to have sprung both from the tears of Ra, the sun god, and of Christ the son of god. In this context, the bee is the messenger of the gods, falling down, like the Hindu tears, towards earth and man to pass on some secret message.

Re or Ra took the title role as the Shining Father, the Sun God, and eventually the various Pharaohs also took on this image as the Sun god on Earth. Other deities became the Shining Stars. The son of the Pharaoh was the Son of the Sun and became the reincarnated Re upon his father's death. Therefore, the Son was his father and the father was the son, literally and symbolically, like the Buddhist dharma and the Christian Father/Son aspect. So with the god being the Pharaoh, the Hermetic, as above, so below was true.

Book of Dead

In the language of the Book of the Dead, or Book of Thoth, we can see that we are permitted to become the Shining Ones or Saints ourselves. When we die, if we are initiated and allowed in, we can undergo the mummification process, which will enable our akh or Shining Soul to be released to the Heavens. Of course, we had to be in the know, be of royal blood or at least very wealthy. This symbolism of everybody being able to reach the kingdom of Heaven through rebirth and knowledge is the same as in other faiths, especially Christianity.

As previously assumed by many Christian Gnostics concerning Christ's teachings, the Book of the Dead was quite specific that the symbolism was to be taken as pertaining to this life; that we can symbolically have this second life of Heaven on Earth here and now. This is the way to the inner circle of the initiated. To be reborn in the current body, as Christ spoke of to Nicodemus. The constant cycle of rebirth starts here and now, initiation of the 'chosen ones', into the 'Shining Ones'.

Text from the Book of the Dead tells us, 'I have the power to be born a second time...I am the Lord of those who are raised up from the dead...he illuminates the earth...I shall come into being in the form of the Lion-god.' The Lion or Sphinx was taken up by the Hebrews when predicting the future coming of their Messiah.

In the Chapter of Making the Transformation into God who giveth Light in the Darkness, we find a familiar Christian aspect to the text. 'I have come to give light in the darkness, which is made light and bright...'

The Book of the Dead has many images of light and darkness, with three streaming rays of sunlight hitting the Shining Soul of the initiated. The seating arrangements are also similar to Christ's words, 'I come forth to Heaven and I sit myself down by the God of Light.' 'I have made my form like his divine form', or, we are the same.

The light/darkness aspect was not solely a later Christian teaching, it was used all over the world and had been for thousands of years. It is clear here that the teachings of Jesus, who spent time in Egypt, were influenced by other cultures, or by the Shining Ones themselves.

In later Egyptian history, there was an attempt by Akhenaton to move towards a single deity, Atun. There were strong resemblances to the god of the Hebrews, Yahweh. Some have said that Atun and Yahweh were the same. This would not be implausible as the Bible even says that Moses learned everything he knew from his time in Egypt. Abraham was in Ur of the Chaldees and huge amounts of influence was shared between these

cultures. To speak the secret name of Ra gave power over the god, in the same way that the unspoken word of god in the Hebrew tradition gave the priest the power once a year in the Holy of Holies. Ra was identified with the Ass; Jesus rode to his death on the life giver, Ra, in a symbolic insult that would have been understood quite easily by those in the know.

The Hebrews will be discussed later, although here we should mention the story of Sargon the Emperor of Mesopotamia who died around 2,279 BC. Sargon rose from being a cup bearer in the Temple to Emperor and ruled his Empire for 50 years. The name 'Sargon', means 'righteous' or 'true king' and his life has since been shrouded in wonderful and magical tales of his prowess, much like the story of Moses. What is important here is the obvious link between the tales of Sargon and Moses in the early years. Sargon was said to have been an illegitimate child and was abandoned in a rush basket only to be rescued by a well drawer. He was brought up by the goddess Ishtar (Inanna). He took power from his overlord, the king of Kish and moved on to take his people into power over Ur, Lagash, Umma and Sumer. Sargon brought Sumerian belief systems into his Empire, and for the first time the Semites had ascendancy over the Sumerians. His daughter became the priestess of Inanna, the moon-goddess of Ur. As we know, this became important for Abraham.

Was Sargon trained in the Temple by the Shining Ones to take power and unite the one religion across a new Empire? Was this one great and powerful plan that had been in place, possibly for decades?

Much later in this book we will look into such conspiracy theories. For now it is sufficient to say that the stories of the Bible have their roots in other cultures and are not necessarily true. Sargon brought the Mesopotamian Empire into a structured and Empire-wide belief system, something virtually untried before, and all eyes would have been watching for its success or failure and for what lessons could be learned for later and much wider belief systems.

We must not forget the archetypal image of the goddess of fertility, virginity and the feminine side of Ra or

Re: Isis. She is like the moon: dark and secretive, powerful and cyclic. Her cult was very high up in the Egyptian religious hierarchy and she played a role almost equal to that of Ra. Just as the Jews had married off their god in tradition, so too had one of the Egyptian trinity married Isis. Her cult has persisted, albeit secretly, without too much of a fight. The city of Paris is associated with her name, Paris = Par Isis or 'grove of Isis'. The oldest church in Paris is built over a large, former temple of Isis. In this church there is a black statue, now called the Virgin Mary, although until 1514 it was worshipped as the goddess Isis. It seems that the cult of the Black Madonna and many Marian images actually relate to Isis worship, which evidently went on, with or without the knowledge of the church, right through the medieval period. Isis even immaculately conceived a child by the god Horus.

Apuleius said of her, 'risen from the middle of the sea...poised on the surface of the waves', "'I am Nature, the universal Mother, mistress of all the elements, primordial child of time, sovereign of all things spiritual, queen of the dead, queen also of immortals, the single manifestation of all gods and goddesses that are. I govern the shining heights of Heaven, the wholesome sea breezes, the lamentable silences of the world below. Though I am worshipped in many aspects, known by countless names, and propitiated with all manner of different rites, yet the whole round earth venerates me.'"

It is interesting to note that the Virgin Mary (the Queen of Heaven) is also known as 'Our Lady, Star of the Sea'.

Here we have an indication of her importance to the ancient and not so ancient people. Isis is equal and opposite to Ra, the Shining One. She makes up the duality of the Yin and Yang, the Mother and Father, Light and Darkness in the Egyptian traditions.

The Egyptian Book of the Dead will become more important to man as the wheels of history turn. Much like the Bible, the book is a collection of various texts written over a considerable period of time (2400 BC to 1600 BC) and its real name is more closely translated as 'The Chapters of Coming Forth by Day'. Parts of the book, or whole versions, were placed in the grave of the deceased so that they could find their way to the Light. The book offers advice on how to get there and how to answer the judges of the other-world once there. There are many hymns, potions and magic spells, said to have been written by the god Thoth.

Thoth will become more important also. His symbol is the cross. A vertical line with a cross bar on the top or alternatively the same as the Horus cross, Ankh or 'crux ansata'. He was traditionally the god of wisdom and the moon, like Isis. His aspect of the moon was the reckoning and calculation of time. He invented writing and was associated with magic, alchemy and medicine because of his power over writing and time. Thoth took on the Greek name of Hermes when Egypt was

Hellenised and is written of in the Hermetic traditions dating from the 2nd or 3rd centuries, where his name becomes Hermes Trismegistus or Thrice Great Hermes. The work calls upon people to become initiated and to receive wisdom and personal vision of the Light of God to attain rebirth. In other words, to become Shining Ones. These works survived and influenced a whole host of Gnostic traditions from Islam to Christianity.

Hermes

Ancient Persia was part of the melting pot and held many of the secrets of the ancients. It seems that this is where many of the ancient Shining Ones were taught their skills. The priestly caste of the Persians were called Magi and are thought by some to have been followers of Zoroastrianism (Zoroaster, by the way, would be born of a Virgin, and return three times in four twelve-millennia periods). Their rituals were incredibly similar to the later rituals of Alchemy and are probably directly related. Chanting over chemical experiments and reading into symbolism were all part of the magician's cloth (the word 'magic' comes from the magi). They appeared to have no temples, leading us to conclusion that the nomadic priesthood did not need one of their own and simply moved between those of other cultures, like the Shaman. Their secret rituals were carried out in Heaven, on mountain tops, the place that is with, if not near, the gods. The priests of Egypt, Mesoamerica and the Far East carried out their secret rituals in manmade mountains: ziggurats and pyramids. Also within the realm of the 'magi way' was the belief in reincarnation, a link to the Shaman/Hindu ways from their past and a sign for the future.

Zoroaster

They were the Wise Men of the East in the Bible story of Christ's birth. They brought three gifts of incredible significance and symbolism, known to them as the gifts to be given to the new king, Buddha, Messiah or Jinas; the new Shining Father on earth, coming from the east, the way of the rising sun and new life. Their gifts were gold, the symbol of royalty and in Egyptian tradition given to the victor in battle; frankincense, the symbol of divinity; and myrrh, symbolic of death, rebirth and reincarnation.

When we understand the meaning given to the latterly named 'Three Kings' we see a little of the Shining Ones coming out. Melchior is 'King of Light' or 'Shining One'; Casper is the White one, remember what the Shining Ones should wear, it is unusual for a Persian to actually be white of skin, unless he was supposed to have been an initiate from a European country, such as England; Balthazar means the 'Lord of the treasures', attainment of the secrets of the Shining ones only possible when we accept the Light and adorn ourselves with the white clothes.

They probably received their ancient training from the Shaman tradition and were most likely just a continuation of that line and tradition. The word 'magi' literally means 'wise men', symbolic of someone who has learned wisdom from Ra, Re, Isis or the Shining gods of ancient times. Thoth, being the god of wisdom, seems very highly regarded.

In the Lusiad, a Portuguese national epic written by Camoens and published in 1572, we see the term Magi used in the same way that denotes the Indian Brahmin, or at least that is where the Magi derived their knowledge, which is exactly what we are saying here; that they were, or shared, essentially the same beliefs and origins.

Ammianus Marcellinus tells us that the magi obtained their knowledge from the Brahmins and Arianus calls the Brahmins, Magi. And the Brahmins got their knowledge from the Shaman.

Every year, those of us who live in predominantly Christian nations, see a Shining One in our own living rooms, positioned on top of the World Tree: the Shining Star of Bethlehem, symbolic of the Shining Father, Sun/Sky God risen above the Tree of Life and knowledge and giver of the same. The originators of this familiar symbolism are the Magi.

This literal event may not have even happened. It became purely symbolic of the Shining Father giving birth to his Shining Son on earth. There were no conjunctions visible in the sky at the time and the only possible conjunction, around 7 BC was of the planets Saturn and Jupiter in the area of Pisces - the Fish.

Chinese astronomers recorded a flared up star in the constellation of Aquila the Eagle and it has been computed

that this may have been visible from the South gate of Jerusalem and would have appeared over Bethlehem. There are many problems with this supernova theory which need further investigation and it is better left to the astronomical experts.

Virgil spoke of the global idea of a coming Messiah, almost heretically letting the cat out of the bag, in telling us of the widespread belief. It was supposed to be the Jewish idea, not everyone's, that fact has been suppressed, even now. Virgil also told us that the 'Golden Race' will have spread throughout the globe and that the mother of this Messiah will be a Virgin Lady, like Isis. Was Virgil more knowledgeable than we are led to believe? He was a poet, something most of the mystical magicians of whom he spoke also happened to be.

It seems most likely that the Magi were the new Shaman and were related to several localities, albeit individual areas of the same group. They were identified with astrology, also popular among the Levant Jewish community at that time; the study and divination of dreams, also a Jewish prophetic practice; and the practice of the hidden ways or Ancient Science. All the old Shaman ways, learnt from the ancients.

The Magi could easily have been attached to the Jewish movement and be part of the overall plan that Virgil revealed, and therefore they are yet another direct Shaman link with the modern world.

Magic, said J.G. Frazer in The Golden Bough, precedes religion. A thorough investigation of the old faiths and new faiths shows us that magic is religion. The secret doctrines and the hidden agenda of the Shining Ones for possibly 50,000 years has moved mankind along in its own sacred way. We have accepted the new front faiths with ease, once we have adapted them. The real leaders behind the scenes of these religions have cared little about any new package of pagan deities or long-eared fairies added onto the old ways, because the old ways are always there; the power is retained in knowledge which is kept secret and only for the initiated. And some would say the secrets are not yet out.

So the Shamans of old, the Hindu Devas, the Buddhist priests, the Egyptian deities and the Persian Magi have common bonds. Their basic beliefs all stem from the same original source, somewhere in central Asia.

The beliefs of the entire globe are now in danger of appearing to have come from the same source, to have been driven by the same group of timeless individuals, to be leading in the same direction, although on the face of it their directions appear to be vastly different. In the end, if they do come from the same source, will they end up back together?

Through the vast array of symbols and coded structures included in the expanding world of the Shining Ones we can begin to see a meaning aimed at all of us and yet at the same time almost controlling us, in the way that any religion can.

There is sufficient evidence to see that once one secret was discovered by our ancient relatives, the whole world got to know about it by any means available, to further or to control mankind, by the semi-nomadic Shining Ones, the Shaman of our past.

In Norse mythology, Odin is crucified on Yggdrasil, the World Tree, Shaman practised crucifixion and Christ was symbolically crucified on the tree. The link of the cross is strong between the years. Mother Goddess has refused to go away. She is called by various names, but she remains. We ritually

follow cyclic patterns, now deeply embedded in our world faiths, and we persist in believing in the deeper mysteries of life. Is there a secret, held for thousands of years by the elite? What was the next step that they took from Central Asia, Siberia, Sumeria, Egypt, Indus Valley, the Middle East, Near East and China? Were they the progenitors of our faiths? Did they spread across the globe to America and Australasia?

We must find out if Judaism, Christianity and Islam stemmed from this early Shamanistic belief system we have discovered to be called the Shining Ones. If they did, then what does this mean to the control factor, which may be a part of our history? Have we been controlled as if part of some big plan? Or does it just seem to be that way? In the next few chapters we shall find out.

Apis, bull god

Notes
Chapter 5

1   Ward Rutherford, p 140. Quoted from The Fire and The Stones. Nicholas Hagger. Element Books. 1991.
2   Dictionary of the Occult. Geddes and Grosset Ltd. 1997.
3   Hinduism in A Handbook of Living Religions. Penguin. 1991.
4   The Great Pyramid Decoded. Peter Lemesurier. Element. 1993.
5   As note 3.
6   Adolf Hitler. John Toland. Wordsworth. 1997.
7   John 14. From New King James Bible. Life Application Version. 1993. Tyndale.
8   Human Antiquity. Feder/Park. Mayfield Publishing. 1992.
9   The Golden Ass. Lucius Apuleius. Penguin. 1985
10   Mysticism, Its history and challenge. Bruno Borchert. Samuel Weiser. 1994.
11   Sevens. Joshua walked around Jericho (the first civilisation according to some and home of the largest group of Shamans) seven times.
Seven heavens - Koran, Bible, Shaman, Druids.
Seven deadly sins and seven virtues.
Life has seven cycles according to tradition.
Massive Hebrew Septenary design in Bible - see Proof. Radikal Phase Publishing House Ltd, Willow Court, Underwood, Notts. 2002
Seven steps to Heaven, popular belief and on ziggurats.
The seventh son of the seventh son is by Jewish tradition believed to have great healing powers.
Magic boots which allow the wearer to walk seven leagues in one stride, goes back to the mythical magic of the giants or men of renown.

Seven days in a week, days in creation.
Hebrew to swear on oath means to come under the influence of the seven (probably planets).
The seven Argive heroes of Greek legend.
The seven champions of English legend.
Seven gifts of the spirits.
Seven Japanese gods of Luck.
Seven joys/sorrows of Mary, seven sacraments.
Seven sages of Greece or Wise Men of Greece.
Seven sciences.
Seven senses - according to the ancients. They are under the influence of the planets. Fire moves, earth sense of feeling, water gives speech, air taste, mist sight, flowers hearing and the south wind smell.
Seven Wonders of the ancient world.
Meanings of seven - scholarly, mystical, withdrawn, dreamy, time, the colours of the rainbow, seven tones of the musical scale, stability and endurance, duration.
Numerology has Jesus Christ as the number seven. Septenary design as 777 (the beast 666)
There are seven elementary hues to the spectrum when blended together they form White.

12   Primitive Magic. Ernesto De Martino. Prism Press. 1988.
13   Intellectual Culture of the Igluik Eskimos. Rasmussen.
14   Toronto Blessing. Supposedly the spirit of the lord coming down on the massed Christians and blessing them so heavily that they fall over, speak in tongues and generally appear as if they are intoxicated.
15   Shining Ones.
        Afrigan Rapithwin, verse 13 says, 'The Star Tistrya, the Shining, majestic one we praise...All stars which contain the seeds of trees, we praise...'
        Yasna, chap 57, verse 27 says, 'Four steeds, white, bright, shining...'

It was, from the beginning the stars who were the heavenly embodiment of the Shining Ones. They could be looked up to in awe and they held power of our future.

Baal

Chapter 6
The Roots of Us

From Central Asia, Tibet, the Steppes, Siberia, and Northern Europe to the Middle, Near and Far East we have links between the various and supposedly different civilisations. History records that these civilisations sprang up from nowhere, almost totally independently; a kind of spontaneous eruption of man and his newly practised social and religious habits.

Of course, there have been many alternative views. There have been explanations ranging from the ancient people of Atlantis, Lemuria or Thule being the cause of our civilisations, to the genetic modification of our species by extraterrestrials, all of which are redundant. The beliefs which we have flowered up over the centuries all share a common ancestor who is neither from outer space nor from some sunken Island the size of Libya.

Humans evolved sufficiently well that eventually there were more and more of them, all locating themselves in the best and most fertile places.

The Shamans' ideas and beliefs spread with these people as an integral part of their culture, as is well documented from archaeological finds.1 The priestly elite became kings, powerful rulers and eventually fell into the social consciousness as gods or demigods, great men of renown from the good and ancient times. The contemporary Shaman used his now mythical ancestor to do his bidding and support his own claim for power within the group.

Sufficient mystical development caused the Egyptian high priests and the secret knowledge power base they had built up to evolve. But this colourful belief system of the Egyptians, Babylonians and later Greeks was to breed a more powerful and totalitarian faith with new high priests who held sway over kings and queens, judges and lay people, and held it by the power of the Law of God.

A Law was created for a nomadic troop to keep them safe, to mould them and see them through dangerous times. But the Law became a stronghold on these people as they began to settle down and new saviours were sought.

This developing faith was Judaism.

The roots of Judaism are to be found in the most unexpected places. They are not solely with the Canaanites, which has been suggested. Neither are they purely the amalgamation of the collected beliefs of a nomadic tribe or group of tribes. They are also, and very strongly, taken from Egypt.

The term 'Jews' dates back to around 63 BC when the Romans incorporated the eastern part of the Mediterranean into their empire and gave the land between Syria and the Egyptian desert the name of Judea.2 This in itself shows how close the land of the Jews is to Egypt in physical terms.

The people of the Jewish Bible are tellingly symbolic figures. Take, for instance, Samson. His name derives from Shemesh (the sun). Samson loses his hair (a woman cuts it off) and therefore his power. Hair is symbolic of the rays of the sun and

when the sun's rays are cut off, its power is shortened. This itself is the real reason that beards are predominantly important to the Shining Ones. The story of Samson may contain some truth, but actually finding the existence of such Biblical characters is difficult. People such as Moses, Abraham, Jacob and

Gilgamesh Epic

Isaac are extremely difficult to find outside of the Jewish writings, though not impossible. There are numerous traditions, rather like the traditions of our own folklore, which contain many truths. These traditions, when tested against archaeological data and other neighbouring folklore and beliefs, can actually be shown to be true or false.

There is much which is accurate within the Bible, and we should take this into account when refuting some of the evidence it gives, although as with any history written by people about themselves we find that it is biased. Many of the Bible's stories come from the surrounding areas, such as Canaan, Babylon and Egypt. The Babylonian Gilgamesh Epic is a perfect and over used example of the similarities between the flood myths.

Some stories and traditions were brought with these people

from their travels. There is evidence to suggest that many of the myths actually came from Central Asia.3 This would explain some of the more rudimentary Shamanistic ideas in the Jewish tales, rather than them having come through the colourful Egyptian net.

There is an idea that some of the Jewish tribes were made up of Hyskos, a Semite sea faring people from the eastern Mediterranean. The Hyskos took power for a time in Egypt and became the first Semite rulers of the kingdom. This may have been when the Jews took root in Egypt, when times were good. Later, when the Hyskos were expelled, the Jews would have felt the need to find their own 'Promised Land'.

All this is conjecture. We do not actually know very much about them as fact. There are some references to them in Egyptian hieroglyphs and temple records. Other cultures also mention them, sometimes in not the most polite terms.

The strongest possibility is that the Jews were an amalgamated group of individual nomadic tribes. They probably came together for strength in the ever increasing world of empires and kingdoms. It may be that they later sided with the Hyskos or were employed by them to take control of Egypt. While they were in Egypt, possibly under Ramses II, part or some of the group were supposedly slaves. Ramses II was a brilliant pyramid builder and much of the knowledge in architecture and planning seems to have come from Semite groups. This collection of tribes then either integrated with the Canaanites or invaded and took control of them. The powerful knowledge of Egypt added to their already vast knowledge of pagan Shamanistic rituals made this group a small, but spiritually powerful force. A fake history provided a good curriculum vitae of the nation and their future was assured.

The religion of the Jews is solely based around the cyclic patterns of Earth. Primitive totemeic is there in small quantities as we would expect from such an old tradition. Fertility rites, moon days and feasts are examples of this.

Gilgamesh Epic

The Jewish tradition has it that the sons of Noah populated the earth. His sons, Shem, Ham and Japheth gave us the major civilisations known at that time.

	Noah	
Shem	Ham	Japheth
Hebrews	Egyptians	Greeks
Chaldeans	Philistines	Thracians
Assyrians	Hitittes Scythians	
Persians	Amorites	Syrians

For reference, the term 'Semite' refers to Akkadians (Babylonians), Assyrians, Arameans, Canaanites, Edomites, Moabites, Hebrews, Arabs and Ethiopians. The Jews are part of all of these, not, symbolically, specifically a nation themselves, but rather the saviours or religious guides of them all.

Reading into the Bible literature, the Father figure is that of Abraham, 'circa.' 2166 BC. He existed around the time of the Pyramid, megalithic and many other great building projects around the globe. He was the son of Terah, a descendant of Shem (Father of the Hebrews etc.), and was thought to be a contemporary of Hammurabi the King of Babylon.

Abraham was born and lived in Ur of the Chaldees, which dates back to approximately 10,000 BC in relation to farming. It was occupied properly as early as the fourth millennium BC. The great ziggurat of Nanna the Moon God and his Moon Goddess wife Ningal is here and the city was called the City of the Moon God. The ziggurat represents the great cosmic mountain of the gods and undoubtedly Abraham would have visited the site. The graves at Ur were filled with elaborate religious objects, some of which were of the 'Ram in the Thicket', the strangely similar image to that of the Biblical 'Ram in the Bush'.

There can be no doubt that Abraham picked up much of what he knew here. If there is any relevance to this at all, then Abraham was most probably at the priest school here, where he learnt his trade as a Shining One, then left the city to move with the nomads of Canaan, and later still moved to Egypt. Abraham took the title role of Father, which he probably won from Lot and this is the reason for their eventual split. The progenitor of the Muslims was Abraham's son, Ishmael, born of an Egyptian slave girl. The symbolism here alone is rich.

That he was given the title of 'Father' implies that he bore a great authority over the people, and this became the future meaning of the title. One of the first instances of the application of this title is to be found in Judges 18:18, 'circa.' 742 BC, when the priest of Micah is made 'a father and a priest to us...and he took the ephod [priest's robe], the household idols, and the carved image, and took his place among the people.' This is a prime example of the title being bestowed by the people, with all the idols, carved images and robes relating to the Shining Ones' office.

In Muslim tradition, Abraham is called Ibrahim and his surname is Khalil Allah or 'friend of god'. His father was a wazir to Nimrod, the great grandson of Noah, who was a warrior, King of Babylon and founder of Ninevah and, reputedly, the builder

of the Tower of Babel. When Ibrahim's mother was due to give birth to him she was led secretly away by angels to a concealed cave near Damascus, referred to by the local community as 'Bethlehem.' These angelic ministrants made the birth painless and the new born babe

Qumran

was placed into the hands of 'Shining Ones' to bring him up in the secret ways.

Again we have an angel and a cave involved in the birth of a child, although this time not in the Bible (See also Judges 13:3, Luke 1:13 and that Angels had wisdom in Sam 14:21). The cave signifies the womb of the Mother Earth, the angel a messenger. The pain was taken away by the drugs and medicinal knowledge of the 'ministrant angels'. The boy was then 'chosen' by these angels for special knowledge. This was the child's birthright due to the high position and ability of his father. The cave near Damascus is close to Qumran, where the Essene legacy lies, the caves where the Gnostic traditions were taught to the ascetic followers of the light and the 'Bethlehem' birthplace of Christ. More on this later.

Later in the story, when Ibrahim could speak, he went outside of the cave, saw a bright star and said, 'Surely this is my Lord', but the star disappeared and he changed his mind. The same happened with the moon and the sun until eventually he cried out to God and asked him to reveal himself. So the Archangel Gabriel came and instructed the young man in the truth. The same Gabriel by title also instructed Muhammad.

Abraham dealt with the Pharaoh and even practised magic against the Egyptians, to bring plagues. His name changed from Abram to Abraham in the tradition of giving new titles and names, as discussed in the previous chapter. In Genesis 14, Abraham, as the 'Father', gave the King of Salem the title of Melchizedek, which meant 'King of Righteousness'. Throughout history there has been only one kind of person who could give names to Kings: a religious pontiff. Was Abraham some kind of great religious leader, respected even by other nations with whom they were sometimes at war?

Does this mean that the Jews were not so much a nomadic nation, but rather a nomadic religious group of special priests? Keep this thought in mind. It may be that the King of Salem was actually a member of the priesthood himself and of the order of Zadok, a later dynast of priests, and that he was given the title Michael (meaning 'he who is shining' or 'he who is like god'), the title of the Chief Angel or Archangel.4

We know that priests within, and external to, the Jewish community actually took on the names of the angels, in the same way that the Dalai Lama takes on his name when he is reincarnated. This, if true, would make the King of Salem a high priest in the order of Zadok and, in the official function of Michael, the Chief Messenger of the people.

Unless the literature is purely apocryphal, we find that in the Bible, the angel figures are simply earthly men. The word Angel ('malakh' in Hebrew, 'aggelos' in Greek, 'angelos' in Latin and in Anglo-Saxon 'engel') means messenger. In Cornish, as in the Semite languages, the word El means 'Angel' and 'the Shining One'. There are many links between both the language and history of Cornwall and the Hebrew history. 5 'England' comes from the Anglo-Saxon Engel.

In the Bible, we do not find angels with wings, there are no original stories of them being supernatural. They are, in fact, quite ordinary. It is always Gabriel (meaning 'man of God' or 'Man of the shining one') who informs the people of a coming childbirth. Was he the Shaman? The doctor? Michael is the warrior and protector, accompanied by angels wielding swords. Each and every one of them has their own specific duty, an earthly duty. People with titles, angelic titles, as messengers and ambassadors of God, just like the early Shaman. The Cherubim means 'exiles' and could be an indication of the origins of the Angels. Maybe they were ordered to leave somewhere, such as Egypt, for not conforming. In Genesis 4:16, the Land of Nod is symbolic also of the people of Israel as Nod means 'Wandering', it is not much of an extrapolation to assume that the priesthood (Cherubim, Angels) were also wanderers. Another example of symbolic titles is that of Enoch, which means 'consecrated'. When Cain and his wife bore Enoch and built a city called Enoch we have the people of Cain being consecrated before God.

Of course, we must not forget the Seraphim of Numbers 21:6 and elsewhere. These are not mystical beings, they have hands, a face, legs, but they do have powers from God, because they are in the Light and they have the symbolic wings of the early Shamans, the bird flight, the dreamtime trance ability to fly. Their name means Shining Ones.

In the Old Testament God is indistinguishable from the angel or messenger of Yahweh. He looks the same and acts as his representative. There is no difference here from Babylonian, Egyptian and Shaman practice.

They are part of the prehistoric 'Heavenly Host' who reside in

the Heavens or sacred mountains which represent Heaven below. This goes right back to the mountains of Central Asia, and comes through to the pyramids, ziggurats or representations of mountains in Egypt and Babylonia. These mountains accept the priests or angels on our behalf, continually in the service of God, full time ministers, the Shining Ones again talking to God for us.

The demons or evil angels are probably threats to the masses to keep in line with the orthodox beliefs or they would 'go to the devil'. These may have been real priests also, administering judgement upon the sinners. In the New Testament, the angels actually take part in the Judgement at the end times.

Mystical Jewish literature tells us that the angels can fly, tell the future, shape shift, speak Hebrew and are emanations of the divine shining light.6

The priestly goings on had by now developed into an intricate system which was highly related to the Egyptian ways and beliefs, especially in solar worship and astrology.

The Hebrews had set feast days based solely around cyclic patterns. New Moon festivals, Full Moon feasts; waxing and waning of the Mother Moon Goddess.

'At the height of your months you shall present a burnt offering to the Lord, two young bulls, one ram, and seven lambs in their first year...;' Numbers 28:11

'And he built altars for all the host of heaven [angels or stars] in the two courts...Also he made his son pass through fire, practised soothsaying, used witchcraft [or old ways] and consulted spirits and mediums.' 2 Kings 21. The host of heaven are said to be the gods of the Assyrians, the stars.

'The children gather wood, the fathers kindle the fire, and the women knead dough, to make cakes for the Queen of Heaven.' Jeremiah 7:18. This is the name of Ishtar, the Mesopotamian goddess. In Egypt in the 5th century BC, there is evidence of the Jews worshipping this Queen of Heaven. 7 In Ezekiel 32:7, we can see that the moon is female and the sun male.

The Hebrews divided the year by the moon rather than by the sun. Twelve lunar months of 28 days, which had to be seasonally adjusted as they lost 10 days per year. Eventually this was altered to make it look as if this was a solar 12 month cycle. It would make sense for a group of nomadic tribesmen to have within their priesthood the knowledge of the stars, if only for use in navigation. This would make the priests more powerful to the group and almost magical in their understanding of the gods of the sky.

It seems that the Hebrews believed that god made and controlled the stars for our destiny. Hebrews and heathens of the time worshipped the stars, as we can see throughout the Bible.

'Lest you lift your eyes to heaven, and when you see the sun, the moon, and the stars, all the host of heaven, you feel driven to worship them and serve them...' Deuteronomy 4:19. A warning against this rapidly growing belief, whilst behind the scenes the priests themselves were involved in the practice.

2 Kings 17 is a reproach from the priests and to the priests for moving towards the worship of the 'host of Heaven' and Baal, the old Canaanite god who shared so much with Yahweh.

In 2 Kings 21:3,5 and Isaiah 45:6, Psalm 50:1, we see that there

is a sundial and that the direction of the sun and moon are greatly important to the Jews.

There are numerous passages throughout the traditional Bible, and other non-Biblical writings of the time, which show us that the Hebrews believed in Solar worship, a Moon or Earth Goddess, the stars as the 'host of Heaven' and various other animal-faced gods.8 The true key in the Jewish success came with the hammering home of the Law, to keep the pattern fixed.

Yahweh was originally believed to be the bringer of rainfall and guaranteed a bountiful harvest. Israel became more and more dependant upon this cyclical god and his name altered to fit every need. God the creator, God the protector, God the saviour. Baal was one of the original names in tradition (Hebrew ba'al from the Phoenician ba'al or 'owner, lord'). Baal took the title of many aspects, Baal-berith, 'the lord of the covenant' and Baalzebub, 'the lord of the flies'. Whilst dealing with the Canaanites, the Hebrews took this style on board. The shrines of the Baal cults were stone altars, with sacred pillars nearby, very similar to, and from the same period as, the huge megalithic structures of the northern Shaman counterparts. Elijah or Elias (9th century BC) fought the Baal cult and engaged in a contest of Shamanistic magic with the priests of the Baal cult, a battle between sorcerers. Elijah had the Baal prophets put to death symbolically and Yahweh sent the symbolic rain after three symbolic years of drought.

Elijah as the 'Shining Prophet' is expected to return. It is said that John the Baptist is the second coming of Elijah, 'come in the spirit and the power of Elijah', Matthew. He is the same idea as Buddha, the returning saviour, and predates Buddha by 300 years. Historical memories of Elijah may have impacted the Hindu priests as contact was often made on a trading basis

between the peoples. It is more likely that the Shining Ones actually trained Elijah in his ways as a magician, Father, leader and the title 'El' for strong, or 'shining', shows where his origins lie.

Elohim is usually translated as 'Lord' or 'God' but it is the feminine plural of the Semitic word el, which itself is found in many ancient languages. The Sumerian 'el' means 'Shining'; the Anglo-Saxon 'Aelf' means 'Shining Being'. So if El means Shining then Elohim literally means Shining Ones and is the most commonly used term in the Old Testament for God and indeed all other gods, as the scribes recognised other gods at that time. Elohim is usually translated as 'Lord'. The Shining Ones are in the Bible, and have been there ever since they put themselves in. If you read the Bible and replace Lord (and don't forget about the added words) with Shining Ones, you will see a remarkable difference, a reading now of how it was meant to be. We now have 'The Shining Light of Knowledge' spoken of in 2 Corinthians 4:6. The Lord God of the Bible is the 'Light' who gives birth to the 'divine spark' of Christ, a pure reading of the global understanding that God was the basis for illumination, the fire, the sun the light and head of those that Shine from that brilliance.

Another thing to remember about El Elohim is that from about the 6th century BC, and most likely well before, he was part of a duality. This male deity was, in tradition, married to Lady Asherah (Ashtoreth), who later became Matronit (Shekinah) who was married to Jehovah. It was well understood that for there to be a creation, a birth of worlds and people, there must be intercourse between the gods. This belief can be traced right back to the early Shaman beliefs.

As we have seen, the male god is almost always associated with the sun or sky and the female goddess with the moon and/or

Earth. According to Laurence Gardner in the Bloodline of the Holy Grail, El had a son called He and the two titles later joined together to become Jehovah. The amazing point of this union between the gods is that from the union comes forth the son. A trinity is created. 'One becomes two, the threefold appears.' (Book of Dzyan- quoted from The Garden of the Golden Flower by Longfield Beatty).

The dual nature of the Jewish god, male and female, is nothing new. It was widespread then, and survives today in Gnostic and Cabalistic traditions. It even survives in the cult of the Virgin Mary in Catholicism. Subtle evidence that no matter what we see on the face of the religion, there is always a continuum of the old ways below the surface. The Canaanite god El, not surprisingly, has the image of a bull, is married to the Mother goddess Asherah, and he is bearded.

Ashtoreth, Asherah, Asheroth, Astarte, Ishtar or Inanna, all names of the Mother Goddess who was incredibly important and who, as Sir James Frazer pointed out, suffered from the attribution of so many names that she was believed to be different deities. The names were attributed to the different aspects of her, as in the case of Jehovah and also the various language differences (Yahweh, or even taken a step further Ra the Egyptian sun god who has so many similarities to Jehovah). In the 'From Fetish to God' by Budge we read about Ra, '...there was no god before him....His unity is absolute. He was a Trinity, i.e. he had three persons or characters.' There are also similarities between Jehovah (IHOH) and IO the name of god the world over including North America and Polynesia; and IO is the symbol of the Ankh in letter form.

The images of these Mother Goddesses are usually bulls or the moon. Asheroth can mean 'grove' or 'single standing stone' or 'pole within a grove'. When we consider that the image of the

Adonis

great goddess was a simple white, shining cone, pole or even pyramid we can begin to see the universal usage. Megaliths, pyramids and various other temples that share common features display evidence of having been whitewashed. In Golgi in Cyprus, conical stones are raised to the Mother Goddess, as in the temples of Malta, in the Sinai, also the tall obelisk or standing stone in the great open sanctuary of Astarte at Byblos in Syria (the city sacred to Adonis), all share this unique shining stone image. In the moonlight the stones shine a remarkable blue colour. They almost come to life. The blue stones of many of the megaliths of Northern Europe shine blue in rain (gift of Jehovah or the male god) and by moonlight.

Ishtar, the great mother goddess, was married to Adonis. Adonis is used throughout the Bible, in the Hebrew form 'Adonai', as a title for the Lord, where pillars or standing stones are erected in his honour. The worship of Adonis was widespread, from Egypt to Babylonia and especially by all the Semitic tribes. The Greeks were using the name seven hundred years before Christ. The other titles of Adonis were Tammuz, or Thammuz, and the Babylonian Marduk. In Babylonian stories,

Marduk

Tammuz appears as the lover of Ishtar and the world's nature is the fertile result. The symbol of Thammuz, Tammuz, Adonis and Marduk is the Tau cross. This ancient symbol was used for many purposes including divination, as a staff of the magi, as a guide to the stars and may have been used as a sun dial. The cross comes from the tree and symbolises the great World Tree. It appears to be central to the cult of Diana, the great Mother Goddess of classical literature, and is associated with all the names of the Mother Goddess.

Diana's sacred groves held great pillars or trees in the centre or at the entrance, which later became the standing stones or pillars of wood. The great Goddess's husband was Jupiter the sky god or shining one, also associated with Adonis. Together they were known as the King and Queen of the Woods with actual human counterparts on earth, acting on their behalf. Sacrifices to the goddess and her consort were made on the altars and a holy fire, symbolic of the spirit, was burned eternally. The wood used was usually oak, which has been found in archaeological digs to be a substance used worldwide for Vestal fires. In German, Swedish, Roman, Greek, Indian, North American, African, Siamese and Chinese cultures, to name but a few, the sacred grove was vitally important in the rituals to the sun and moon deities. The groves differ slightly, but all are basically the same. In many of them, sacrifices are fastened to the trunk of the great centre tree, just as Jesus was sacrificed on the centre tree of the three.

Diana is associated with the moon, and her name comes from the Aryan root meaning 'bright' or 'to shine'. This root occurs in all the names of the Greek deities.

In ancient times the Aryans worshipped the oak as the World Tree. To the druids of ancient Europe, the oak was incredibly important. The tree has strength, longevity and hardness, useful for buildings, weaponry and later ships.

The origin of the tribal Jewish god can be traced back to Tammuz, an idol-god who died every year and then came back to life again in spring.11 As did Jesus. The cyclic patterns of existence are at the root of one of the world's largest faiths. Ideas and stories of these gods are reminiscent of the Hindu Agni, god of fire and shining, when Abraham and Moses see Jehovah as shining, bright fire or light. The burning, but cool, bush; the bush of light, is the same scenario as the Druidic god striking the mistletoe bush and lighting it up. The Ram in the thicket is symbolic of the fire of Ra (depicted as a Ram) in the tree. In Egyptian, the phrase 'Amun-u-El' means 'Amun is God' or 'the shining one'. This eventually became the Jewish Emanuel 'the shining one [or god] is with us'.

So who put all this together? Who crafted such a marvellous and symbolic book, which would stand the test of time and war? The one person in all Jewish history who can lay claim to having written much of the Bible is Moses.

'Moses was trained in all the wisdom of the Egyptians.' Acts 6:22

Jewish tradition and folklore claims the first Great Magician to be Moses, who probably lived around 1,400 BC. Mary, the sister of Moses, or Maria the Jewess, is said to have founded Alchemy. The Key of Solomon dates to around 1,000 BC and is one of the oldest magical works in existence and the root of much Alchemy and magic.

Tradition has it that during his stay in Egypt, Moses was an initiate in the mysteries of Osiris and helped to build the pyramids, with the non-slave help of Semites. 9 Moses also carried a staff or rod, as did Isaac. Some have claimed that

Moses was the Pharaoh Akhenaten who also carried the royal sceptre which was topped with the Caduceus-like coil of a snake. The rod is attributed magical powers and wields authority. As with the staff of Merlin, the magic of the ancient Shaman and Druid was represented by this, often rowan, staff. Symbolic of the World Tree and the Caduceus, capable of divination, as in Hosea 4:12, the rod or staff was wielded only by the powerful Father of the Shining Ones.

The snake also has symbolic meaning. The snake was always involved in the worship of the Sun God and was often the symbol of the sun. Sun ake (Snake) actually means 'Great Sun'. Nachash, the Hebrew for snake resolves into 'on ach ash' or 'One Great Light'. Another meaning of Nachash is 'to become wise'. The Greek for wisdom was Sophia, the Virgin of Light, and can be traced back to 'is ophis'; 'the light of Ophis the serpent' or 'light of the living light'. Almost Hermetic in origin, but too old.

The idea of Moses being the Egyptian Pharaoh, Akhenaten may hold some truth, especially when we consider that he was banished and had to lead his people from Egypt because of the worship of one god, Atun or Yahweh. A point to note is that Tutenkhamen was Akhenaten's son.

Josephus, the Jewish historian, claimed that Moses was a Helipolitian priest and an initiate at the temple of On, the Egyptian centre of the Sun cults. And it is here that he is credited with building an open-air prayer house or stone circle

to the sun god. This is also the place that Joseph married Asenath, the daughter of Potipherah, a priest of On.10 Plato was also an initiate at this temple years later.

Because of a mistranslation, the name Moses was given the image of horns in the painted forms associated with him. In Exodus 34, we find that Moses came down from Mount Sinai (Heaven) with shining and radiant skin. This 'shining forth' can be translated as he either 'sent forth beams' or 'sent forth horns'. Not surprisingly, the rest of us have been given the horns translation, whilst the initiates of Gnosticism were given the shining version. Maybe we should take a good look at everywhere the word horn is used in the Bible, we may find a new meaning.

Moses is also credited with having led an Egyptian army as their General. Although this has been criticised by a few, it would quite easily fit with the fact that druids and Shaman were responsible for leading men into battle. The famous stance of Merlin, with magical battle staff in hand, which allowed Arthur's men to do battle against the raging foe, is not a million miles off the mark.

The final ingredient in this mix was the Jews. All the ancient beliefs were brought to life in the people of the Book. No more changes and alterations, no more big leaps, the Law would stop the fickle people changing their minds. The beliefs and customs of the Egyptians were now too fanciful. Kings needed to be gods, or hold the power of the gods in their hands. The priests needed to come under the sway of the king and we see this in the battles of Jewish magicians with the Pharaohs, and in King David's Kingship taking little notice of the priests, even though he paid the price. Yet this comes through as just another front; the basic elements of the Shining Ones' religion are still there. The prophets are magicians who practise trance-

state operations to reach god. Daniel and Jacob in their dream quests are prime examples. Divination, star, sun and moon worship, blood rituals, sacred mountains, bulls, crosses, they are all familiar to us now.

When we look at the European traditions of the period we also see a highly organised pagan belief system, which held the same beliefs as the rest of the world. From tree worship to solar worship, the rituals and core beliefs remain the same. The light had already spread to Europe. The gods may differ slightly in title, but their names still meant 'to shine' or 'be bright'. The ancient Shaman ideas of the World Tree, of reincarnation and rebirth, the worship of the sky with all the host of heaven and the great Father and Mother deities were all there. It would, therefore, have been no great effort for the people of the Book, the people of the Covenant, to have moved in with their fellow priests and kings.

Around 1,000 to 900 BC (the date is uncertain) the tribes of Israel dispersed. It is highly uncertain as to where these tribes moved, although new evidence is coming out all the time. Among these, were the people of King Omri. In old English, King is, 'cyn', meaning 'nation' and 'ing' meaning 'of'. Therefore 'cyn mri' can easily translate into 'Cymri ,or nation, of Omri'. Israel was actually called Omri's Land by the Assyrians, and King Omri traded far and wide, especially with the Phoenicians who are known to have traded with the tin mining communities of southern England.

By tradition, the priesthood of ancient England and Northern

Europe at that time were called Druids. They share similar beliefs to all those discussed previously. They practised divination, astrology, tree worship in much the same way as the pre-Druidic peoples of the area. The name 'Druid' may derive from the word 'truth' or possibly 'oak'. A branch of the Levite priests were called 'the Truth' and this may be where the title came from.

The sons of Isaac may have been translated as 'Isaac's son' or 'Saxon', and Angels or messengers as 'Angles'. Therefore the Anglo-Saxons become messengers of the Sons of Isaac, or people of Israel.

The word British, according to some extreme ideas, may have come from the translation, 'B'rith' which is Hebrew for 'covenant' and 'ish' which means 'men and women'. Therefore the British may mean 'people of the covenant'. The invasion of the Anglo-Saxons and the Britons was, therefore, by the warriors of the people of the covenant.

The supposed founder of the third incarnation of Stonehenge was Hu Gadarn Hyscion (or Isaac's son). 12 He was an Egyptian Hebrew and is the man who supposedly led the K'Omri, the people of the covenant, to Britain. It is he, the present Druids claim, who set up the people of Truth or Druids. Hu is Egyptian for protector and is used in the element of the Sphinx. The Kurgan link of Hu is helpful in the fact that these were the people of the burial mounds and this fits in with the various mounds scattered across northern Europe. These mounds were called 'S'iuns' by the Druids and means mounds of stone. The Hebrew term Zion, which sounds very similar, also means mountain of stone.

In Druidism there is a priest called Linus, which means 'white robed'. The Druids not only wore white robes, but also grew beards. Musaeus was another priest, whose name means 'knowledge'. The Druids also had their own trinity. The Druid Triad, as it is called, includes Belie (Teutates), the light or sun, Taran (Taranis), the bull or Jupiter and Yesu or Esus, the Saviour or Oak. Together these are shown as three shining rays of light in the Cymric cross and every Druid wore this emblem. The Triad is symbolised by three white berries from the mistletoe of the Oak; the gods of the tree of life, the spirits within the tree. The unspoken name of the godhead was Awen or Om and in the spoken word it was Du-w, pronounced 'Doo-weh', phonetically similar Yahweh, and Du-w means 'shining one' or 'one without darkness'.

Seth, the Egyptian brother of Osiris, claimed that Druidism was founded from the Shamanism of Asia. He may have been right, although the journey was a little longer in time, probably by way of the Americas.

In Ireland there is some evidence that Cuchulainn (called Cuthullin, by Ossian 13), the Irish hero of myth, may be linked to Kukulcan, the sun-god of the Mayans, especially when we consider that this god was closely related in symbolism and association to the Aztec Quetzalcoatl.

Quetzalcoatl was one of the main gods of South America. He was bright of skin or white, his symbol was a cross and he had come from abroad with others. He was said to be bearded and to have reigned in the 'Golden Age'. Apparently, he disappeared across the

Kukulkan

eastern sea and promised to return. He was the creator and sky god, as was Kukulkan.

Kukulkan or Quetzalcoatl was the plumed serpent, able to fly and shape shift. He was born of the Virgin, Queen of heaven, and he invented the calendar. He brought much insight to the people in the form of law, time, inventions and civilisation. Just as the Shaman had brought similar things to the fertile crescent. He carried the spear of the 'morning star', a title from the Old Testament and attributed to Jesus or Esus. He carried a rod, or staff of life (reminiscent of the Tree of Life), which held magical properties. He was at the same time a man and a god, like Jesus or Krishna. He travelled to the other-world and was the Light of day. When he had done wrong, he decided he was to pay for his sin and ordered an imitation cave to be erected where he stayed for four days. In Jewish tradition, to rise before three days would have meant that the sin had not been paid for. Jesus rose on the third day, from a cave. After his time in the cave, Queztalcoatl was risen up on flames to the heavens, where he literally became the morning star, or Venus.

He is also linked with the resurrected sun, who dies and rises every day, as did Ra of the Egyptians. He sent out disciples and overcame temptations, he descended to hell and is promised in a second coming. The parallels are obvious.

The promised land of the Aztecs was 'Anahuac', 'the Place of the Circle', reminiscent of the Grove and circles of the Hebrews. The brothers (like Moses and Aaron) who were leading them had a magical staff (like Moses) which they had acquired from the holy land. They drove the staff into the sea and, yes you guessed it, the waters parted. The staff was red (like the Red Sea) and the people walked across the now dry land. One of the brothers in a later story enters a mountainside cave (or, symbolically, the womb of the goddess in heaven) as if in death, and to everyone's amazement he is risen again in glory.

Of course these stories can be traced back through the much older Olmecs and, according to Pierre Honore, to China and Indo-China. He does this through language similarities and the art of the various cultures.

Olmec

In the 'History of Central America' by A.B. Jaurequi the Mayan 'Hele, hele lamah sabac ta ni' or 'I faint, I faint, and my face is hid in darkness', bears a remarkable resemblance to the supposed last words of Jesus on the Cross, 'Eli, eli, lama sabachthani'. Is this proof of an ancient, secret, ritual or language of life and death, known only to the Shining Ones?

The evidence from the archaeology and mythology of the Mayan, Aztec, Toltec and the Olmec civilisations is varied. Every year, something new emerges which links the cultures together. Recent finds of mummified remains, similar to the Egyptian and central Asian mummification techniques, has shed new light and doubt on the emergence of the culture. The emerging similarities will soon force standard history to be re-written. Of course, we must not forget the incredible likeness between the pyramids, more of which later.

There is some evidence that the Celts of Wales actually went to America. There were, to the surprise of many, Welsh speaking Indians in Virginia in 1666 AD. Although this may be from some later Welsh ancestry or even a mistake of the person interpreting. The Mandans of the Missouri River area were said to be white skinned, made Welsh style coracles and used remarkably similar names for many items.

It appears to be highly likely that there was a trade route to the Americas from as long ago as the height of the Egyptian reign. Research into the possible early travel between the continents has demonstrated that ancient man was quite capable of trading across the oceans. Even Plato said, 'it was possible for the travellers of that time to cross from Atlantis to the others islands and from the islands to the whole of the continent over against them which encompasses that veritable ocean (Atlantic).' It may be that the memory of these other islands was the memory of Atlantis and this became the other-world of popular culture. When we discover that Columbus was himself an initiate in later years, it is no surprise to find that he also went to the Americas, using maps already in existence.

In North America, there is the Chokia Mound, or Monks Mound, with extremely similar architecture to the South and Central American Pyramids and the Babylonian style temples of the Middle and Near East. The mounds are astronomically aligned, and the whole site has been named The City of the Sun. 'Great Serpent Mound', a huge mound in the style of a serpent on the east coast of North America bears a close resemblance to many European, central Asian and African mounds. Petroglyphs of the Algonkian people are exactly the same as Russian Petroglyphs, which shows that travel across the ice-links between the continents was highly likely.

In Chaco Canyon, New Mexico, there are strange circular stone Kivas or chambers. Rituals were carried out in these circles, as in groves and stone circles. It has been suggested that the local Anasazi Shamans were more aware of the Earth's current in these highly radioactive granite chambers. Around these chambers are long lines. It is possible that they reveal earth energies as Ley lines or dragon paths. The Anasazi

people are said to be a mystery themselves, with their strange almost Atlantean knowledge. It is not known where they came from or where they went.

The world's ancient building sites are places of mystery and wonder. So much has been written about them and yet we seem to be no closer to the truth. Now, with the information we have collected so far and the slowly revealing story of the Shining Ones, we may be able to discover the purpose of these sacred places and find out who built them.

Notes

Chapter 6

1   Human Antiquity. Feder/Park. Mayfield.1992.

2   The Sacred Chain, a History of the Jews. Norman F. Cantor. Harper Collins. 1994.

3   The Fire and the Stones. Nicholas Hagger. Element. 1998.

4   Bloodline of the Holy Grail. P 68. Laurence Gardner. Element. 1996.

5   The Fire and the Stones. Nicholas Hagger. Element. 1998.

6   The Book of Ceremonial Magic. William Ryder and Son. 1911.

7   All Biblical quotes are from the New King James Bible. Tyndale.

8   Other places to look into for Sun, Moon and Star worship of the Hebrews. 2 Kings 21:3,5. 23:5. Job 31:26,27. Lev 26:30. Isa 17:8, Gen 1:16. Gen 37:9. Deut 4:19.Gen 1:14 Ps 104:19.

9   Folklore of the Holy Land. J.E. Hanauer. The Sheldon Press. 1907

10   Ancient Egypt, Myth and History. Geddes and Grosset. 1997.

11   The Golden Bough. Sir James Frazer. Wordsworth. 1993.

12   The Fire and the Stones. Nicholas Hagger. Element. 1998.

13   Ossian or Oisan, the 3rd century Gaelic bard.

Chapter 7
Sacred Places

I have visited many of Europe's stone megaliths in the course of my research, and each time I am overwhelmed by their mystery. None of them, however, has filled me with awe more than England's Stonehenge. On my last visit, I tried to imagine how it might feel to witness the site put to its proper use.

I pictured myself standing there at dusk, watching modern-day Druids walk slowly around the ancient cathedral. They are dressed in white and carry long staffs. They chant as they circle the stones. The sky is painted with orange flames as the sun sinks. The gathering falls silent.

Then the scene changes, slips backwards in time thousands of years. The stones are whitewashed; bright colours mark significant aspects of the sky above them. They shine like stars under the rising full moon. Great wooden fences emerge from the ground to surround and protect the spirit and power of the Shining Ones within the circle.

The Druids pick up their pace. They are Shaman, performing an annual rite of sacrifice, their screaming victims symbolic of death. The all-important cycles of life and death played out in ritual. The floor is painted to mirror the sky. Dances and processions follow the patterns of the gods on the ground: as

above, so below. Flames are lit around the holy place and rainbows of colour erupt from within the stones. Everybody gasps in fear and wonder.

This may be a fanciful image, but it is based on sound research, which can be gleaned from the pages of tradition and mythology.

Many modern historians mock the Druids, but research carried out for this book shows that their beliefs and rituals may be closer to the truth than any of the guesswork currently available. Even though thousands of years separate modern druids and their ancestors in spirit, the imagery and traditions are very similar.

Stonehenge, the pyramids of Egypt, the burial mounds of America, the temples of the Middle East; these and other such amazing structures have always been the subject of much

debate as to who built them and why.

To discover the people and the purpose behind these sites we will need to note the similarities between them. To begin with we should look at the origins of some of the shapes we find in ancient sacred sites. In the stone monuments massed around the world, there is a wealth of information, previously hidden from us through a different understanding of them. Many such stones are of meteoric origin and are said to have 'fallen from the heavens', such as the Islamic 'kaaba'.

Kaaba

We have seen that the influence of the Shining Ones came from Central Asia, Africa and Siberia under the title of Shaman, priest or magician. The Shining legacy was thereafter hard to kill. The ancient priesthood took a strong hold, and developed ancient monasteries, universities and places of learning all over the world. These centres took their influence from the surrounding natural world. The vast and mysterious mountains of Tibet and Central Asia, with misty tree lines and strange night-time noises, spectacular sunsets and the power of the mountain forests all had a part to play in ritual and in town planning.

The cycle of life could be manifested on the mountain itself. In Tibet, on Mount Kailash, the ceremony of 'Parikrama' is the process of cycles. By circling the holy mountain, the mind is

Mount Kailash

sent through a cycle of death and life. Glastonbury Tor, in England, is said to have a turf pathway all around the holy sculpted hill where the ritual of life's cycle is carried out in ceremony by walking around the hill (In Syrian, 'Tor' means 'mountain' and in Britain it means 'conical hill').

Muslims consider the resting place of the meteoric 'Kaaba' stone to be the most sacred spot on Earth. The story goes that Abraham and Ishmael built the shrine on foundations already laid by Adam, the first man. All Muslims are expected to visit this black stone, which is held in a sacred sanctuary at the centre of the Great Mosque in Mecca. This is the spot all of Islam faces to pray, and upon completion of the pilgrimage to this holy site there is a special ceremony of circling the great stone.

Mecca

In Madhya Pradesh, India, there is a small mound, very similar to Glastonbury Tor, which is called the Great Stupa of Sanchi. As far as we know, it was built around the 3rd Century BC. On top of this small mound is the 'yasti', which is a spire with three 'chatras' or discs. The mound is surrounded by a stone fence in the form of uprights and cross lintels, reminiscent of how a complete version of Stonehenge would have looked. All around, there are symbols of the trinity or triad. To pay their respects to Buddha, followers must circle the Great Stupa. If we look around the world we will see this circumnavigation of the sacred mountain to be a regular practice in places ranging from the Americas to the mystical temple of Borobudur in Java. In Egypt, the king, who was the Sun God, had to walk solemnly around the Temple to help the sun make its way.

Borobudur

The top of the dome at Sanchi represents heaven. Mountaintops, spires, pyramids, ziggurats and towers all represent heaven, or man's attempt to reach the heavens. Moses went up Mount Sinai to retrieve the tablets from God in heaven, and the folklore of the world is filled with such tales of the holy ones visiting the heavens on top of mountains.

When the Shining Ones came down from their homes upon high and brought with them the mysteries of the mountains, they also needed to emulate the ancient heavenly realm on the plains. As you will recall, the beliefs of the Shining Ones were handed down partly by the Kurgans or Mound Builders.

One of the earliest types of mound was the dolmen. This consisted of two or more huge stone slabs placed edgewise against the earth and topped with a capstone. They were then covered with earth and stones. A large proportion of these

false hills were surrounded by stone circles, as if in symbolic completion of the cycle of life, the stones represented the person. This would look very similar to the Great Stupa, and is found all over the world, from America to Europe and Japan to North Africa. Some of these dolmens are burial mounds and others are simply for ceremonial purposes, but even so the rituals were still carried out regardless of whether an actual burial had taken place, the point being that it was considered a place of rebirth. This is a point we should remember when dealing with the Great Pyramid of Giza, which did not include a burial, just a large and rough hewn stone coffin which had probably been used previously in the very same ritual for which it was now intended, although Egyptologists maintain that it had probably been robbed.

Burial tombs are by far the oldest universal structures in the world and hold many secrets. From these burial tombs we can learn much about our past, especially from the symbolism implied.

From the barrows of Europe and the Mound Builders of North America to the Mycenae beehive tombs and the importance of the Egyptian Valley of the Kings, we can see how much effort and wealth has been poured into the idea of rebirth into either another being, the afterlife or the next plane of existence.

The Native American Mound Builders laid down their legacy over many thousands of years (8,000 BC to 1,800 AD). The wonderful and huge examples are strangely similar in design and are produced to such remarkable accuracy that they are worth a second look. 1

In Koster, Illinois, a burial mound dating from 6,400 BC contained an infant, which had been dusted with red ochre, in much the same style found elsewhere (Skara Brae, Orkneys, Swinside, Cumbria, Swaziland and all over Europe), as if in some sort of rebirth ritual. Finds from burial mounds in Ohio (which include circles, octagons, crosses and pyramids) and the Mississippi  valley have revealed that bracelets were buried with the burned skeletons. This was a similar practice to those of the Hindus, and the jewellery itself resembled bangles made in Persia and Hindostan. Why would this be? There can come a point where the coincidence of similar beliefs arises too frequently, and we must ask whether this can surely be just another freak emergence.

Another point of note is that as with Stonehenge and thousands of other sites around Europe, the earth and stone used at some cairns in Ohio was brought a considerable distance even though there was suitable stone and earth in the locality. This could have had something to do with the earth energies, an idea which has been put forward for the European sites. The theory is that earth or stone taken from elsewhere reveals a better earth signal than local materials, and it is said that the ancients knew which material to put where and how to read the signals.

The circular mounds of America are surrounded by stone circles. Close by are settlements, which resemble the European earthworks of our ancestors. The majority tend to be aligned to solar and lunar patterns as well as some star alignments. The native Indians believed that they could reach the Great Power or Spirit (the one god of the Senecas) by climbing the mound of heaven. Alongside the Mississippi there is a rock known as the Spirit Rock. During a whole moon, the natives dance around this stone, as in a May Pole ritual of Old England. The stone is often painted white, red or blue and sacrifices are carried out before it. This too is a global practice. How did these similarities come about? Did ancient man travel to the Americas? The South American tales of the Great Feathered God, Quetzalcoatl, demonstrates the beliefs that white men visited there and influenced the belief systems.

In the early pioneering days of the great West, the Shawnee natives of Northern America told some European colonists that the ancient forts and mounds had been built by white people and it was only after many years of wars against the red skins that they were beaten. The Delawares of Northern Ohio and Kentucky say that they were called the 'Tallegewi' and that they did indeed leave the country after long wars.

A cavalry officer claimed that in the country west of the Mississippi he had seen a tribe of white Indians who had reddish hair, much like the Celts of Europe and the image portrayed of Quetzalcoatl. These Indians informed the cavalry officer that their ancestors had landed in Florida from a foreign land. A companion of the cavalryman was a Welshman who claimed to be able to understand the language of the Indians as being very close to Welsh.

The period of these 'white' Indians is open to debate. There may be no truth in it at all. All we know are the stories and the archaeological evidence of the mounds themselves. It was only as recently as 1986 that modern historians finally accepted that it was the Scandinavians who actually discovered America and not Columbus (and now it could even be the Chinese). These Scandinavians could have been red haired, and certainly would have known about mound building, although some of the examples of mounds pre-date these Scandinavian intrusions.

There may also be some truth in the 711 AD escape from Spain of a group of Christian bishops, who fled the Moorish invasion. In some traditions, this group of seven bishops never returned, but they went wearing white clothes, with red crosses adorning the front, and wore beards, as the image of the South Americans' god shows. The problem with this, however, is that not all the traditions surrounding Quetzalcoatl can be synchronised with those of the obviously early Christian ideas of the bishops. There were not seven of them, and the early Americans were not so uncultured as to be unable to recognise a man when they saw one. After the long Atlantic journey the bishops would have been dishevelled and in a poor state. The language barrier itself would have been a problem, unless somebody had been there before. Some of the sites, both north and south, predate this occurrence, if indeed it happened at all, so therefore any pre-bishop times are left unaccounted for in this scenario.

The mounds of America were commonly conical or pyramidal and served many purposes. The early burial mounds certainly held important individuals, some of whom may have been the local priest-deity or medicine man. Temples were built on top of the mounds in some areas and show similarities with South American mounds and the idea of a temple and mound in the Egyptian delta.

Similar examples of these mounds can be found in

Silbury Hill

the rest of the world. Silbury Hill in England has a prime example, which on the face of it looks like a large circular mound. When we dig a little deeper, however, we find a complex stepped construction, like a ziggurat or pyramid. Silbury Hill is the world's largest manmade mound and remains almost untouched by archaeologists, although in 1967-70 Professor Atkinson led an excavation with the BBC and found nothing. There is nobody buried beneath this great mound, so it must have been a temple. The daily gauge of the shadows of the Great Pyramid and the Silbury mound are identical (Cox, A Guide to Avebury). It is amazing to think that this temple mound should once have been the site of the Shining Ones' great rituals of life and rebirth just like the temple mounds of Egypt, Mesoamerica, South America, North America, Siberia, Central Asia, and the rest of the world.

These temples were often positioned in relation to a natural feature, such as a sacred mountain, to be close to heaven, or a river for purification and rebirth. Many believe that they were built only on Ley lines or earth energy spots. There is much speculation, along with results from dowsing techniques, which circumstantially back this theory up, although until modern science decides to take a look we cannot say for sure. (For Ley Lines and other such mysteries, see note 14).

Uxmal

The pyramids of Mexico were known as

'teocallis, teo calli', meaning 'House of God'. At Uxmal, there are seven pyramids grouped together in the form of the seven stars of the Great Bear, just like the star alignment of the pyramids at Giza (as above, so below).

In, or just outside, each temple there is a stone or wooden altar, a universal requirement. Ritually, the altar was used only by the priest, shaman or magician.

There were two kinds of temple. The first is the hill type, which brought man closer to heaven and probably made the priest look as if he was god himself when he walked the lonely steps home again. The second is the tomb, or chamber temple. This began as a cave, much like those of the Zoque in Mesoamerica, where rituals were carried out in the womb of Mother Earth who accepted the human sacrifices with joy. Eventually, these two styles merged and we end up with the greatest kind of temple: the Great Pyramid at Giza.

Greek Temples were literally a hill city or acropolis and people looked up towards the white-robed priests. Pliny tells us that the worshippers of the Sun God were responsible for the great obelisks, which are symbolic of the Sun's rays. Roman temples stole much from the Greeks and were almost always set upon platforms to raise the sights of the masses.

As we have seen, the Indian, Hindu and Buddhist temples represented the heavens in all their symbolic glory and the world mountain, Mount Meru. The schematised tree of stone, which usually accompanies these temples, represented the human self. Within this mountain or heaven we find the cave-hall, the interior or womb. There are freestanding tower temples in Hindu systems and we can see that towers became common around the world with the advent of Islam. Islamic tombs also took on the sacred mountain aspect with huge domes representing heaven.

All these temples, tombs and mounds are aligned to the sky, and take their lead from the power of the heavenly host, the Sun, which dies at the end of the day and rises in the morning as if born again. This natural, daily ritual became the central theme for thousands of years of religion on our planet. Although it was taken to have slightly differing meanings, it remained an essential element to all thought, creed and building.

Symbols adorn the temples and burial mounds, and secretly tell a tale of life and death. Modern historical research has shed new light on ancient writings, but still the meanings behind the majority of glyphs remain hidden to us.

Colour was one of man's first symbols, and each had its own secret or clear meaning. Red, for example, stood for war or blood. Each of these elements had their own meaning and would have to be related to something else to turn the key. Red with a symbol of a womb meant blood; red with the symbol of a weapon would mean war. More and more layers added to these symbols made the message increasingly difficult to understand, and only those with the eyes to see could interpret it. Now, thousands of years later and living in a completely different world, we find the data very difficult to translate, especially with the myriad messages buried within the layers. Only in the last 100 years, and even more recently, have we finally begun to interpret the Bible through all of its remarkable layers, which remained hidden to us through prejudice.

In Barclodiad-Y-Gawres, Anglesey, Wales, there are a number of large stones upon which are scattered mysterious patterns. The most universal and basic symbols from ancient times is the

spiral and in many photographs of the site it can be seen that the spirals upon these stones and on various items of pottery have been filled in with white paste. Evidence from such sites prove that the builders and users of these rock temples used colour in their rituals. White was the most commonly used colour, and many standing stones were whitewashed so that at significant times of the year, such as summer and winter solstices, the stones would shine brightly as the angled sun struck the pure white image of gods.

The spiral is a universal symbol for the sun and the cycles of its power, spiralling to death and back to life again. This symbol was also linked to the cycle of woman and snakes.

At Le Petit Chasseur in Switzerland we find what is probably the earliest (3,200 BC) image of a Shining One priest. The statue-menhir stands firm at the front of tomb 11 (although it originally stood at tomb 6). This stone slab has no head, just a small half-circle in place of the neck. There are two long, spindly arms which fall down towards the belt, below which hangs a sacrificial knife. Around the priest's neck is a necklace with two large spirals, which resemble ovaries.

It is a well attested fact that the female cycle was probably the second most important cycle to any tribe. The birth of children was paramount to the survival of the clan. Young ones were needed to carry out the work for the elderly and to continue the name of the group. Everywhere, all over Europe, this symbol of the Sun in the spiral echoes across tombs and stones which have more in common with the Mother Goddess than the Sun God. The spirals are often at the entrance to the womb-like tombs, as they are at Newgrange in Ireland, and inside, where the sun penetrates only once a year in a universal cycle.

In Castelluccio, Sicily, there is yet another stone slab which once blocked a chamber. This time the image is more blatant and firmly backs up the idea that these spirals are indeed images of the Mother Goddess. Here, the two spirals are at the top of the slab and a small slit below and towards them is caused by a phallus pushing upwards. With this image, there is no doubt that a sexual ritual is in process and is related to these chambers: new life being created where old life is buried.

Another idea about these spirals is that they brought Earth energy to a point in space required by the priest. Any electrician will know that energy can be directed via such shapes, so there may be some truth behind this effect, although, again we would require the helping hand of the scientists to research such claims. The solar power of the sun or the power of a menstruating woman may have been inferred by the priest in these circumstances. At the West Kennet Avenue, England, the alternating shape and size of the standing stones is thought to be 'raising a form of energy, through coils and spirals'. 2

Another widespread image of the Mother Goddess was the horned bull. At Anghelu Ruju in Sardinia, the bull's horns were painted with red ochre, symbolising the blood of menstruation and fertility. At Haga Qim in Malta, and all over this area, effigies and images of a large fertile Mother Goddess can be found. These are not the simple items of a needed fertility, they are a systematic and specific language of ritual and a message to each other. They are the tools of a language hidden from us because of our present belief in the

Mother Goddess from Malta

simplicity of early man, our idea that all he was interested in was bringing in the harvest and procreating. These things are and were important, but at one level only. All these pictures and images have other levels of meanings. The idea of reincarnation, rebirth of the soul is rife throughout these areas, and this doctrine later became more deeply hidden in the mainstream religions. Today, the Hasidic Jews of Eastern Europe are the direct descendants of those who first believed in the doctrine of reincarnation, which they called 'gilgul'. 3

This idea of rebirth is never more firmly placed than in the Tree. The image of Jesus dying on a cross is rooted in nearly two thousand years of myth. As we saw in an earlier chapter, the Bible never mentions a cross, instead the original word was 'tree' and almost all early Roman crucifixions were on trees, also, the Jewish way of executing a criminal was by stoning. The cross was an early symbol of execution by crucifixion. People were often impaled or nailed to a pointed stake or tree and left to die. So where did this cross image come from? And who added it into the Christian passion?

There is an enormous variety of cross forms, all of which come from the same root. The Egyptian Ankh, Tau (from the Greek letter T) cross or 'crux ansata', a T shaped cross with a loop above, represents life and is held by a deity or king as a sign of his power to issue life. This cross was held to the nostrils and life returned to the departed, in the same way as breathing the breath of life into the nostrils, noted in the Bible and just about every other creation myth. Without the loop, this cross represented eternity to the Egyptians, and predates the Christian cross, which was introduced into Christianity 300 years after the death of Christ on a tree. The reason for this was so that this new Shining One, enlightened king-priest-deity, could be linked with the old ways, just as he was in so many other ways. Those with the eyes to see and the ears to hear would have understood the vital symbolism involved with this link. The legend of the true cross of Christ is linked with the Tree of Life, because symbolically it was upon the Tree of Life that Jesus died.

The cross is found in all cultures and, mostly in the magical context, it has power. The various words for cross (crux, cruz, crowz, etc.,) come from 'ak ur os' meaning 'the light of the great fire'. In many doctrines the four stations of the cross stand for air, earth, fire and water. The permanence and alchemical significance of this is obvious to the enlightened.

The Aztec weather goddess carried a cross, and at Cozumel it was an object of worship. The symbol of Quetzalcoatl is a cross. Americans marked their boundaries with the magic cross. The Swastika cross, 'fylfot', 'manji' or 'crux gammata' is formed from four Greek gammas joined together. It was widely used and is found on many stone monuments around the world. Regarded as a symbol of good fortune, it derives its name from the Sanskrit 'svastika' ('of well being' or 'blessed'). It has been used by Mesopotamian, Cretan, Mayan, Navajo, Celtic, Hindu, Jain and Buddhist cultures. It is believed that it represents the movement of the sun through the heavens and the cycle of life.

The swastika (German 'Hakenkreuz') arose more obviously under Hitler's Nazi Germany when it was turned counter clockwise to represent evil and negative forces. Hitler, as we have seen, found the swastika on a Christian Monastery doorway, and it also became the symbol for his Thule Society which was responsible for the Nazi movement. The swastika was originally a sun symbol, a symbol of the Shining Ones and of the Earth Mother, the two important deities coming together in one symbol.

The cross is unique in its all-inclusive symbolism, which covers cyclic patterns, the sun god, the earth goddess, the life giver, the great tree, and as something which is in touch with the earth energies. In many cultures the cross was placed upon the sacred initiate's chest as a symbol of rebirth. In the Christian mysteries, the cross of Christ, the standard and most widely known cross in the Christian world, is symbolic of the universe, the cyclic patterns of life and death. It tells of the coming of the next man of light or Shining One and in this respect is similar to the swastika. The Celtic cross, the standard or Latin cross of Christ but with a circle behind, is remarkably similar to the majority of stone circles when viewed from above. A long alley or passageway through which the sun rises up in new life giving vigour to the altar at the centre of the circle which is the place of the chakra or pineal gland on the head. The centre of the circle is the place to receive new life, the place of the sacrifice, as Jesus was sacrificed at this place on the cross. Therefore, as above, so below, the sacrifice on the cross as is effected in the rituals of the stone circles on the ground. This is also evident with the Pyramid. As Peter Lemesurier pointed out, at summer solstice, the Great Pyramid forms a huge cross on the ground, matching the circles at the centre being the place of ritual for rebirth and renewal. Many places the world over, with or without connection to Christianity, have set out the pattern of their sacred buildings to the form of the cross, from Hindu to Aztec, all in the same style as the circles and the pyramid with the ritual centre at the head of the cross.

Many of these cross shaped buildings, especially in the Americas, are that way because of the earth, fire, air and water and the four corresponding directions of north, south, east and west. Many burial mounds around Europe are laid out in a cross-shaped pattern, obviously due to the rebirth aspect of the cross. The West Kennet Long Barrow in England is cross-shaped with the entrance facing the rising sun from the east, symbolic of new life. Carrowmore, Newgrange and Knowth are the same and there are many more.

Another point to make about Celtic crosses is that all over Europe there are images of pagan gods, woodland creatures of the night and old pagan or Druidic tales of cyclic natures, which adorn the standing stone crosses. This merging of beliefs and ideas is partly the reason why it is so difficult to get to the underlying elements of the various faiths.

In 100 BC, crosses were set up above the graves of the elect by the Scandinavians who also used them as boundary marks (as did Americans), and the staffs of the Scandinavian priests were crosses mixed between the caduceus. 13 The Tau cross without the loop (a T) is the 'crux commissa' and is probably the oldest type. It is the cross of the god Thoth (later Hermes) who became the god of the alchemist, the magician, the inheritor of the Shining Ones legacy. It was also the symbol of the god Thammuz (Tammuz), a Sumerian, Babylonian and Assyrian god who died every year and rose again in the spring (at the same time as the Christian Easter or rising of Christ), matching the cycles of the sun.

Thammuz is identified with Adonis and Marduk. The Jews obviously knew about the cyclic nature of Thammuz, as he is spoken of in Ezekiel where the 'women weeping for Tammuz' is alluded to. The early 4th century Gnostics took this old pagan symbol of the sun, the earth and the cycles of life, and made it represent the man who was to symbolise all these things and more. Jesus may have died on a cross symbolically, but in truth, the truth of reality and symbolism he died on a tree. All crosses originated from the most basic of altars, the sacrificial tree, which in the case of Jesus was, significantly, placed upon a mountain with two others as a trinity sacrifice.

The tree as the image of death and rebirth is universal to all cultures. In South America, sacrificial victims were invariably fastened to tree trunks. In China and Japan there are sacred groves and trees standing at or just outside the entrance to their villages, offerings are pinned to the trunks of these trees. The worship of trees is fundamental to an understanding of the supposedly mysterious images we have around us now. Grimm pointed out that the word for 'temple' taken from the Teutonic background pointed to them being natural woods or groves.[4] The druids held special interest in the Oak, indeed the Druid word for 'sanctuary' matches with the Latin word 'nemus', and means 'grove' or 'woodland glade'. In Sweden, Greece, Italy, India, America, Australia, all Europe and Africa the worship of trees is so deeply ensconced in the origins of their beliefs, we must wonder how these beliefs came to be so universal and so similar. It is, therefore, no wonder that the idea of God dying upon a tree was absolutely fundamental to the plan of Jesus' death.

Worship, especially the more sacred and secretive worship, seems to have been carried out in groves. The natural grove would have been modernised with the sacrificial tree being placed at the centre or entrance. Upon this altar, the king-god or son of the king-god would have been sacrificed. This is well attested to in several books on the subject. [5]

The grove would then have been fenced with posts, poles or trees, this eventually led to the small stone circles: a more permanent structure. The altar or sacred tree would then have been transformed into a large stone monolith and all the attention diverted towards it. In conjunction with this, knowledge of the stars and the cyclic patterns of nature would have been taken into account and suddenly we have the most useful temple in existence. People would come from miles around to pay their tithes to the sacred priesthood, see the prophecies, enact the rituals and learn.

Around these magical circles arose great centres of learning, stone age universities of the initiated. The great white horse of Uffington, for example, signposts the way to the Shining centre. We can see from archaeological evidence that these great centres arose.

In places like Skara Brae, the buildings alone show that these were no ordinary farmers. There were few trees on Skara Brae 5,000 years ago so the buildings were made from stone. The place is linked with Ireland's Boyne Valley tombs (Newgrange), Spain, Portugal, Woodhenge and Durrington Walls, so the late Neolithic site is of great importance. The trade was taught in the quiet surroundings where the learned passed on the sacred magical skills which were then taken on to the big city. Traces of coloured pigment were found, which may have been used for painting themselves or other items.

There are many other such sites and even larger ones around Europe. Chysauster, Cornwall and Carn Brae in Cornwall show the south of England as being important, probably from the point of view that the priests could move easily across the European continent from this popular tin mining area. The most famous priest of all time, Jesus Christ, is said by tradition to have visited Cornwall with Joseph of Arimathea who himself is reputed to have owned tin mines in Cornwall. Did he visit the old universities of the Shining Ones? And did he bring Jesus with him?

The Shining Ones came to Northern Europe and set up large stone monuments. In Ireland they left the legacy of the 'Tuatha de Danaan' or 'People of Anu' which means 'People of the Shining Ones'. (Anu is the feminine version of the Mesopotamian god Anu and was worshipped by the

Anannage). These Danu people probably gave rise to Denmark also.

The God of the Tuatha de Danaan was 'Ogma', whose name derives from the same root as the Biblical Gog, Magog. The stone building expertise of the Biblical figures was now global and the same rituals were being carried out.

At Les Pierres Plates in France, the Allee-coudee passageway offers indications of the skills of those inside. In his book Megalithic Mysteries, Michael Balfour puts it like this, 'The place is like a deserted teaching hospital; the reception area is in on the left, and prehistoric medical illustrations have been left on the walls - ribs, hearts, lungs, livers, stomachs, below collar bones and neck recesses, with spinal cords, channels of life.' Those who used and are buried in this place were medicine men and were quite practical ones by the sound of it. The signpost of the horse, similarly the one at Uffington, England, is intertwined with the whole concept of the Shining Ones' ancient symbolism. Across the globe the horse is always associated with the solar force and is generally involved in fertility rites, as are most such land markings. In Blyth, Colorado, there are stone circles, a horse and a man laid out on the ground. In the south of England we have a man, a horse and stone circles. Strangely, in Colorado, and in fact North America, the horse died out around 10,000 years ago, leaving the people who idealised its image something of a puzzle, as according to history's version they never came into contact with one. The horse was not introduced into America until the 1540's by the Spanish. Who laid down the image of the horse in America? Why are there stone circles across America? The Big Horn Medicine Wheel Circle is 10,000 feet up on Medicine Mountain, again a sacred mountain. This has proven to be a precise astronomical observatory, with sunset, sunrise, summer solstice and at least three major star orientations included. Who were these people? Why is their knowledge so similar to that of other parts of the world? Why, without the actual existence of the horse, was the animal important enough to be raised in stone or marked upon the ground?

The horse takes a special place in the minds of the Shining Ones for various reasons, such as travel, freedom to move around. For a nomadic culture and a livelihood that necessitated speedy travel the horse was literally a godsend. The Gaulish word for horse was 'epos' or the 'Eye of Light', a hint of the deeper meaning to come of the horse symbol. Like the tree, which provides all round sustenance and symbolises the cyclic pattern of life, the horse also provides sustenance. Even today in many parts of the world the horse is ridden and eaten. Leather for clothing and all manner of useful implements comes from the horse. The durability and manner of the horse has inspired so many over the centuries, so much so that early man must have been equally inspired. Although its use as a means of transport can only be traced back over a relatively short timescale of only a few thousand years, it is beyond doubt that part of the relationship developed beforehand.

The Japanese god Kuannan is the white or bright horse god, in China Kwan-yin is the same. The sun god, Helios, is depicted as a bright shining horse. Actaeon, the famous Greek horse of mythology, means 'shining one' and the horse of Diomedes (the hero of Troy), was called Lampon, or the Bright or Shining One. Aethon is fiery red, Lampos is shining like a light, Phlegon means the burning one and Purocis is fiery hot. Aurora's horse is called Phaethon and means the Shining One. Pluto's horse, Abaster means to come away from the stars. Mohammed's horse Fodda was a white mule and Buddha's Kantaka horse was white.

In Norse mythology, Skinfaxi was the Shining Mane. Zeus, in the form of a white, swan loved a maiden called Leda who gave birth to an egg (symbol of fertility) from which came the two twins, Castor and Pollux, who are represented as riding upon white horses. Of Castor and Pollux, Macaulay said, 'Safe comes the ship to haven, Through billows and through gales, If once the great Twin Brethren, Sit shining on the sails.'

Tacitus records that in Northern Europe, snow white horses were reared at the expense of the public for use in the sacred groves of the Druids, and their snorting, when they were tied to the sacred chariot or post, was recorded and used as omens for the tribe. It was firmly believed that these horses knew the plans of the heavenly powers. The Druids and the Magi practised divination via the horse, showing a remarkable link across two magical traditions, which of course we are proving were not so separate. In Japanese Shinto Temples there was the albino sacred horse known as Jimme. In the temple of Nikko there are three snow white horses.

A white horse is symbolic of innocence and this has been taken into that mythical creature, the Unicorn. This is simply a horse with a horn, which symbolically means a horse with light shining from its forehead (pineal area), thus making it divine. The Unicorn is global. In China they call it the Lin and it 'appears when sages are born.' They believe that like the messiah, the Lin is 'to come in the shape of an incomparable man, a revealer of mysteries supernatural and divine, a great lover of all mankind.' Sometimes the Lin is called the Lu which could come from el Hu or shining light.

In Sanskrit the word 'harit' means 'horse', it also means light of the morning (morning star), bright, shining and resplendent. In the Vedas there is an entire hymn specifically to the Sun in the form of a horse. It may be that the Horse was the symbol of the

Mother of Ra or Re the Sun God (mare = Ma Ra or Re - consider also, Mary).

In Greek the word 'ikkos' means horse and 'great light'. In Saxon, 'ehu' (compare Great Hu god of Shining) meant horse and is similar to 'Ayhu' or Shining.

White, bright or shining are all indicative of the solar Shining Ones' way of truth. White appears again and again in stories related to our ancient and mystical monuments. In popular myth and traditional fairy stories white ladies usually dwell in great white towers or atop mysterious snow capped mountains. In the German White Lady myth she is called Bertha which was the name of the Great Goddess of Nature. In the city of Megiddo in ancient Palestine there is a horned altar from around 2,000 BC, the stone is white lime. The Great Pyramid at Giza was covered with white washed plaster and topped with gold. The Egyptians called it the Light and it would have been visible for hundreds of miles, calling and reminding people to worship the Great Light or Shining One.

At Borobudur, which means 'Temple of the Countless Buddhas' or 'Temple of the infinite enlightened one', we have a huge almost ziggurat (ziggurat = Mighty Light) shaped pyramid with three stone circles of bell shaped stupas on top. The idea of the temple was for the initiated to walk around the false mountain and read or 'see' the reliefs which stretch five kilometres around the lower square base. When the initiated had understood the reliefs he could move on up to the top of the 'heaven' mountain and be holy. Their shape is derived from a plain central Asian burial Mound, indicative of the rest of the burial mounds of Europe. Seen partly as a Mandala (Sanskrit for 'circle'), the circles symbolise wholeness and the cycle of life. The cross between the stone circles, the pyramid, the burial mound, and the procession running up to the top, links

all the major constructions of the globe together, as if those who built the structure, in around 900 AD, knew the various paths of religion around the globe and indeed were party to their planning and sacred architecture.

The people of Borobudur moved on further east and influenced China and Japan, or at least that is what the archaeology shows. It may of course be that they were all from the same root anyway and just did things ethnically different. A similarity which occurs in mystical thought is that the ancient stone sites in Java, including Borobudur are claimed to be situated on earth energy spots and to be in lines, as the Ley Lines of Europe show our stone monuments to be. One remarkable thing to remember about Borobudur is that when it was first built it was painted white and shone like a celestial city in the sky.

In North America, it is said by tradition that upon mountains, sacred and holy people exist called the Great White Brotherhood. These are the Lemurians or people from the days of the past who are advanced souls and who help us through our evolution. They are guiding us through the generations, with a set goal in mind for mankind. They inhabit etheric monasteries and make themselves visible from the light at certain important times in our history. Could there be a subtle clue in this old tradition as to the influence and historical identity of these people who hold our lives in their hands? What is their goal and how do they carry out their purposes? If they exist, and conspiracy theories are impossible to prove incorrect by their very nature, then they have produced Buddha, Jesus Christ, Muhammad and any number of other enlightened beings, all for our improvement.

Hassan ben Sabbath, the mystical Islamic figure, was known as the Old Man of the Mountains and he later went on to set up

the Assassins who worked closely with the Templars in the thirteenth century. The evidence for their existence is growing, albeit without the mystical element attached to it by time and man's elucidating. From the oldest stories of the return of Vishnu on a white shining horse we have, through the centuries, linked the white horse with good and god. This may then be a sign to the whereabouts of the Shining Ones in our past. Wherever the horse is depicted was where the ancient priesthood were situated. Not only that, we need not split up the ideas of sun worship and horse worship and get ourselves confused as to why there should be so many differences. These ancients believed that the horse was symbolic of the sun god, the image was placed upon the Mother Earth in union and it depicted the presence of mystical learning.

It would follow that the Shining Ones themselves or their employees would, therefore, be wearing garments of white, although we must be careful not to include everybody as Shining Ones just because of the colour associations. The situation, the role and the time must be taken into account. Ancient Bards wore white, they were the tellers of tales, the keepers of our history. It was these people who made our history and religions become real in the minds of the ordinary and not so ordinary folk. The stories they told, the morals they put across became real and we then went on to live lives according to those tales.

The tales of King Arthur and his round table inspired thousands of knights and kings, and moved nations into action as well as being used and abused by the ruling class to feed the age old propaganda routines to the masses. Bards were employed by the ruling class, they were also wandering oracles who held the people in awe of them and in many cases it became a crime to even upset a Bard. They were surely deeply involved in manipulating the people.

The Romans noted that the inheritors of the stone circles, the Druids, also wore white. With the background to the Druids steeped in myth, and the fact that in all probability their ancestors were the people who built the stone monuments all over Europe and Central Asia, there can be no doubt as to the reason why they wore the Shining colour.

Elsewhere, the priests of Osiris were adorned with a white crown, over their pineal gland, to guide them. The Priests of Jupiter, the almost Druidic magicians, wore white. The Magi and Persian priests wore white and said that their gods did also. The Romans carried the Caduceus, which, not surprisingly when we take into account its significance, was white.

From discoveries of chalk and lime stones and balls at or around stone circles it may have been that the stones were painted white to shine like the Great Pyramid. In Ireland white quartz central stones occur in a number of circles.

Even today, many stones, when struck by the sun on the solstice, shine a brilliant white without any paint. The chalk may have also been used as a marker for the floor, so that our ancient friends could map the shadows for their predictions and time calculations. The Mandala of the Hindu and Buddhist beliefs was a circle of life. The priests frequently drew the Mandala on the floor with special powder for the initiation rites. Was this practice carried out on or around stones circles? Was this a nomadic stone circle? A kind of travel pack Stonehenge? Was it universal?

The psychologist Carl Jung said that the Mandala was a 'universally occurring pattern associated with the mythological representation of the self', and it is still used today as a therapy tool. The Maoris of New Zealand represent their

deities as standing stones in the ground, the Kafirs of India worshipped stones, the god of Israel was a 'rock', Mithra the great bull god was born of a rock and Moses said we all came from a rock. But what were their uses?

Clues as to the actual uses of the circles are held in the most popular book of all time, the Bible. It should follow that if the people of Israel had been influenced by or led into the way of the Shining Ones their writings should include evidence. It does, in abundance.

In Exodus we find out why these stones are so rough in appearance. 'If thou wilt make me an altar of stone, thou shalt not build it of hewn stone: for if thou lift up thy tool upon it, thou hast polluted it,' and in Genesis we see Jacob buried in a 'cave in a field'. The area was flat, no mountains, hills or any way that a cave could be hewn out of the rock. The only way for a cave or, if interpreted a different way, 'tomb' to be in a field is if one is built. Newgrange is a prime example of a cave in a field. A large circular stone tomb, erected for the burial of the 'elect'. This 'cave in a field' of the Bible can be traced right back to Abraham (c.2,166 BC) which almost brings it in line with Newgrange but certainly in line with thousand of other 'caves in fields' all over Europe, North Africa and the Middle East.

In Judges 9:5, there is a Pillar at Shechem and a Ziggurat called Beth Millo. Sacrifices took place here, just like the ones on the ziggurats and stone altars or pillars of the Americas and those of Europe. We must not lose sight of the fact that sacrifices were not the sole act of the Shamans or Medicine men of the Americas. All over Europe, and especially in Scandinavia, discoveries dating back thousands of years have been made of sacrificial offerings in the form of men, women and children who were put to death as an offering to the Earth Goddess Nerthus. The 'Cimbri' (sounding remarkably like 'Cymri' of

Wales and 'K'Omri' of Israel) and Teutonic tribes roamed Europe overcoming Roman armies and pillaging various localities.

It was these people who brought with them the appeasement of gods, such as Ishtar and Astarte, from the Middle East, where such practices were common. The sacrifice had to be held on the right date, at the right time and the planets had to be in their correct place. All the more need to understand the heavens, or at least that is what the priest would say. It may also have been chosen priests who were sacrificed as the victims often showed no sign of hard labour, had a 'special' last supper and occasionally wore jewellery, all indicative of being high in status in their society. Tacitus the Roman historian told us that these sacred priests were the only ones who could commune with the great goddess, making them the most holy of Holies. No one was to go to war, rejoice, or sacrifice unless the priest gave permission. Tacitus also told us, 'Their holy places are woods and groves'. Historians tell us that these people were derived from the Battle Axe people of Indo-European tongue who migrated from Central Asia over 4,000 years ago; the very same place we are building up that the Shining Ones originated their Shamanistic ideas.

Another thing Tacitus tells us is that these people had fierce blue eyes and reddish hair and although most men went clean shaven, the priests probably had beards. When we look at Quetzalcoatl of South America we may find that this white man who came from the East with red hair and all the rituals of the Shining Ones may have been a Cimri or K'Omri or Cymri.

According to Cyrus H. Gordon of Massachusetts' Brandeis University there is sufficient evidence for there to have been old world voyages to the Americas. He points to the one-roomed domed stone structures of Vermont which correlate

with those in the Mediterranean and Middle East, implying that they were all built by Bronze Age masons who evolved from a worldwide culture which was somehow, and for some reason, in existence and appeared over 5,000 years ago. Pottery from Japan matches that of Ecuador and many ancient stone buildings of America, such as Mystery Hill in New Hampshire, match those of Stone Age Europe. Roman and Arabic coins over 1,000 years old were discovered off Venezuela and markings found on a stone in Georgia match those of Minoan origin. 6

Across the globe, discoveries of earth energies at ancient sites are increasing by the year. Both scientists and pseudo-scientists have used all manner of equipment, from Kirlian photography to ultrasonic and radiation devices and have shown a mixed response. The conclusion to be drawn from much of this data is that more research, especially from a non-aligned aspect, is needed. There is no doubt that monuments have been built in lines, on large water deposits, on granite, on places that had increased electrical activity as the sun rises and on fault lines.

The work of Professor Alexander Thom, Norman Lockyer and Gerald Hawkins was fundamental to the understanding of megalithic monuments. It was they who discovered the astronomical links, the solar and lunar connections and the amazing calendrical systems tied up in the stones. Thom discovered the 'megalithic yard' of 2.72 feet which was in common usage across Europe, Britain and North America. They also discovered that pi had been used at Stonehenge, a serious problem considering Pythagoras was not to discover 'pi' until 2,000 years later. Not a problem if we then discover that Pythagoras was a Shining One. A philosopher and early alchemist, who had supposedly been reincarnated several times, once as a fisherman (see Jesus), used a looking glass for divination, visited the underworld or cave (as did many others including Jesus, Muhammad, Buddha etc.), lived in Egypt, spent ten years in Babylon learning arcane knowledge, used Shamanistic powers over animals, and had many other attributes which link him strongly with the initiated including the use of numerology.

Many traditions survive around the megalithic monuments. The Isle of Lewis has strong traditions which claim that the Callanish stones were erected by a world priest-king, wearing priestly robes, who came in large ships from abroad with large gangs of black men. All such traditions need backing up with hard evidence though and we do not have any here.

We need to look towards links, universal uses of the sacred sites.

Universally, the specific timing of cosmic events is vitally important. In Exodus 24:4, we have Moses building an Altar at the foot of a mountain or just below heaven, with twelve pillars for the tribes of Israel. This kind of timing unified religions. Offerings were burnt collectively and we see the images of a huge procession of elders up the mountain to heaven. All this had to be done at the right time and the right place. The imagery of this long procession of elders or chosen ones who were 'good enough' to trek the path to heaven, all dressed in white and all with beards, carrying their own symbolic item such as a caduceus, cross or branch of a tree must have been tremendously awe inspiring to the people massed at the foot of the mountain.

This Biblical 'stone age' stretches back to an almost forgotten time for the people of Israel. The 'large stone of Abel' was in existence before any records, and is spoken of in 1 Samuel. In this same book we have the people of Shemesh reaping the harvest and sacrificing on a large stone at the Autumn equinox. In 1 Samuel 14:33 Saul built sacrificial altars, and 1 Samuel 2:8 says that these pillars of the Earth are the Lord's. The dimensions of Stonehenge give the same canonical numbers as the Temple of Jerusalem and the 'Teotihuacan' of Mexico.

Genesis 28:18 shows that Jacob rose early in the morning, took a stone and raised it at Bethel. This is unusually specific about having to rise in the morning for such an operation and as we know all astronomically aligned stone erections are used mostly at sunrise. The place 'Bethel' means 'House of God', and Jacob called it the 'Gate of Heaven'. Bethel has also been called 'Luz' which means 'Turning Aside'. Later, Jacob revisits the site and adds an altar. In Genesis 31, Jacob and Laban set up a pillar and tell the brethren to gather stones and make a mound. They then ate on this mound and called it 'Jegar Sahadutha' or 'Galeed' which means 'Heap of Witness' or 'Cairn of Witness'. Cairns number in their thousands across the world. American Indians used them for social occasions, such as eating, and as watchtowers.

This site of Jacob was also called 'Mizpah' which means to 'watch'.

Joshua also built stones circles at a place called 'Gilgal' which itself means 'stone circle'. There are Gilgals all over the Middle East (Take Gilgal apart and we have 'ag il ag al' which means 'The Mighty God', and in Brittany the word used for stone circle was 'galgal'). Joshua understood that the meaning of these stones would be forgotten when he wrote, 'What do these stones mean to you'. The people were already forgetting. And yet in Deuteronomy 27, we have instructions on how to raise the stones and, importantly, how to paint them with lime. Lime comes up white and here is clear evidence that the ancient megalithic monuments were indeed supposed to be white.

'When you have crossed the Jordan you shall set up these stones on Mount Ebal, as I command you this day, and cover them with plaster. You shall build an altar there to the Lord your God: it shall be an altar of stones on which you shall use no tool of iron. You shall build the altar of the Lord your God with blocks of undressed stone, and you shall offer whole-offerings upon it to the Lord your God.' (The New English Bible version). As we can see from this one sentence alone, we have an altar built from undressed stone.

When we look around at the altars of Europe, in stone circles or standing alone, we see plainly that they are, on the whole, undressed. The stones were to be set up at Mount Ebal, a sacred mountain and gateway to heaven. The stones were to be built to 'your' god and to be plastered white.

We can now see with the text from the Bible and various other sources, comparisons with modern cultures and looking towards the Egyptian examples just how the ancient monuments were used. Painted white to be like the heavenly host on earth, the Shining stones beckoned the people to their rituals. The planets foretold the weather, the hunting and tales of the future. The priestly shamans of the stones entered trance states, walked through fire, produced magical divination, became gods before the eyes of the bewildered masses. The elders walked in long processions, dressed in white, sometimes riding on white horses. They ritualised the great world tree with a sacrifice of the king, the king's son or symbolically in animal form, pinned the sacrificial 'lamb' to the tree, utilising the symbolism of the threes for rebirth, and the sun rising for new life. Strange languages were spoken and even interpreted by the shaman who prophesied from within the holy of Holies. The earth energy was tapped by the power of the magician with his tree-like staff or caduceus and songs of the earth were heard through the wondrous vibrations of the energy at the solstice, causing healing powers to come through the god-like priest. But all this ritual, in whatever changing format it took, in all the different locations around the globe, was to be eradicated and rationalised.

In 2 Judges 23, we can see that the authorities were moving on, and in line with their new way of symbolically ritualising their worship and probable dissipation of followers (or in modern language, a drop in the polls), they started to destroy the stones and the idea that these now so-called false gods should be worshipped. 'He suppressed the heathen priests whom the Kings of Judah had appointed to burn sacrifices at the hill-shrines...as well as those who burnt sacrifices to Baal, to the sun and moon and planets and all the host of heaven.'[7]

Considering the centuries of blight against the reasons for the monuments it is no wonder that myth has arisen. The Christians of the eighteenth and nineteenth centuries did their best to eradicate the existence of the stones, but so too did the writers of the Bible. Myths have arisen, probably in symbolism of the truth, that the ancient giants built many of the monuments. Taking the idea of the giants actually having been the men of renown from ages past and having been the priesthood who actually did build them, then the myths are not so far away from the truth.

If we look across Europe, we find over 40,000 earth mounds, hundreds of long barrows and in England alone 1,500 hill forts. Even without taking into account stone circles, standing stones and many other earth works, we can build up a map of the ancient states of the Shining Ones. Their centres, schools, the most important astrological sites and even their mines have been discovered. Transport was no problem. Ships capable of carrying stones suitable even for Stonehenge have been discovered in Holland dating from 8,000 years ago, and many modern investigations have come up with any amount of ideas as to how ancient man could have transported his cathedral stones. In the mountains of Turkey there are fossilised remains of the most massive ship, claimed by Christians to be the Ark of Noah. If not the Ark, then it at least shows that ships of that size actually did travel the oceans. 9

We are building a picture of a large but secretive church (for more information on links between Bible, Stonehenge, Egypt see the notes 10, 11, 12 and for energy lines see 14), with centres across the globe, sacrificial rituals, knowledge of the heavens and earth powers; but more importantly an acute awareness of how to manipulate people.

They watch the changing moods of nations. As technology and rationality has increased, so too have their methods of power control. We see this remarkable process in action when these priests discover that the people need and want a leader. In return, the priests actually become that leader and king themselves. In the Bible, when the people of Israel cried out for a king they got one, albeit one chosen by the priests. When Europe needed unity in the ages of darkness, a new light was born and used in symbolism, and in reality through his children as they became kings.

When Arab speaking countries were in a void of pagan beliefs they too had a new leader, one adapted to their needs and one, as we shall see, born to be a Shining One. In central Asia the spiritual void was filled by one who became enlightened under a tree and who united the people amidst their mass of idols. When spiritual leaders and kings were no longer required, because they could not be 'voted' in democratically, the new favoured ones were the politicians, who were the landed gentry and royalty anyway. When the politicians became boring, the superstars of television were placed before us to keep hold of our excitement. Now we are given false ideals via the medium of the Internet. Where there is change it has been created to keep power. Who holds this power and why?

We have seen so much information, dates, beliefs, buildings, energies, powers, magic and lies. Now we need to reflect upon what we have seen before we move on to what became the next and biggest step for the Shining Ones - Christianity.

Notes
Chapter 7

1. The Ancient Earthworks and Temples of the American Indians. Lindesey Brine. Oracle.1996
2. Megalithic Mysteries. Michael Balfour. Parkgate Books. 1992.
3. The Great Pyramid Decoded. Peter Lemesurier. Element. 1993
4. The Golden Bough. Sir James Frazer. Wordsworth. 1993
5. The Golden Bough. Sir James Frazer. Wordsworth. 1993. Sir James Frazer's incredibly detailed account on the subject is still highly relevant today, especially when we consider that the research was carried out without the vast archaeological data and sometimes blurred perspective of technology.
6. The Giant Book of Lost Worlds. Damon Wilson. Paragon. 1998 citing evidence from Cyrus Gordon.
7. The New English Bible.
8. The Atlas of Holy Places and Sacred Sites. Colin Wilson. Dorling Kindersley. 1996
9. Proof. P. Gardiner. Radikal Phase Publishing House Ltd, Underwood, Notts. 2002 Tel: 01773 764288
10. Some Biblical Stone references and links.
    Joshua 4:3 'Take you hence out of the midst of Jordan, out of the place where the priest's feet stood firm, twelve stones, and ye shall carry them over with you, and leave them in the lodging place, where you shall lodge this night...That this may be a sign among you, that when your children ask their fathers in time to come saying, What mean ye by these stones?...and these stones shall be a memorial unto the children of Israel for ever... (all of them? Even Europe?) And the children of Israel ...took up the twelve stones out of the midst of Jordan, as the Lord spake unto Joshua...set up

twelve stones in the midst of Jordan...and they are there unto this day.'

'Gilgal' means 'Stones Circles', 'Gilgul' means 'reincarnation' which is still believed in by the Hasidic Jews, heirs of the Essenes. The Essenes, therefore, are the heirs of the truth of the stones and the ancestors of the Hasidic Jews who now hold it. All the mysteries of Egypt and magi are held by the heirs of Gigul.

Saul was made King at Gilgal or at a stone circle. The captain of the Lord of Hosts told Joshua that the place was holy, Joshua, Chap 5. Bullocks, Sheep and Oxen were sacrificed at Gilgal, Hosea 12:11. Angels of the Lord came from Gilgal, Judges 2:1. Samuel travelled year on year between Bethel (House of God), Gilgal (stone circle) and Mizpah (Watchtower) and judged the people. A wandering, shining priest, using the powers of the Earth's energies?

11.   Other Links -
Stonehenge links with Egypt. The trilthon ring diameter 97 feet or 1164 inches, the diameter of the Egyptian year circle or quarta aurora is equivalent to 1163.8 inches of nearly 97 feet. The angle of latitude of Stonehenge is 51 degrees 10.8' N. The angle of slope of the Pyramid is 51 degrees 51' 14.3. Maybe the originals were exactly the same, the similarities are enormous. The Stonehenge outer circle can be used to construct a triangle which has almost the dimensions of the Great Pyramids cross section. The Aubrey holes of Stonehenge are planned around an isosceles triangle. The Stonehenge circle is basically a circular image of the same sacred mathematical formula of the Pyramid, built at the same time, on behalf of the same priesthood who shared the same information.

The Egyptian counterpart of the Greek 'Kronos' (Cronos = time) was Keb the Great Orb. Kronos when

dissected becomes 'ak ur on os', the great fire, the one Light and Keb has its root in the word 'Kebla' and means stone circle. In Latin the term 'Septum' means stone circle, however taken apart, 'is ep tum' it actually means the Light of the Orb. 'Tum' meaning time. The time and light factor of the stone circles are inextricably linked. Tum is also the root word, 'wor '.

Temples. We also find that later on this idea was taken forward. 'Temenos' was the word Diodorus Siculus used to describe Stonehenge, it means 'enclosed circle'. In Wales the word 'tommen' means 'barrow' or 'Stone Time'. The Israelites used the term 'Shiloah' or 'Shiloh' for their stone monuments which actually is the word used for the expectant messiah. It was also used for 'Tower'. The monument in the Cornish hills called 'Carn Menelez' means 'Stone of the Lord of Light', 'Menelik' being a royal Assyrian name.

12.   The dating of the Sphinx.

Due to recent problems involving the dating or re-dating of the Sphinx at Giza we have to take a quick look at the problem here. The re-dating that Graham Hancock and various others claim should be put into the history books of about 10,000 BC would affect our Shining Ones theory. This would lead to the problem of a civilisation existing prior to the known history of the early shamans of Northern Europe, Central Asia, Africa and elsewhere.

The evidence put forward by Hancock and others is simply the water erosion of the monument. They claim scientific evidence that the erosion must have occurred over a much longer period than previously claimed; however, there is no need to re-date the structure to such a date as 10,000 BC. We have the demise of a civilisation at Santorini or Thera in the Aegean Sea due to a huge volcanic eruption in around

1,626 BC. The intense culture of this highly civilised place was so advanced that many have put across that this was probably the Atlantis of Plato.

There are images close by at Akrotiri of Bronze Age seafaring trips to distant places, evidence of telescopes and more evidence of the seafaring skills of the inhabitants probably venturing as far as England. But this is not why I have brought up Thera. Scientific research has shown that the fall out from this massive explosion caused a huge amount of acid rain. Particles from the frozen wastes of the Earth's ice stores has actually given us the correct date.

There was an explosion equivalent to several hundred hydrogen bombs. The Island itself was buried beneath 100 feet of ash. The wind spread this ash over an 80,000 square mile area. Tidal waves a mile high crashed around the globe at 200 miles per hour, smashing into Crete and the Egyptian delta less than three hours after the explosion. The scattered survivors of this lost race probably took their knowledge with them to neighbouring civilisations and continued the work. The acid rain caused by the explosion, however, had severe effects upon the Sphinx. Just as our modern day acid rain is crumbling the fabric of the great cathedrals of medieval Europe, so too did the acid rain of Thera crumble the sand stone of the Sphinx, making the weathering seem older.

There are of course some problems with this theory. Other buildings close by do not seem to have taken such a beating from the acid rain. If these buildings were from the same period as the Great Sphinx then surely they would, whether by acid rain or time erosion from water. The buildings may have been built at different times, there may have been a different volcanic eruption which caused the acid rain depletion of the Sphinx or the close by buildings may have simply been repaired or covered by outer erections at the time.

13.　　Cicero. De Divinatione, ii, 27 and 81, 81.

14.　　Energy Lines

According to many paranormal experts Ley Lines or Earth energy lines have been known about for thousands of years. They claim the lines of Earth magnetism are the reason for the positioning of ancient monuments in straight lines. 'The Old Straight Track' was published in 1925 by Alfred Watkins and is the first modern idea of this phenomena. Since then, energy lines have been traced all over the globe. Scientists tend to ignore their existence, although this pseudo-science will not come into the mainstream until serious scientific investigation is carried out. With the existence of the power of our pineal gland and the knowledge that we can prove ancient man possessed, there should be no doubt that if the power is there then ancient man may have known about it. To what use he put to the energy is debatable. From healing to the Feng Shui idea of finding the most balanced place to build, the geomagnetic energy of the energy lines is probable and should be investigated by reputable organisations, there may even be an energy power from which we could make a living.

The Nazca lines in Peru are said to be energy lines. Modern archaeology, however, has shown that these were some kind of rain ritual device, although it may also be that this ritual of bringing down the rain from heaven had to happen on an energy line, and taking into account the way all things are connected (See 'Gaia') then this may have somehow actually brought the rains down. There is no need to presume the involvement of aliens in all this as we have seen so far that mankind was developing sufficient knowledge of the way of the universe without the help of extraterrestrials.

New World Order

Chapter 8
Reflections

"In very truth the myth is truth, symbolic truth, while reality is error." Groddeck, The World of Man.

We have travelled a long way in the past few chapters, and have covered uncharted territory. The story of the Shining Ones explains the reasons why we believe in deities, the science behind some of the more paranormal aspects of faith and the evolution and development of the magical activities of ancient man. All the information offered so far is an attempt to give everyone, including those who know little about religion, the early history of mankind and the nature of our planet in relation to ourselves a fair chance of understanding about the Shining Ones and the reasons for the links between them in their various settings.

Before we move onto the next and most important stage in the story, we should take a little time to reflect upon what we have learned so far, which will help us move towards the important aspects of where we are now.

In the first two chapters we found that our bodies, the chemistry and physical nature of ourselves is intrinsically linked with the universe around us. It has been this way ever since there were humans. After all, we were created from what was already in existence, namely the universe. But more than that, our minds are also as one with this universe, although not in some strange mystical manner. The mind is linked because of the nature of ourselves, we are of the same chemical constituents, we are in tune with the cycles of the world, just like the oyster, which opens and closes with the high tides. We may not realise it, but our mind reacts to the seasons, to the pressure of the moon and to the electromagnetic energy which is all part and parcel of the earth and the cosmic affects upon it. All things are inter-linked.

Earth energies are found to exist in specific places, to emanate from trees and stones. The brain has a fascinating way of tapping into these magnetic energies and can even lead us home. We discovered long ago that we could use these tools of nature for divination and thus begin the journey to power.

We have now come to realise that ancient man understood more than we had previously given him credit for. Some of the most basic elements of life - the sun, the moon, the stars, trees, mountains, water and the cyclic nature of life and death - have become the most enduring symbols of our religious life; but more so, they are also woven inextricably into our social structures, our philosophies and our politics. They are the universal aspects of man's search for truth. Local ethnic alterations and thousands of years of manipulated myth (more in the last 2,000 by the Christians than by anybody else), have blurred the meanings; however, now we know what we are looking for we can begin to see the similarities.

Trinities feature widely across the globe, from Hinduism to Christianity. There is evidence of tree worship in every culture; also mountain temples, burials and platforms raised to the heavens; the circling of the sacred mountain, standing stones, may poles and temples. The symbolism of the shining Heaven's Host is to be found in stone circles; white clothing, horses and buildings; the sun father, earth/moon mother, the holy spirit.

The old men of renown became the giants of our history and folklore, they held a misty respect, an understanding that exists in our own minds today, we hark back to their ideal and dream. We find that they wore white (like the first images of Santa Claus), had beards, used magic, held caduceus staffs aloft and worshipped the same gods as each other. Their gods were Shining Fathers, they were the Shining Sons. The stars represented them in the sky or even vice versa, as above, so below. They became known as Shaman, medicine men or magicians. They evolved into priests and kings, or both.

These developing spiritual leaders held for themselves the secrets that could control men; which, therefore, enabled the priests to gain more power. Eventually, a large structured and global power base, in a flexible and open to evolution manner, was set up. Like local authorities, these groups retained control in their region but travelled abroad to the main centres of learning at On, Helios, at the Great Pyramid, Ur and many other places around the globe we have already named. They moved and altered their 'faces' with the continuing evolution of the ordinary man and woman. To us, the main story was in the king or the war. When we read history, we read about the main men, the battles and who won them and on what date. We do not read that there were people moving in the background, manipulating the game. Sometimes, this game-playing does come to light, and when exposed it is discredited or the historical record altered.

The truth of the origin of our societies is hidden within the folklore, traditions and basic tenets of our faiths. When we consider archaeological records and anthropological data with a lateral outlook, we can see that there are incredible links between all cultures. It may be that because we no longer have an interest in religion we do not research the similarities, and added to that, how many people who do know about religion also know anything about science and archaeology?

The truth of these links was waiting to be discovered. Now in this modern age of information and technology we can research at the push of a button, I know, I have done quite a lot this way. This technology enables us to gather information faster and to understand more. Therefore we start to see the links in existence more clearly. As recently as 100 years ago, people in England would have been lucky to have read one book in ten years. They could not even afford the extravagance and luxury, if, indeed, they were able to read. Small children were working hard in factories or sweeping chimneys. But, just as in the time of Plato, there were thinking men and women, who had the time and the financial resources to be able to look into such things.

Sir James Frazer was a prime example, and he too discovered connections, although he chose to follow a classical path which did not necessarily lead him to the real truth. But because of the early research of people like Frazer we can now see the mass of collated work he and others produced and can work on them ourselves. The information has been there for a considerable period of time and it is almost as if it has been kept away from us. We have to ask ourselves, why, for so long have we been fed the idea that all the various religions emerged separately? Is it due to religious intolerance?

This would imply a lack of understanding on the side of those who were intolerant as they would surely understand that all faiths come from the same place. The only credible answers are that either nobody actually knows about the existence of the Shining Ones, (although the evidence of their actual historical existence is beyond doubt) or the Shining Ones still exist and still have an agenda. There should be nothing sinister in this as their history does have many examples of good, almost superhuman kindness and peace. Jesus was a prime example. We do, however, have to look to the foundations, as Jesus himself pointed out, there must be good foundations if the building is to stand the test of time. We have seen that the foundations of the Shining Ones are built around magic and our physical connection with the universe around us. They used their intuition of these powers to enable them to hold power. This shows strong leadership skills and quick thinking. It also shows deceit.

In chapters 5 and 6 we went through a mass of information, collated by myself and hundreds of others like me who knew in the pit of their stomach that there was something. In chapter 5 we saw new evidence from China, which has shown that red-haired Shaman of European origin lived and traded in the far east. The Hindu beliefs of reincarnation and all their symbolism is deeply rooted in the religions of the globe. The idea originated in Africa, the cradle of mankind, and developed on its way up to the Central Asian provinces. There it grew and developed, keeping open its links with the African Shaman, who would later meet up again, century after century. The travel path of those early Asiatic Shaman moved across the globe, eastward towards Japan and China, westward to Europe and south to India and then to meet with their African brothers once again.

We considered the secret teachings of the world's oldest documents in India ('Upanishads' = secret teachings) and the sacred universities of Egypt where the men of renown passed on their knowledge to Moses, Abraham, Jesus, Plato and many others. Buddha, one of the greatest Shining Ones, is shown to be a good signpost and one to watch out for. His teachings are reflected in those of supposedly unrelated religions.

The giants, the Anakim, who were possibly the Anannage of central Asia and Angakok of the Eskimos (who came from central Asia anyway) were the myth makers, the men of fables. They moved across continents as the Great Sons of Anu or the Great Sons of the Shining One. They came from Shaman stock and influenced the whole world. They moved into Egypt, Babylon and then onto Europe to inspire Ireland's mythic heroes and England's giants of folklore. They travelled through Earth's great catastrophes, such as the floods, and entered our tales as Noah and various other flood survivors. They fathered nations and wrote the law ('Mankind learned from the Shining Ones; they set things in order', Sumerian creation myth). These early developments have spawned a mass of Atlantean and Lemurian myths, which speak of great, tall and brilliant people from ages past, who knew more than we do and gave us our civilisations. Millions of books have been sold, adding to the tales and dangerously destroying valuable evidence of the identity of these people.

Actaeon
being attacked

The recurring name of the Shining Ones in all cultures is shocking at first sight. The Devas of Hindu myth, the solar gods of Babylon, the Anannage, the Egyptians, the Americans and the Europeans; at face value, the names appear to be different from each other, but they all translate into 'Shining Ones', 'Shining Father', 'Shining Soul' or 'Shining Sons'. The Biblical

magi are from the land of the rising sun, the east. They are the shaman, the magicians, the Shining Ones. They are later made into three and given names which have a deeper meaning and purpose. The gods of the Jews, the Elohim, are the Shining Ones and Shamanistic rituals and creeds abound within the Bible. So much so that the Bible can be taken to be a Shining Ones training manual, and bearing in mind the infinite levels of the Bible, it probably was.

The New Testament is a continuation of their theme, part of the plan. Jesus on the cross and tree. The ancient symbols of new life, of Mother Goddess, of cyclic patterns. All these and more are within the pages of the New Testament.

Through Judaism and the Roman Empire, Christianity spread across the globe. It was good for several types of culture, and was adapted by each of them. For those who could not follow this new 'Way, Truth and Light', the religion of Islam was created. Both came from Judaism, and the way of the Shining Ones can be found in this faith which hides secrets of the words and meanings. It hides the origins of many nations and possibly even Britain's. There is divination, shape shifting, speaking foreign languages, raising and conversing with the dead, astrology, sun and moon worship, how and when to use stone circles, and the secrets of the numbers used across the globe, Mother and father Gods, sacrifices, trees, mountains and human messengers called Angels. Most notably, we have the mythological stories of those most magnificent of Shining Ones Moses, Abraham and Jesus. Their story is told in hidden messages, their way shown in symbolism. They hold staffs, produce prophecies, learn in great centres of the Shining Ones universities and fly. All the ways of the Shaman are in the Bible.

Later, we find that Druidism was founded in the Shamanism of Central Asia and they too are the inheritors of the truth. Their

names are symbolic also, their creeds have trinities and trees and they also wear white, hold up crosses and staffs and have god names strangely reminiscent of the gods of the Hebrews. They are a marker in our history, a spotlight which we can recognise easily as being of the Shining Ones.

In the Americas, we have the same thing. 'Kukulcan' the sun god associated with Quetzalcoatl the white skinned, bearded Shaman god who could shapeshift, fly, was born of a virgin and invented the law. He carries a staff of life and a spear called the morning star. He was a man and a god at the same time, he visited the other world, he entered a cave and was risen to heaven on flames. In the ancient buildings of the Americas we also see these beliefs coming through. The stone circles, mountains and tree worship structures are everywhere. Across the globe there are similarities, not just in style; style can be a distraction.

We look at Borobudur and say there is nothing like it anywhere else. This is true if we are looking only for something that was built by the people of Java in their own style. But we are not just looking at the artistic similarities of the various peoples of the globe, we are also looking at the religious similarities; the belief's structure in the building's structure. Borobudur is a useful example, in that it has a pyramid or ziggurat style with stone circles. It is circumnavigated and interpreted by the initiated. It was white and shining in the sun. The religious path to enlightenment is a common theme across the continents.

The Great Pyramid at Giza, alternatively called 'the Light' by the Egyptians, was also white and was used as a ritual path to enlightenment or rebirth, which eventually equates to the same thing. In Glastonbury Tor we have a large sculpted dome with a route for those who wish to become enlightened, as we do at the Sanchi Stupa. Modern research shows that with a

pyramid structure, a great healing power seems to be released, and I personally know of management centres which are now building on mountain sides because they have shown by market research that the teaching is much more effective on these sacred mountains.

Sacred mountains were built in towns and cities and on the supposed energy lines in the form of ziggurats, pyramids and large mounds. Temples and sacrificial platforms were built and the whole thing was made to shine brightly. In the groves of Europe, the circles of sacred trees developed into stone circles. They were painted white to shine, and circumnavigated in rebirth rituals and as centres of great healing.

We are building a picture of a great and massive worldwide priesthood which started small some time before 5,000 BC, and used nature's attributes for temples. Groves were everywhere in a world full of trees and this made it possible for the priesthood to be nomadic and spread their news and secrets far and wide, recruit eager new initiates and forge a strong power base before civilisation itself began. After 5,000 BC, we have the knowledge of this global priesthood enabling civilisation to erupt in several places such as Sumer and Egypt. People were immediately put to the task of manufacturing these natural temples, firstly out of wood and then stone. The stage for the Shining One had been built, and he had the power base sewn up because he was there from the beginning as a man held in awe and respect, a magic man who brought the rain and sun, a man who could also very easily be king or make kings.

Eventually, these separate temples of the globe would compete, just as local authorities do now for money, but they would be essentially the same, would come from the same place and almost all of them would lead mankind in a direction

that would seem daunting to you or me. There were dissenters, but these created natural variations, which adapted themselves to the very human habit of desiring change and wanting to be different. Behind each more and more structured religion, there were priests who all believed in the same basic ideas. They occasionally rebuked each other, as do Members of Parliament who still sit in the same House of Commons and lead the country. From the writings of early Christians we can see their supposed confusion. On the one hand they believed in their Christian God and on the other they practised the black art of alchemy. It was the same for everyone. The day job, and the hobby.

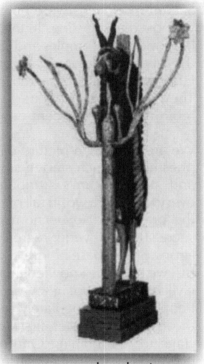

The most important thing of all is the recurrent theme, which is the reason for this book. The Shining Ones' name crops up in all cultures, whether hidden through mistranslation and myth or by intent. There is an

Ram in the thicket

understanding in all religions, by all Rabbis, priests, pastors and witches that the Shining Ones have been there all along. Each individual religion has known about them in their own particular area, but because their outlook on the subject is insular and they are interested only in their own faith, then they see only that faith.

A Christian will see the basic message of the Bible telling us how to live, and the straight value of the stories. He may see a little deeper and start to believe he has had a revelation himself. This in turn gives the church a stronger hold on this particular Christian because he is excited by that revelation and searches for more. This usually takes a person all his lifetime. By the time he has discovered the Bible's deeper or secondary meanings he is ready to die and take with him all of those marvellous gems of 'seeing'. This is what is intended, and is something that is not just common in writing but also in buildings. If the searcher looks hard enough he will find numerology, alchemy, magic and all manner of fantastic truths hidden in the pages of a book or carved on the cathedrals of Europe. This is an important part of the ancient craft of the Shining Ones. Only a small part of the craft is seen by any one person.

A Christian sees some of the marvels of the Bible, and the architect sees the sacred geometry of an ancient building and interprets it accordingly, a magician is sworn to secrecy in his magic circle because the small part he plays as a modern-day sorcerer is big enough for him and is not to be passed on to everybody; the power is to be kept within.

This is how the Shaman, magicians, medicine men and priest-kings collectively known as the Shining Ones have maintained their power hold for thousands of years. What we must ask ourselves is whether these people actually have a long term plan, which must, by the very fact of historical activity, stretch over many hundreds of years. If they did or do, then the next step after these old civilisations of Egypt, Rome, Greece and Ancient Europe would be to find a unifying priest-king, who holds all the symbols and upholds all the various beliefs of their kind. This priest-king must have a trinity, he must be god, he must be sacrificed on a tree and cross, he must fulfil prophecy in so many ways, he must be the sun and the son, he must defeat evil and be everything to everybody. Such an amazing challenge would be impossible for us in our modern age to pull off; unless we held the power base of the nations without the nation's knowledge. By keeping ourselves out of the history books, we remain outside of the minds of the people and therefore whatever we did would go unnoticed, we would be the civil servants of the government, the manipulators of the pawns of power.

Two thousand years ago, in a political turmoil, in a nation with seemingly religious splits, in a highly varied culture of beliefs, in a world where human sacrifice was still practised and yet philosophers had died out 200 years previously, into this world the impossible was arranged. It was planned to the last detail in a military fashion. The plot was put through without a hitch. But not only the plot, the story thereafter was carefully developed, nurtured by those who knew how for the correct long term ends. This was not the first time, they had done this before in different countries and had effected change on vast continental scales. The small tribal Shaman had come a long way, he was using the same language but it was now symbolic, he was still manipulating the tribe and the king but it was now on a larger scale altogether. And this was not to be the last time that the Shining Ones showed us the light.

Chronos

1.	Similarities and Links

Shining Ones - The remnant of the Raphaim was Og the giant (Bible, Joshua 12:4) linked with Ogma from Sumeria which in turn was linked with Cerne Abbas which in turn is linked with Dyaeus which means 'the Shining Ones' - therefore King Og of Bashen in the Bible is the remnant king of the Shining Ones. Dyaus Pitar means the Shining Father and links to the Indo-European Shaman where sacrifices were held towards the great Shining Father.

Devas of Hindu tradition means 'Shining Ones'. Buddhist Bodhisattvas regarded as the Shining Ones and saviours. Agni the Hindu sage means 'Shining One', he was father, priest, king, protector and messenger. The people called the Anannage (linked with Angakok of Greenland and the Anakim Giant race of the Bible) means Great Sons of the Shining One after their God Anu the Shining Father. Ra the Egyptian God of the Sun took on the role of Shining Father and the kings the Shining Suns. The Egyptian akh means Shining Soul. Isis governed from the 'shining heights of heaven'. Melchior, the magi king of the Shining Ones. These magi supposedly derived their knowledge from the Brahmans. Virgil tells us that the Golden Race will spread throughout the globe and produce a messiah who will be born of the Virgin Lady.

Archangel Michael means 'he who is shining'. In Cornish the word El means Angel and the Shining One. The Angel Seraphim means Shining One. Elohim, the Jewish god or lord means the Shining Ones. The host of heaven or stars in Sumer and Israel were the Shining Ones. Egyptian Amun-u-El phrase means Amun is the Shining One. Moses is Shining Forth when he comes down from the mountain or heaven. Quetzalcoatl is the 'Light of day' meaning he is very bright. Helios is depicted as a Shining horse. Actaeon means Shining One. Lampon the horse of Diomedes is the Shining One. Skinfaxi the Norse mythological horse had a Shining Mane. Buildings became Shining when the were painted or plastered white and the priests became the Shining Ones when they too adorned this sacred colour.

Fatima (the daughter of Muhammad) means the Shining One, she said to be virginal and her title is 'bright blooming'. The Nile is said to be the healer of mankind who 'shines when he issues forth from the darkness...' The word 'Saint' probably comes from the root 'san' which primarily means 'Light of the One' and 'shining'. The Great Hu means shining light and Hu is the root word of so many other religious divinities such as Dyu which is where we get the word dew from for the shining wetness of the morning.

Also - Lugh, llew, Dyhu, Taou, Huish. Waldensian pastors called barbes or Shining Lights.

Beards - Giants are said to have beards and as we have seen this means stature, power, manhood, enlightenment and is common throughout the history of the Shining Ones. Shaman, medicine men, kings queens and priests. Pharaohs of Egypt (including Queens) wore either real or false beards. Baal wore a beard which comes down to our image of the Christian god having a beard. The men of Islam wear a beard. Samson loses power when his beard is destroyed, Samson was a member of the Nazerites (Jesus etc.) who also had beards. The Essenes wore beards. El the Canaanite god also to become the god of the Jews is the Shining One who has a beard and is the image of a bull. Jupiter is associated with Adonis, the other title used by the Jews for God, was the Shining One. Quetzalcoatl had a beard. Druids had beards.

Crosses - North American Shaman are suspended by their wrists in the style of crucifixion, taking them in a trance to the other world and coming back with powers. Odin sacrificed on the Tree of Life and visiting the underworld. Hindu Temples in the shape of a cross, burial tombs all over Europe in the shape of a cross, the Great Pyramid at Giza forming a cross on the ground at summer solstice, Hindus form a cross by outstretching their arms as an initiate tries to gain salvation. Quetzalcoatl's symbol was a cross, South American cross worship.

Celtic crosses with winding snakes are same as the Hindu images and as the caduceus (which is mercury linked with Thoth - Hermes and we also find that the Shining Seraphim of the Bible were sent down as 'fiery serpents' in Numbers 21:6 and therefore a note should be made of the importance of the snake in symbolism). Jainism has the cross and swastika as do Hindu and Buddhist beliefs. The same swastika chosen by Hitler. The symbol of Tammuz and Thoth and therefore Hermes is the cross and this is the reason that Mercury who is associated with all these has the cross/tree like caduceus.

The ram in the thicket of the Assyrians is Ra the Shining One being lit up by gods lightning strikes or light from heaven.

Trinity (for seven see chapter 5 notes) - Three Shaman worlds. Three kinds of Devas or Shining Ones in Hindu. Triad of Hinduism, Brahman, Vishnu, Shiva. The Christian Trinity, God the Father, the Son and the Holy Spirit (Ghost - being an old pagan idea included). Book of Dead in Egypt with three streaming rays of Shining Light hitting the soul of the initiated. Thrice Great Hermes comes out of the balancing act between Thoth, Tammuz, Hermes and Mercury.

Zoroaster would return three times. Three magi who brought three gifts. Jesus crucified on a mountain with three crosses, one either side of him. Three chatras on Hindu temples. Buddhist three fires and three marks built into all existence. Buddhist trinity of refuge, three bodies of Buddha and three jewels. Three foundations of the universe of Simon Magus. Druid holy Triad. Taoist three giving birth to creation. T'ai-chi represented by three candles. Asgard three thrones. Classical trinity of Zeus, Poseidon and Hades or Jupiter, Neptune and Pluto.

Fatima the Shining One and daughter of Muhammad gave birth to three sons. Druidic Harps made from a triangle, three strings and three turning keys - all symbolic of the Great Trinity of the Druids and Bards. If the people had been true and honest to the 'three grand articles of religion' then the Bard may sing a requiem which would enable the people to enter into heaven or have salvation via the trinity of the harp.

The Babylonians represented the Supreme Deity as an archer shooting the Three headed arrow. This became the archer Sagittarius. The English arrow being 'arewe' or the Light of Ewe and the Sanskrit for arrow being 'ishu' or the Light of Hu.

Duality - Shaman ideas of light and dark, good and evil, the balance. Japan, China yin and yang duality. Mother Father relationship in all cultures.

Bull - Shaman bull image for sacrifices. Egyptian sun god Ra in the image of a bull. Bull throughout old testament. El in the image of a bull. The Latin Apis meaning Bow is identical to the Apis, the sacred Bull of Egypt.

Rebirth - Bhagavad Gita, 'I have been born many times', Bible 'You must be born again', Egyptian Book of the Dead, 'I have the power to be born a second time'. Christian belief in reincarnation before 500AD. Egyptian rebirth rituals abound. Magi believed in reincarnation. Zoroaster, Osiris, Horus, Adonis, Dionysos, Hercules, Hermes, Baldur and Quertzalcoatl all descended into hell and were risen again on the third day. Vishnu said 'Every time that religion is in danger and that iniquity triumphs I issue forth for the defence of the good and the suppression of the wicked; for the establishment of justice I manifest myself from age to age.' Resurrection is all part of Mithraism, the Orphic mysteries and Isis worship (and not surprisingly these were the very religions, Christianity had to compete with).

Virgin Birth and cave instances in birth - Isis immaculately conceives Horus. Virgil said the messiah would be born of the Virgin Lady. Zoroaster was born of a virgin. Abraham in a cave. Muhammad enlightened in a cave. Jesus given birth to in a cave. Fatima the Shining One gave birth to three sons and is said to have been a virgin. In China the Virgin birth consists of treading in the footprint of God which the mother of Hou Chi did and was born like a 'lamb'. He was born amidst sheep and cattle, just like Jesus. (Hou sounding like the Great Hu or Shining Light and part of JesHu [Jesus])

Circles - Mandala in Hinduism, Stone circles, groves,

Borobudur circles, America, Europe, Asia, Africa in fact everywhere. Chakra wheel is tied up in energy points of the body and may be similar to the wheels on the ground of energy points. Promised land of the Aztecs was the place of the circle or Anahuac. Stone circles are named in the Bible as Gilgal. Ancient traditional belief that evil spirits may not pass through a circle of candles.

Wearing white - Jains. Knights Templars. Druids, Bards, Priests of Osiris, Jupiter, Magi, Romans. The Persians said that the gods wore white. Carmelites or White Friars. Cistercian Nuns and Monks, Magdalenes, Order of the Sisters of the Presentation of Mary, the Congregation of the Daughters of the Holy Ghost, Congregation of the Missionary
Sisters of Our Lady of Africa and the White Fathers.

Chapter 9
The Greatest Plan of All

'This means that the whole community, through the sorcerer's redemption, may also be redeemed and attain salvation.', Primitive Magic, Ernesto De Martino.

According to Hugh Schonfield in his book the 'Essene Odyssey', there is 'an individual of substance' behind all the major faiths. A man who merged through literature and time into all the aspects of Muhammad, Buddha and Jesus. He is only partly correct, however. This man of substance is not one man. It is the experience of the Shining Ones played out in the game of history. Their influence has been shown in all the areas previously mentioned and now we can see how they intended to hold power by introducing a new leader or messiah into each age. This is a natural step for them. They believed in the resurrected or reincarnated soul, or spirit, and that they had the divine right to be the power brokers. Each new time should have the new 'Mahavira' or Buddha or whatever you want to call him.

There can be no time without a new prophet, no time without the strong influence of the Shining Ones. In the 2nd century BC, prior to the greatest influence we have known in the last two thousand years, there was a schism in the Holy Land which was created with a purpose; to see through the predicted birth and death of the Sky God, the Shining Father. A group was created or evolved from the main group, given a cover name

Qumran

and, utilising major Shining centres of learning, went about planning his coming. This group was called the Essenes.

On the breastplates of the Jewish High Priest were twelve precious stones, called 'logeion' by Philo. These stones were arranged in four rows, like the seasons

and were symbolic of 'Reason which holds together and regulates the Universe'. Josephus called these 'logeion' 'the Essene' which means 'One Essence' or 'One Light Shining'. This was Josephus telling us something about the Essene, of which he was a member. They saw themselves, the One Light Shining, as the regulatory body which holds the world together, they were in charge.

The Essenes were a Jewish sect, probably as large as the Pharisees and Saducees. Their real name comes from the historical 'Hasidim' or Pious Ones who marched out of Jerusalem because of the Hellenisation of Jerusalem. Suddenly two camps were created, the Maccabees who set up their own priest and king

and the Hasidim, now known as Essene who began to manipulate their own dynastic order. They were renowned for their asceticism and almost communistic way of life. It was these zealous individuals who were responsible for the now famous Dead Sea Scrolls discovered at Qumran (Qumran or Khirbet - is Hebrew for 'stone ruin' an indication that there may have been an importance to the stone here). They, like the local Qumran community of the time, as a whole, were against the Hasmonean high priesthood who held power in the 2nd century BC.

They considered themselves to be the true Israel, or chosen people, waiting in the wings. If the written history of the world is anything to go by, then these individuals were about to change the world, they were to prove that they were the chosen ones. According to Hugh Schonfield in his book 'Essene Odyssey', the Essene 'would compose speeches for their characters, where these were not available, in terms deemed appropriate to the individual and the circumstances. And sometimes in the interest of propaganda, they would credit such characters with sentiments favoured by the writer...' It seems that a person's eminence was exalted and his skills increased by the harmless little pen.

There are various suggested prototypes for the Essene community. The 'Hasidim Harishonim' or 'ancient saints of elders' and the 'Had Da'ath' or the 'pure of mind' are but two. Of the many strict rules within the community many are similar to the prototypes named but not all. They included washing in cold water and wearing white garments. It has been reported that the Essenes were also against slavery and were said to have bought slaves and then set them free. This would ring true with the words of Jesus when he said that the Lord has set us free.

The strict practices and ascetic ways of these Essenes were too hard for some to take and only the elite remained. It has been said that their ways were much akin to those of Jesus and his disciples.₁ They had names for the various parts of their communities. The 'Governor' was called the 'Crown', the 'Council' the 'Multitude' and the 'Way' was how the 'Community' should live. These followers of the 'Way' were called the 'children of the light' or 'shining ones'. 'Kittim' or 'Babylon' stood for the 'Romans', and 'Lepers' were those not

allowed into the fold as were those called the 'Blind', who were not part of the 'Way'. All of these titles are found richly in the Bible and all the writings of the Qumran finds.

The Essene codes and ciphers are now famous in the world of the scholar, but we need a little guidance if we are to understand what the Essenes were talking about. We have to understand that they were hiding valuable information within their publicity material. Hiding it, not only from the eyes of the Romans (who if they were initiated into the Shining Ones would have understood anyway), but also from the High Priesthood of the mainstream Jews, or at least those who had bargained power with their powerful overlords.

The faithful were called the 'poor' and were the ones Jesus told would inherit the world in his great political and world changing speech. The wealthy were 'sinners'. Amongst the 'poor' were the 'Ebionites', which actually meant the poor, and they too were amongst the initiated, and joined with the Qumran community and the Essenes in general to see the plans through. In the Book of Enoch, written at the time of the Essenes, we have not only the idea of the reincarnating messiah but also the titles given to earthly men, which are

plainly the names of Archangels and Angels.

Therefore Gabriel, which means 'Man of God' or 'Man of the Shining One, was actually the title of a man within the Essene order. John the Baptist's other title was Zadok the priest, his inherited role, and Michael. He was, therefore, the contemporary Michael-Zadok or Melchizedek, the King of Righteousness, if this is true then he may also have been the present True Teacher having inherited the title from the previous one. Also within the Essene group were the top three men, called the Father, The Son and the Spirit.7 The Father was the leader or Papa (Papa = Pope) and was elected. His deputies were the Son and Spirit.

One very important title to remember was the 'Word of God' or more simply 'the Word'. This was the title given to Jesus, and any reading of the New Testament will show this. Why then, do we have the 'Word of God' appearing again after the supposed death of Jesus? Acts 13:7, '..and desired to hear the word of God' or listen to Jesus speak. Acts 6:7, '..and the word of God increased' or maybe had children. The very beginning of the book of John says 'In the beginning was the Word and the Word was God and the Word was Jesus.' This is an unsubtle way of telling us that Jesus will from here on be known as the Word. In one part of Revelation, we find not only the allusion to Jesus as the 'Word' but also that he will be riding a white horse upon his return, just like Vishnu.

'And I saw heaven opened, and behold a white horse; and he

that sat upon him was called...and his name is called The Word of God.'10

This 'Word' is Logos. Logos is Greek, Hermes was known as the Greek Logos, and comes from what the Greeks called the Gaulish Sun-god, 'Lugus' the alternative title of 'Lugh' the Irish Sun-god or Shining One. Also equated with this Sun-god Lugh, Lug or Logos, is the Welsh term 'llew' which means light, shine or lion (Lion of Judah could therefore now mean Shining One of Judah 11), and is a corrupted version of the god the Great Hu which in turn may come from the Egyptian word khu (ak Hu) and you will not be surprised by now to find that it means the 'shining one' amongst other things such as translucent, intangible essence of man and spirit. From this Great Hu (which is also a name for Horus, the 'Craftsman who lighteneth the darkness...', taken from the 'Ritual' of Egyptian antiquity). We also have the Indian and Greek 'Dyhu' or 'Dyu' meaning the bright or shining. From this we developed the Tao of the Chinese. In Mexico, this was taken as 'Anahuac' (or 'Mexico') coming from 'huaca' meaning 'sacred and artificial hill or 'heaven'. In central America we have the Quiches worshipped the 'Ak Huishes' and in Avebury we have the Huish Hill. In ancient Britain we find that the people worshipped 'Hi ik' and were called 'Huicci'. In Slav legend we have the 'Niezguinek' which may come from 'on iz ag Hu in ek' which in turn may mean the 'mighty shining one or Hu.' In the legend of Niezguinek we have the description regarding the horse of lightning, 'Marvel of strength and of beauty so white.'

The word of god was later to be taken a step further and turned into a sword of god. A corruption of 'se-word' or 'is-word' meaning 'the light, or shining, of the word' or 'shining'. In Anglo-Saxon (Isaac's Son) the word for sword is 'seax' and means the 'fire of the great fire'. In Italian this sword moves into 'sepada' which incredibly means 'the fire of the Shining Father' and in German 'sabel' means the' Fire of Bel, the shining god'.

As we can see the ramifications of the various language differences between these titles shows quite clearly that Jesus was meant to be the Shining One. These various titles, however, the translations between Hebrew, Greek, Latin and Aramaic, along with the ciphers, numerology and codes employed throughout these early scriptures makes the real meanings all the more difficult to see, especially when we consider that for two thousand years now we have been fumbling around hoping to find the truth through the one level arguments of the literal Bible. Now we know about the Shining Ones' influence on religious societies we can begin to see some of the deeper truths, although it will take many more years to actually go through all the data again. In fact, how can we now believe any translation that we have ever heard? These new facts bring the whole foundations of religion, and especially Christianity, to the ground.

The Gabriel who saw Mary was a priest, the 'trinity' an elected group and the 'poor' those elect. What else are we to find?

From contemporary writings we can see that the Essenes had communities all over the Holy Land, including Qumran as what appears to be the main centre, and without doubt elsewhere. Qumran has shown relics dating back to 3500 BC 9 and the area was called 'the wilderness', so when Jesus went into the wilderness he went simply to Qumran. We are also told that it is now possible that there may have been some influence form Alexandria, as part of the Dead Sea Scrolls were in Greek (see The Elixir and the Stone by Michael Baigent and Richard Leigh). Just outside Qumran is an old monastic centre where the children of the Essene were brought up. This place was referred to as Bethlehem of Judea and is the real place that Jesus was born, not the other and more well known Bethlehem. Children born out of wedlock were generally brought up here and Jesus was no exception; however, due to the fulfilment of the prophecies and the correct lineage (that of his father's side), the problem of his illegitimacy was resolved.

In these centres scattered around the known world, they practised some very Shamanistic type spiritual roles, including sun worship and dualistic philosophy; Pythagorean2 ways; healing or practising medicine (consider Jesus taking up the clay and healing the blind man) and flying3 (Jesus flew back to Heaven after his resurrection). The Egyptian influence on the Essenes is obvious. The words placed by them into the mouth of Jesus come directly from the Egyptian Book of the Dead. In the Book of the Dead we find the 'Chapter of Making the Transformation into the God who giveth Light into Darkness' we find not only that god has a solar disk (shining light) around his head (taken up by later Christian iconography around the illuminated Saints etc.), but we also have this passage, 'I am the girdle of the robe of the god Nu, which shines and sheds light...I have come to give light in the darkness, which is made light and bright by me...I have come, having made an end of the darkness, which has become light indeed'.

This is remarkably similar to many sentences attributed to Jesus. Becoming a priest of the Shining Ones, or akhs, in the Book of the Dead was spoken of thus, 'Behold, I have come forth on this day, and I have become an akh [Shining One].' 8 Jesus was to be portrayed in this way, as the coming Light of the world, the Morning Star, shining brightly as the returned messiah.

Their main doctrines included this idea of the messiah. This is not, as we have seen previously, a new idea. Consider, for example, the Jains, who believe in the Mahavira who was the son of a King or god whose seed had been implanted into the womb of his mother (a young Queen) by heavenly angels and is said to reappear as a saviour. In Kashmir there is a tomb located in the Khanyar district of Srinagar where Yus Asaph is laid. In the typical Jewish way this tomb is aligned east to west with the feet facing the Holy Land. It is said, 'he was a prince by descent' (Certificate of Rahman Mir) and that he 'had given up all worldly affairs and was a lawgiver.' Yus Asaph has also been called Yusu which sounds remarkably like Yesu, another term for Jesus or Jesu. It may also be Joseph or Jose (Yusaph) as this is the common term for Joseph. We do not really know who exactly is in the tomb. It may be one of the characters of this story or it may not. The date may be correct for the tomb of Christ, but that is insufficient evidence for his body to be there. The fact is that cross cultural links were in effect between these Asian arenas and the Middle East. The place has been revered and kept holy as a shrine, albeit now Muslim. At the time of the Essenes there were huge cross cultural links and teachings and trade. Support from around the world was sought for the evolving plot that was to take shape.

The leader of this growing band of Essenes seems to have been the one who had the title, Teacher of Righteousness or Teacher of Truth (Moreh-zedek which sounds like the Old Testament Melchizedek who was the King of Righteousness - compare John the Baptist who had the title of Michael-Zadok and it may well have been his father or grandfather who was the Teacher of Righteousness at the time the Essenes were set up). This teacher taught that there would be two messiahs; the priest and redeemer, the suffering and sacrificial one who would be of the line of Levi, and the Royal messiah who would be just, wise and have power and authority and be of the Davidic line.

This teacher has eluded identification ever since these writings were laid down and probably will forever, as nobody can be sure of any of the evidence. It is known that it was he who brought the pious Essenes out from Jerusalem and the main religious centres because he was supposedly sick and tired of the trouble with the mainstream priests. He took them to refuge in the hills of Qumran and to their old centres of learning in Egypt. This True Teacher, the illusive and unidentifiable leader, drew up a code of discipline and law and led the way forward. There never was one individual called the True Teacher. The reason he is spoken of throughout the Bible, across vast periods of time is because there was probably always a True Teacher; one given the job of seeing in the birth of the next enlightened or anointed one. In this age, the True Teacher had the use of the Roman roads and the written word.

Islamic Angel

Qumran itself became a publicity bureau and

sent out press releases across the world, hidden in cipher and code. Some of its members returned after a while to their normal lives, like fully trained MI5 or KGB agents going back to spread the word. They became Nazarenes or Virgins. Jospehus, the famous Jewish historian, spent some time at Qumran, but according to the standard histories could not make the grade and left. Considering the good publicity of the Josephus record for the Qumran community and the bad press given to the mainstream community it is highly likely that Josephus was one of these initiated spies, the elite spiritual force created out of hard work and discipline.

Josephus maintained the mainstream party line, although his influential writings were spread far and wide and did not suffer from the insulting manner of some of the other critics of the day. It is also said that in later years the Egyptian Essenes or Therapeuts actually influenced the Christians, Muslims and Jews in a way that shows how much authority these people had. Along with the teachings of these early religions, Gnostic and Hermetic literature was produced which became the undercurrent of the world's religious societies. The secret name of the True Teacher, Asaph, became known throughout Jewish, Christian and Muslim thought as a seer and master of the secret arts. Asaph also became the Builder and Architect of the Temple and was therefore highly important to Freemasonry. This name of the True Teacher was a title, given to many men through the ages. Only the initiated have known that Asaph was another name for the Great Thoth, and only the initiated would know who this person actually was at any given time. Later, one of these was Asaph ben Berechiah who produced a now famous medical treatise.

The Essenes were excellent healers and, according to them, their medicinal skills were inherited from the long priestly line of Shem the Shamanic medicine man. As we have seen, Jesus himself was an excellent healer and thousands flocked to his healing evangelisms. The Shaman, in their early and prime method of helping the tribe, used many medicinal techniques which we are only recently rediscovering. The knowledge of the Shaman and in this context, the Essene, seems to be excellent. Some of the more spectacular healing produced by these people can only have come from a knowledge of the cycles, currents and subtleties of the planet on which we live. In all Shamanistic practices, a god or spirit power is invoked, either by prayer or meditation. Sometimes the laying on of hands or anointing the person would be required, as would sacrifice. All of these practices are to be found in the Bible, and were performed by Jesus.

The True Teacher of the 2nd century BC was a prophet, a lawgiver and was highly literate, sharing the attributes of Thoth/Hermes. Much of that written about this individual has been utilised again and again over the centuries, for John the Baptist, Jesus and Muhammad and for many prophets of the Old Testament. He is said to have been anointed, a messiah who had been reincarnated as an inspired seer and in whom dwelled the Holy Spirit.

Indeed all High Priests and kings were said to be messiahs or anointed ones. This is because the writers of the various scriptures were all initiated into the same club, the Shining Ones. To be associated with the True Teacher or Lawgiver was a privilege and honour. Josephus said of the Essene, 'After God they hold most in awe the name of the Lawgiver.'5 The Lawgiver's other title was Hermes or Thoth, or the very Biblical Tammuz. This True Teacher was merged with the Egyptian God in the Shamanistic style of the old days. In fact, this had been happening for a very long time, as Moses had been the Lawgiver when he came down from the mountain (heaven) with the stone tablets of the law. Moses had learned his trade

in Egypt, the home of Thoth, and had come to the Israelites to give the law. It may, of course, be true that Moses was a Prime Minister of Egypt or even a Pharaoh, we will have to await confirmation if it is ever forthcoming.

One thing about the Essene organisation should be added here. They actually set up their community constitution along the lines of Israel under the specific guidance of Moses, the one of Egypt. It seems that Moses was the True Teacher, Asaph, and designated Thoth. The role of Lawgiver has, therefore, been around for some time and the True Teacher of the Essenes was just filling the gap for a short period as an initiate. This True Teacher was expected to return with each generation, the promised prophet and maker of the New Covenant, but this time around he was to sow the seeds of a New Covenant that would last for a very long time. The fact that this Teacher was to return with each generation shows how it was expected that the line should carry on as it had always done, just as the various other lineages were inherited with each new generation. It was the True Teacher of each new generation who was to pass on the correct interpretation of the Bible, as the spiritual monitor of the people. (One other point to note about the Dead Sea Scrolls is that there are many parallels with Iranian concepts and Zoroastrianism, showing the depth of linkage involved here.)

Among those initiated into the Essenes were Joseph, the father of Jesus, and Zecheriah, the father of John the Baptist.4 This is not surprising when we consider they were to go back into the world to prepare for the coming of the two messiahs. The time was right for the coming and had been predicted (in fact the date had also been changed a couple of times because he had not yet come). The stories which surrounded John the Baptist (and still do with the believers called Mandaeans who say John was the messiah) were eventually rewritten into the plan as if they were for Jesus. John was said to be the child of Light, born in Bethlehem, planted out of the heights and laid in Elizabeth's womb. Even when he (John) was born the famous Magi came to worship him, of course, following a star all the way.

Zechariah was warned by an angel (messenger) that Herod wanted John dead and they took him away into the 'wilderness' (Qumran) to safety. The best parts of the story, the most symbolic and effective, were used in the story of Jesus.

This does of course also explain the conflicting reports in the various Biblical and non-Biblical gospels of the birth of Christ.

The messiahs of Jesus and John the Baptist were to try to usurp the mainstream kingly and priestly messiahs of Jerusalem. They planned a spiritual battle which would inspire not just the Jews but also the Gentiles. Along the way they would employ the Gentiles in their work and their plan proved to be more powerful than any other standard office of messiah so far.

The Essenes had set up a separate power base to undermine the mainstream. They exiled themselves, or distanced themselves from Jerusalem, claiming power spiritually, rather than physically. They made Bethlehem part of Qumran and acted out the passion play in or near Damascus. The plan was clever and had taken nearly one hundred years

to see through. John, the son of Zechariah, the Melchizedek of his age, was of the Levitical lineage. Jesus the son of Joseph

and Mary, both initiates of the Essenes, was of the Davidic line. Finally, after altering the predicted dates twice, the stage was set for the coming of the two messiahs.

We should note here that Mary was said to have conceived by the Holy Ghost through her ear. There was a popular superstition that lizards also conceived via their ears. Lizards adorn many Cathedrals, which attests to this link. The Italian for 'lizard' is 'lucerta' which means 'shining light' and is of the same root as 'wizard'. The link here is that Mary, the mother of Jesus, was considered to be a shining one.

Just as Jacob had built an altar to Elohim, the Shining Ones, at 'El Beth-El' ('God of the House of God', El being Semitic for Shining One), and had revered the Shining Ones in doing so, the Essenes now revered the Shining Ones in their writings and their planning. The Elohim of the Essenes were the creating gods, plural in aspect, they created light out of darkness. They shone brightly in the sky and Jesus was to be the manifest Shining Son. For some, Jehovah was above the Elohim.

In Isaiah 43:10 we have, 'I am he: before me there were no Shining Ones, neither shall there be after me.' 6 The whole plan was built around the Shining Ones, their history and their prophecies.

John the Baptist was associated with Elijah (the Shining one of Jehovah) because he was to be the returned Elijah, as predicted, and as part of the normal and accepted way of these Shaman. Elijah went away with the Shining Ones. In 2 Kings 2:11 he is taken up in a chariot of fire. The Seraphim or Shining Ones accompanied him and it is they who were to return him. As we have seen, the Seraphim were the Shining Ones and the word 'saraph' in Hebrew is a form of serpent or

the essence of light. In English this serpent was sometimes called an eel which comes from El.

In England we also have Stonehenge, whose stones are said in legend to come from Kildare, specifically a place called Naase or the One Light. Naaseni means the good serpent and Naas is the Semitic term for serpent. Are these old linkages between the languages, between and across continents purely coincidental? Or is it more likely that these Shining Ones were actually all over the globe, shaping the names of places, with their usual way of hiding more meanings within the words? The Semitic links alone are startling. Remember that these stones of Stonehenge, apart from coming from the home of those in the light, supposedly, originally and mythically, came from the remotest parts of Africa, the home of some of the earliest Shaman and Shining Ones.

The reason for my occasional divergence into other legends, places and languages is simple. We need to understand that when Jesus told the Apostles to send the word to the Gentiles it was part of a large plan. The whole story and essence of the Jesus saga had to be all encompassing. It had to take on board the subtle differences of the world's belief systems. Or did it? The reason his story rang true to the known world was because the basics and legends of the Shining Ones, the languages and hidden myths, were already there.

The idea of the duality of the messiahs eventually fell into trouble as John the Baptist was caught out and killed. Maybe he had gone too far for the authorities or maybe it was all planned and he did not die, the question will forever remain unanswered. Whatever the case may be, Jesus was now to take on the dual role of both priest and king messiah. The lineage did not prove to be a problem and minor alterations were made, as can be seen in the gospels with the conflicts between the lineages.

Jesus had been born to a virgin. This was so as to fulfil prophecy and not to alienate him from the other Shining Fathers or Sons who had also been born of virgins. Mary was not a virgin at all. The word for 'virgin' is 'almah' which in fact means only 'young woman'. In Latin, 'virgo' simply means 'unmarried'. In fact, Jesus could not have claimed the correct lineage on his father's (Joseph) side unless he had been sired by him. The Virgin Birth was nothing more than, and was well known to be, a symbolic statement. Mary may have been a member of the now infamous Virgin Cult which prevailed at the time and could well have been set up to bring, as virgins, the new Shining Ones into the world.

The community at Qumran, Bethlehem in Judea, may have been the birthing spot of the children born of 'virgins', or unmarried women. As we have seen, Bethlehem was the place where children born out of wedlock were trained. Indeed, we have to ask if Vishnu or any other such returning messiah was going to be born in this place, especially as it had been occupied since 3500 BC by nomads, who were the early Shining Ones. If there were world-wide training centres, centres of trade, mining, building, learning, writing and any other such industry employed by the universal Shining Ones, this could have been the spot that an upcoming messiah should be born. In the Gospel of Philip, surprisingly not in the Bible, we have the obvious statement, 'Some say that Mary conceived by the Holy Spirit. They are wrong. They do not know what they are saying.' The words of one who knows the truth, but not entirely forthcoming. He simply attempts to realign the facts.

Traditionally, it was the job of the Abiathar priest to approve the marriages of those in the correct lineage, especially when one is found to have conceived out of wedlock. This Abiathar priest had another title, Gabriel - the man of God. It was this Gabriel who spoke to Mary and Joseph and worked between them, as tradition dictates, to bring about this predicted and planned birth and subsequent wedlock.

Mary also had other children. James, Joses, Simon and Judas, along with the unnamed sisters (Mark 6:3 and Matthew 13:56). All were to play a part in the saga, and all were equally trained for service at Bethlehem and Qumran. None of these were the first born, however, and religious tradition globally states that the first born must be the sacrifice.

Joseph, quite clearly the father of Jesus (Luke 2:27), has been called a carpenter. The word used is the Greek 'ho tekton', a Semitic word, 'Naggar', which means scholar or teacher. It may be that this use of the word and the role taken by Joseph as he spoke to the human angel Gabriel indicates that he was the True Teacher or at least one of them. It also shows that he was a respected person in the society, and the word indicates that he was master of whatever he did.

The word 'carpenter' can be taken to mean 'master of the craft' which is remarkably like the later title of the master Freemasons. The word 'carpenter' in Zend13 is 'Tashan' which means 'creator' and this may have been a subtle, symbolic way of saying that the father of Jesus was the creator god, which was Elohim, the Shining Ones.

Mary gave birth to Jesus in a house, not a stable, and much of the myth of the Nativity began. Part of this Nativity was the gifts given by the Magi (Magicians of Persia who were Shining Ones and who came from the East, the land of the rising Sun-Ra god, and symbolic of the new life that the messiah was to bring). The gifts themselves were subtly symbolic. Gold was given by Egyptian Pharaohs when they had been defeated, an indication that Jesus was the conqueror. Myrrh was embalming oil, a pain relieving agent which was symbolic of the relief of pain that Christ would bring and the death he was to suffer. Frankincense was used in anointing a priest and was simply to say that Jesus would be the priestly messiah in the place of John who was to die. Jesus was born into a sect of the Essenes called the Nazarenes. He was not born at Nazareth, which may not even have existed at the time of his birth. 'Nazarene' comes from 'Nazrie ha-Brit' which means 'keepers or holders of the covenant'. These were the ones who had been given the secrets of the plan and were the ones to carry it out. Not surprisingly, we find that Jesus' brother, James, and John the Baptist were also members of this sect.

Any investigation into this sect will show that the rules were strict and the teaching rigorous. Any secrets, that were intended to be kept that way, would stay with the individual until death. When we look at how our own intelligence services train the spies of tomorrow we can see that good discipline is essential.

The absolute knowledge that a secret once given, is a secret kept. In the Fifth Book of his Memoirs, Hegesippus stated, 'Now Jacob, the brother of the Lord, who, as there were many of that name, was termed the Just by all... He drank neither wine nor fermented liquors, and abstained from animal food [a very Hindu thing to do]....A razor never came upon his head [beard];...He alone was allowed to enter the Holy Place...He never wore woollen, only linen garments.'

Jacob (James the Just, brother of Jesus) was a Nazarite and was brought to his death because of it by the high priest, Annas. The names of Jesus and others were highly important. In the old ways of the Shaman to issue forth a name was power. To speak a name and utter a request would bring about some reaction. There truly was power in a name, especially in ancient times. The true names of almost everybody in this tale are not told. Jesus was not his real name at all. In the Acts of Thomas, the Gnostic paper, King Misdaeus says, 'Thou canst not hear his true name at this time; but the name that was given him is Jesus Christ.'

The early years of Jesus are not spoken of in any detail in the Bible and we can deduce from information so far discussed that he was busy preparing his future and raising the global support required to become the next messiah. After his training was complete, he chose those who were to aid in his attempt to gain power. Regardless of popular Christian opinion they were not fishermen or simple men.

The term 'fishers of men' is symbolic of a certain section of the priesthood who actually baptised in the rivers or lakes. The Gentiles were to undergo this kind of Baptism and it was these baptisers of Gentiles whom Jesus recruited. Part of the process of baptising the Gentiles was to walk along a ritual walkway placed just above the water, the ritual was called 'walking on water'.12

The disciples' names differ at various times and between various gospels, but it is sufficient to say that those chosen were not ordinary men. They were nobles and high ranking officials, both within the secret sect of the Shining Ones or Essenes and like spies within the established church, even to the point of being tax collectors. Again we see the use of alternative titles so that those with the eyes to see will be able to discern the real background. James and John were described as the sons of Thunder. 'Thunder' was a title of a minister in the Sanctuary. The sons would inherit a great estate from their father, although where the title 'sons' is given it actually means 'to inherit' and, therefore, James and John were simply to 'inherit' the titles. Even the names given to these people in the gospels differ from those issued at birth, which explains the various name changes seen between versions. 'Jesus' was the name issued by the Essenes, by Gabriel, in fact, and 'Christ' the title. He would have had a birth name also. This is seen when people from his own town reject him as they literally say 'this is not (the) Jesus'.

The political rival to the Thunder title was 'Lightning' and this was bestowed upon Simon Magus. Simon had other names too, such as Zebedee and Simon Zelotes. He was the head of the Samaritan Magi and chief magician. When James and John were to inherit the titles of Thunder, Lightning was also one of those titles to be inherited. James and John were also 'Fishers' and were capable of baptism. The 'Fishermen' were different. They were the ones who brought people to the 'Fishers' and were a little lower on the social rankings because of this. The 'Fishers' of men is symbolic for a much deeper reason than to simply 'fetch' fish out of the ocean.

The identification of the saviour with the fish is universal. In the Talmud the messiah is called 'Dag' or 'Dagh' which means fish. Dag comes from 'Dagon' the Solar Fish God of the Philistines. Dagon was sometimes called 'Odakon (O'Dagon)' who in turn was sometimes known as 'On', the same god that various Shining Ones worshipped at the Temples of the Egyptians. Vishnu, in his first form as the saviour who led mankind to safety in an ark, was as a fish and the word 'fish' is equated with the first letter of Vishnu. Vishnu is sometimes translated as 'born of a fish' and we have already seen the many links between Hindu and Jewish myth, especially the myth of the returning messiah. Vishnu is said to have spoken of the times when religion is in danger, and that when iniquity triumphs 'I issue forth for the defence of the good and the suppression of the wicked; for the establishment of justice I manifest myself from age to age.'

The Babylonians, Phoenicians and Assyrians held the fish in high regard and almost as a god. Jesus is said to have been born under the astrological sign of Pisces, the fish, and in the early Christian catacombs the sign of the two fishes is in abundance. The very secret symbol of Christ is the fish. Paulinus said Jesus was the 'fish of the living water' and Tertullian referred to Christians as 'fishes bred in the water and saved by the one great fish.' Prosper said of Christ, 'the Fish dressed at his death - the great fish who satisfied for himself the disciples on the shore and offered himself as a fish to the whole world.' It has been said that the secret term of the fish used for Jesus, the Greek 'Icthus' or 'Ictheus' means fish, but it also means 'ik theos' or Great God and we find that in Old Irish the similar word 'ischa' is the Eastern form of Jesus and means fish.[14]

In Arthurian and Atlantic legend, we have the all-pervading power of the Fisher King. Many say that this alludes in myth to Jesus himself. It has now become clear that throughout the myths of the world, the fish has played an important role and, symbolically, equates with the messiah. Considering that there are many messiahs, then there have been many fishes and many Fisher Kings.[15] Bacchus had the same 'mystery-name' of fish as did Jonas (taken from 'IO' the name of the global god), who was swallowed by the 'fish' (the word in the Bible simply means large fish) and was resurrected by the fish. Jonas is depicted on reliefs as the 'fish man' as is the chief guide of ancient China, 'Fuh Yi'.

The disciples were chosen one by one until they numbered twelve, which was specified by the Qumran Manual of Disciples and was essential for the preservation of the faith in

the land.16 Simon Magus, or Simon Zelotes seems to have been the most important. In Acts he is spoken of as representing the power of god; and if he was the Magi, the magician, then he was indeed God's tool. His powers would seem great and, like a Shaman's, to have come from god. So it follows that the Samaritans would send a Magi to uphold the attempt at power by Jesus and the Essenes. These were the wise men of the East, the very same who had supposedly been there at his birth and had previously plotted the whole power struggle. All articles regarding Simon speak of a master of the art, of cosmology, levitation17 and natural magnetism; the full works of any Shaman or Magi. The title 'Zelotes' comes from the fact that he was a leader in the martial Zealots. In German, 'zeal' transfers into 'seelig' which is 'se el ig' and means 'fire of god almighty'.18 Hardly a surprising title when we consider that the Romans considered them to be bandits.

Without going through each disciple in detail, which is not the role of this book, we will cover the basic elements of each one. Judas was the Chief of the Scribes.19 His second title 'Iscariot' was probably 'Sicarius' which actually means 'Assassin' or the 'dagger' of a Zealot assassin and alludes to the fact that he was the part of the plan to have Jesus sacrificed. Incidentally, the verb 'skariot' is the same as the Hebrew word 'sikkarti' to deliver up. The 'sacrifice delivered up' or the 'assassin the deliverer'. In Islamic lore Judas is shown to be a defender of Jesus, not a betrayer and in the 14th century theologians were suggesting that Judas actually took the place of Christ on the cross.

Thaddaeus (Judas) was a leader of the Zealots and a member of the Egyptian Essene order 'Therapeutate'. Matthew was a tax collector and is also called 'the Levi' in Luke. This was a deep cover, as the taxes collected were to be transferred to the Temple at Jerusalem (the plot had to be funded somehow).

The collection of taxes was hated by the Pharisees, who saw it as the role of those who were not pure. James was Jonathan the 'Thunder' and held the title of 'Jacob', a very high position in the Temple. Bartholomew (John Mark) was head of the Proselytes and also probably a member of the Egyptian Essenes. Philip was a Gentile Proselyte and head of the Order of Shem which in itself is rather peculiar when we consider that Shem was the originator of the Semitic people. Unless of course Philip (lover of Horses) and all Gentiles were thought in some way to be related to those early Semites (which would be true in the eyes of the Shining Ones).

Simon Peter and Andrew were Essenes and were ritualised lay people involved with the 'Fishers of Men' scenario. Peter, entitled 'the guardian', was probably the bodyguard of Jesus and other members, if not indeed the head of the bodyguard, truly the 'rock' on which to build the Church. Thomas (one of his official titles, his birth name being Crown Prince Philip) was the son of Herod the Great [20] and Mariamme II. He married Herodias (Herod's granddaughter) and had a daughter called Salome, who later on was to request the head of John the Baptist. The political intrigue builds. It was the brother of Thomas, Herod-Antipas who was to move on and become Tetrarch of Galilee.

Because of this, Thomas was called Didymus (twin) or Teoma ('Thomas' and 'twin' in Aramaic), after the style of the story of Esau who also lost power to his brother. There is good strong reason and bad feeling here to see why Thomas would join with a group who were intending to take power, one way or the other. Of course, there may be another reason for Thomas being known as the twin. He may simply have looked like Jesus and taken his place on the cross; this would truly make him the designated 'twin.' Another element we should not forget is that in ancient times the twin was supposed to have been blessed.

He was credited with immense magical powers. This is the reason why the constellation of the Twins is thought to be lucky. This idea comes to us through the fertility ideals, where giving birth to two children at once was thought a gift from god.

As we can see there is much more to be read into the gospels than we ever thought. Even the so called miracles performed were symbolic. Just as the ordained ministers of Gentile baptism were called 'fishers' the official Levite ministers also had a title, 'loaves'. Only Jews could become 'loaves'. The uncircumcised non-Jews were called 'Ham' and were not allowed to be called 'loaves'. They also numbered five thousand. When the 'five thousand' were fed 'loaves and fishes' it was the Essene way of saying that 'you are all accepted and can become members of our elite club.' These stories, including the feeding of the five thousand, are steeped in symbolism and are worth looking into at a later point.

There is a huge story to be told here; however, I am choosing only that which relates more directly to our current story.

Jesus was baptised by the other messiah, although I believe this to be an added story to show that John was passing on authority, due to his unfortunate death. At this baptism, the Spirit of God came down like a dove. A candidate or initiate in the Temple in Egypt would be anointed or baptised by Anubis (meaning 'the One Orb of Light') and the spirit would descend upon him like a dove (the spirit being known as 'Dove of the Spirit' or akh, shining one).

It is important to note that Jesus had a beard. This was relevant to the sect of the Nazarene, which was part of the Essene (Hasidim or Chasidim) or Shining Ones. We have previously

seen how important the beard was to the symbolism of the age. In later times we will find Christian Pastors (Waldensian) known as 'barbes'. In French, 'barbe' means 'beard' and 'barbes' means 'shining lights'.

The name 'Jesus' (Jehu, Jeshu, Iesus etc.) has other connotations. 'Jes Hu' possibly comes from the Great Hu which means Shining.

The fact that Jesus married, and had three (a significant number) children has been written about in some length by others (see notes). It is highly probable that his wife, Mary, took the children to Europe, where there were others of her kind, and settled down there. Early Christian (and Pagan) holy places show signs of Mary having had influence in a number of places, as would any Queen.

It may also be that Jesus married his sister, one of those spoken of but unnamed. This was the custom (as it is for many nations) of the Egyptians, to whom the Essenes (Shining Ones) were closely related. Although this was not the general practice of the kings of Judah, it would have made symbolic sense to everyone at the time that Jesus was of the spiritual order, from the Egyptians, a true king and deity just like the Pharaohs. This would also have made the sons of Jesus true heirs to the throne later on.

It may also have been possible that Jesus had to marry in order to fulfil another rule. The age-old poetic marriage of heaven and Earth, Sky God and Mother Earth goddess. In the psalms we have an allusion to this possibility, 'Mercy and Truth are met together; Righteousness and Peace have kissed each other. Truth shall spring from the earth ; and Righteousness shall look down from heaven.' The idea of this union of deities was an age-old custom. Jesus the Son of God, the Word and God's representative on Earth marrying the Mother Earth Goddess, Mary, would have been an almost Shamanistic reconciliation union. A ritual so sacred and old it remained part of the secret of the group and covered up more with each passing century. As the Polynesians say, 'Up to this time the vast Heaven has still ever remained separated from his spouse the Earth.' 22 Now the union was made, a truly symbolic gesture, and one powerful secret held by the Gnostic.

For three years in his ministry, Jesus showed his prowess as the sacred Heart at the sacred art. He was truly a Shining One, and like our politicians of today he had a number of very clever, skilled and useful advisors and spin doctors.

Their job was to see him through the plot and ensure that all the symbolic acts were carried out. Those that were missed were simply added into the narrative later on (three wise men etc.) and nobody was any the wiser.

Many of the things that were added in went unnoticed as there were times when Jesus was alone with his advisory staff. The codes within the Bible were kept secret and it has taken two millennia to sort them out. Some are so misleading as to be ridiculous and others are 'red herrings' (Bible Code, for instance23). There are several 'truths' about the real Jesus portrayed today, from the bloodline of the Jesus lineage being the Holy Grail to the Buddha being Jesus. There is truth in all these. Buddha was Jesus in a way, because he was simply another messiah reincarnated into his inheritance of earthly kingship and enlightenment. The Holy Grail or 'san graal' is possibly the bloodline as many have shown.21

The one major area which would make Christianity fall, is the resurrection. If, however, the resurrection had never happened at all, because Jesus did not actually die on the cross, then we would be into the arena of altering the history of the western world.

We have already seen that the advisors employed by Jesus, the spies sent forth by the Essene, had huge influence and power in the Temple, in the military and within the Royal family. We also have the renowned magician, Simon Magus. There have been literally hundreds of modern-day magicians or tricksters who have claimed and proven that today they too could pull off the illusion of the resurrection. Without doubt, the efficiency and skill of those people two thousand years ago was tremendous. If we are to believe that they could produce such an awe inspiring set of documents now known as the Bible then we must also believe them capable of such a plot. The intricacies of the Bible and those books still kept out of Holy Scripture, are fascinating. I have spoken to endless Christians and Jews alike who feel that the Spirit of God has spoken to them every time they have experienced a new revelation from the Bible.

This was the writers' intention, and it shows an almost unparalleled, unique intelligence. The reason for such immense knowledge is simple. The Shining Ones are behind all religions and have been around for a long time. They organised great centres of learning. They travelled extensively between continents, passed on learning, discussed new movements and discovered new ways all the time. They would have had meetings in which they discussed movements in world opinion, in the various differences between cultures and would have gradually implemented the same controls.

The apostles were not poor people as we have been led to believe. They were quite the opposite. They had no need to work hard for a living, and they had a faith which moved them forward. They had years of learning under their belt. Jesus was

not ready for his ministry until he was thirty, which shows a long term training implementation in process. We can see from the same periods involved with Buddha and Mahavira that they too probably underwent similar training periods for their role as messiah.

Jesus was perfectly aware of the plot, he shows this in the scriptures when it is said that he knew that the crucifixion was coming. He could rely on his men completely; they were a professional group who had all the plans in place. The stage ready, all that was awaited was the leading actor. He rode upon a white donkey into Jerusalem with palm branches scattered on the ground as a carpet for the coming Lord. The palm itself is symbolic of several important myths. Firstly, it was the sign of the Flaming Column found on the coinage of Carthage, in the foreground was a great horse. The palm also stood for fire and, even more in keeping with our story here, the Tree of Life. The leaves were never changing and in this they signified the unchangeable lord.

The Phoenicians also held the palm in high esteem, and their coinage displayed the serpent coiled around its trunk. The 'Baal Tamar' meant 'Lord of the Palm' and 'Tamar' means 'resplendent Sun Fire'. In Greek, 'palm' is 'phoenix' which has obvious connotations with the resurrected Light or Fire of God. This palm spreading activity may or may not have actually occurred, it may simply have been the disciples playing out their plan and symbolically informing the people of Jerusalem that this was the Christ. After he entered the Temple, Jesus did not find too much of a stir and we find in Mark's Gospel that nothing much occurred. In fact, the disciples were reprimanded for causing a disturbance (Luke). Therefore Jesus went on to Bethany. The prophecies that the messiah would not be recognised came true, and the total rejection of the people for the expected messiah was complete. It was not surprising that he was not recognised. He had spent little time in Jerusalem and was, after all, an Essene, with a group of anti-establishment spies in tow. The people were not expecting symbolism in their messiah, they were expecting force. As history has shown, force, in conjunction with the messiah, has been highly unsuccessful. Any attempt to take power by force, before or after Jesus, proved impossible.

The people did group behind the self-proclaimed messiahs, but never in enough strength to ensure a lasting self rule. With Jesus, the plan was not a power attempt by force, it was one aimed at the mind and the soul via subtle symbolism.

The next step was for the 'assassin', Judas, to make his move and bring the Priests of the Temple into the knowledge of Jesus' struggle for power. This had the desired effect and the play was truly begun. At this stage, there was no turning back. Next, the Last Supper, the story of so many Gnostic traditions, was planned. In this alone we can see how rich these people were. In one of the most hectic towns of the area, at the busiest time of the year, Jesus and his entourage took their supper in what must have been a huge room. Symbolically, it was an Upper Room, pertaining to the Heavens, and the taking of a meal was reminiscent of the ancient practice of eating on top of mounds.

Here, we have to ask, if Jesus was supposed to move to Bethany after his entrance into Jerusalem, then why is he suddenly back there again? The answer is simple. The Qumran community left Jerusalem, as we have previously shown ,and set up in or around Qumran. This new 'Vatican' was called Jerusalem also.

They began the ritual of the Feast of the Messiah or 'Last Supper', which just so happened to be at the same time as the

Passover, because the tradition had stayed with the Essene[24].

Close by there was a place known as 'Mount of Olives', an old monastery. These similarities of names to those of Jerusalem are no surprise. When the English emigrated to the Americas they too started to name the new places with the names of their old land (York/New York etc.). That night, Jesus prayed alone in the place known as Gethsemane and in obvious symbolism showed how he was the messiah. He endured the darkness, where his disciples could not. The act of being alone before a sacrifice is one typical of the Shaman, who would be alone to talk with the spirits before any such practice.

Judas betrayed Jesus as specified in the plan. The trial was short, due to the fact it was a mock trial, under Essene influence and that Pontius Pilate was given power to execute this man. In all the writings regarding Pontius Pilate the stark fact comes across that he had no dislike for Christ and in fact wanted to let him go as he had done nothing wrong. The priests, however, pressed for his execution under the law of the Gentiles. There would be no point in executing him themselves, people would obviously know it to be a fraud and never believe him to be resurrected. The crucifixion had to be public and properly authentic. The sacrifice on the Tree took place.

On the two trees either side (significantly, three in all) were members of the group also placed there as part of the plot. In the books discovered at Nag Hammadi, we find the discourse known as The Second Treatise of the Great Seth. In this we find the words of Jesus, after his crucifixion, 'As for my death - which was real enough to them - it was real to them because of their own...blindness.' We also find a certain Simon of Cyrene who was the one to switch with either Christ himself of one of the others during the walk along the 'way of sorrows' (Via

Dolorosa). It may have been Simon the Magi, who was also

involved in the deceit, and much has been written regarding this Passover Plot already (see notes). We must not forget that it is still an Islamic belief that Jesus did not die on the cross.

It is sufficient for us to say that the following occurred. Either Jesus or Simon the Magi was switched with Simon the Cyrene. A mixture of gall and vinegar was issued to Jesus on the Tree and this had the effect of providing unconsciousness (gall is snake venom and vinegar is poor or soured wine, both symbolically significant items).

Normally, any crucifixion would take at least five days to kill someone. This time Jesus appeared dead within hours and he was taken down and given into the hands of his brother, Joseph of Arimathea. Joseph was an honourable member of the Sanhedrin and a secret disciple of Christ. He had inherited his father's title of the name 'Joseph' because Jesus had already been issued his title by Gabriel. Jesus was David, the kingly title, and James his brother was Joseph, the next in line to the title. In this, James was the Crown Prince which translates as 'Rama-Theo' (Divine Highness) he was therefore Joseph of Arimathea (his father's title and crown prince). There is now no confusion as to why Pilate should hand over the body of Jesus to a stranger. Jesus and the other two were taken away to the family tomb which had already been rigged with sufficient escape holes.

Keeping watch over the cave-tomb were angels; the men with official authority. Indeed, those who visited the tomb actually thought that these angels were just ordinary people. If anything, these angels were guarding against spectators and

hiding the fact that a conjuring trick was in progress and were most likely to have been Essenes as they were dressed in white and it is known that the Essene were excellent medicine men. In John 19:39, 'He (Joseph) was joined by Nicodemus, who brought with him a mixture of myrrh and aloes, more than half a hundredweight'. Later, Mary of Magdala (the wife of Jesus) said, 'They have taken the Lord out of his tomb.' First Nicodemus brings myrrh and aloes and then, Jesus is 'gone' because 'they' have taken him. Myrrh is a sedative and brings pain relief. The juice taken from aloes is a powerful medicine used to expel unwanted poisons, such as snake venom, from the body's system. Together they were precisely the tools needed by any good 'medicine man' such as Simon or Nicodemus. A great earthquake and an angel appeared. That is, two people appeared, and Simon the young man in a white robe had made their plan come true. The cast of the whole play had brought about one of the world's greatest mysteries which is still with us today.

In traditional Shaman style, Jesus then showed he had brought back the power. Flying was a key aspect of this Shamanistic practice as he flew to heaven at the 'Ascension'. Three days after crucifixion his wounds were healed by 'Marham-i-Isa' (Ointment of Jesus), a salve referred to in old medicinal papers and in all likelihood one sold by the Essene to the populace. As we would expect, his return was promised and as we shall see a new leader was chosen by a later Gabriel.

The symbolism of the whole story of Jesus Christ is the richest on the planet and worthy of a much greater study than allowed here. The point is that for two thousand years we have followed this story as literal truth, then we altered slightly and modern rationalism made us see it in the sense of 'good teaching', and now we must see it in the context of not just this good teaching but also a deeper teaching. Within your old Bible, stuffed in the bottom drawer or up in the attic, there are pages of real truth, pages of the real history of mankind. That same history has been hidden from us by the tabloid garbage of the official historians. There is more to history than the kings and queens, the wars and battles, the famines and gold rushes. Behind all power bases there is another story; the story of the ones who do the work in the background and take no credit, the ones who manipulate and cajole those in the public eye.

What we have seen, for the first time in some detail, is the working of the Shining Ones to bring about change. Never before in the history of the Shining Ones had they attempted such a radical departure from the normal low key secretive ways. This operation was huge, the secrets had to be tied up, a specific spy training school had to be employed and for almost the first time these Shining One trainees were to take leading roles. Not only that, decades were wasted trying desperately to establish the correct lineage for the whole thing to come to fruition. Whether the plans went correctly the whole way or not is another matter. The point is that change was brought about. It seems from the historical settings that the Shining Ones, Moses, Abraham, Buddha, Mahavira, and as we have seen a much larger list, had learnt much from their ancient dealings. The skill, knowledge, sheer determination and bravery of such a plot must have seemed daunting at times. But with the military chiefs, intelligence officers, assassins, teachers, ministers, princes, Baptists, Gentiles and magicians, there were sufficient numbers of highly skilled operatives in and off the field to enable a

complicated plot like this to be worked out. If ever there was a 'mission impossible' then this was it.

As Ernesto De Martino pointed out, the Shaman was the redeemer for the tribe. The tribe relied solely upon this one man to bring them salvation. So too did the Essenes and the Shining Ones put this idea into practice with the plot of the symbols, the literally 'spiritual war' that they fought. They had one huge advantage: nobody knew who they really were. Their identities were protected by men and women sworn to secrecy and murdered if they broke the confidence, just as they were murdered when they fell out of any covenant they had entered. We have only to look at Ananias and Sapphira and see that they were 'struck dead' for walking among the idols of their hearts. There was no time here for self, this was a time of great movements, of the great 'plan'. For the root knowledge and symbolism of this great plan see Note 25 which gives information relating to other 'people' in history who were influential in the making of this Jesus 'story'.

An early complaint against the Gnostics was that they hid their true identity. They conformed to the religions of the nation they were living in and kept their secret ideas to themselves, thus avoiding detection and the loss of their secrets to the world. This was a dangerous business to be in, it was power. Iranaeus said, 'Neither can they be detected as Christian heretics, because they assimilate themselves to all sects.' They formed esoteric schools around the globe, either that or they simply carried on in their esoteric schools as they always had.

Tertullian said, 'They undermine ours in order to build up their own.' This was a true statement of one who understood that the power of such a group would be, if it wasn't already, massive. Nevertheless, Christianity was placed over the old religions and beliefs of the world like a thin veil. Always we could see the old ones shining through and occasionally the two would merge into one picture. At times like Christmas, we have a period which has nothing to do with Jesus and yet he has altered his true birthday in accordance with old pagan ideologies. The merge was not difficult, after all the aggressive take over bid was being funded by the mother company anyway.

The Shining Ones had been under the skin of Judaism all along. In the copy of the Pentateuch from the 2nd century, owned by R. Meir, we have the text from Genesis 3:7 which instead of the usual and later reading of loincloths or coats of skin actually reads 'coats of light.' Adam was truly the idea that man was created from god as light and moved into darkness through his sin. The Shining Ones were the ones who were sinless and enlightened and who were now to transform Judaism into something new and up to date.

Philo of Alexandria was greatly influenced by, and indeed did influence, a group of Jews called Therapeutae or Greek Essene. They dressed in white garments and became one of the 'think tanks' for the way forward. Philo tells us of the all-night festivals of  these almost Shamanistic people, 'This is how they keep it. They all stand up in a body, and in the middle of the banqueting-place they first form two Choroi, one of men and the other of women, a leader and conductor is chosen for each, the one whose reputation is greatest for a knowledge of music. They then chant hymns composed in God's honour in many metres and melodies, sometimes singing together, sometimes one Choros, beating the measure with their hands for the antiphonal chanting of the other, now dancing to the measure and now inspiring it, at times dancing in procession, at times set-dances, and then circle-dances, right and left.'

The word 'Choros' or 'Choroi' comes from the carole of the Troubadours meaning to dance in a circle or form a circle and relates back to names attributed to stone circles. Dancing and forming circles, chanting and beating is all very reminiscent of typical Shamanistic rituals. Philo and the Theraputae together developed the assimilation of the ideas of Plato and Stoicism, reworking them into current ideas to make them more acceptable to the Hellenised world. The Logos was the way god 'radiated' or 'shone' his being into the world. The idea that everybody in one way or another could become Shining Ones or illuminated was introduced and taken on with great excitement. The way forward had been discovered, but the old ways needed incorporating and adapting.

The prophecies incorporated into the Bible, both the face value prophecies and those with a hidden agenda, were universal. The birth of the messiah from a virgin had already taken place time and again across the world. It was a necessary act to begin the cycle of life, that God was the instigator of the life of his counsel on earth and essential as God's show of power. The Light of God was to reach everywhere. The long term and intense training of the young chosen one was not just specific to Jesus, it had happened to all the others (Buddha 29, 30 or 35 before he began his ministry, Jain 30, Zoroaster, Muhammad and see also the modern day Dalai Lama who was trained for years from his childhood for godhead). Jesus trained with the Shining Ones in the 'wilderness', and at other times he moved around the globe like some modern-day politician gaining support prior to an election.

There is sufficient evidence from tradition around Europe and ancient writings to show this to be the case. Walking on water, turning water into wine, casting out demons, prophecies, death on the sacrificial tree and raising up three days later to fly to the mountain or heaven; all these things and many more are simply part of the way of the Shaman , and the universal understanding of the initiated.

The real understanding of the gospel has been hidden from us. The king of kings, was and is a symbolic attempt at power and it worked. He chose his successors and it was they who moved on to create the 'kingdom of heaven' here on earth. Two lines of descent emerged from this daring plot. The bloodline of Christ, which took hold of the Royal power of Europe and then the world, and the Holy Church under the elected powers of the disciples (whose lineages have also continued). With the basics now in place, small mini cultures developed around the world and on the face of it appeared to be schisms. The main power brokers, however, had their way for a very long time. The Catholic church had power unmatched by any other. Until Islam.

Chapter 9
Notes

1   Dictionary of Phrase and Fable. Wordsworth. 1993.
2   The Holy Blood and the Holy Grail. M. Baigent, R. Leigh, H. Lincoln. Corgi. 1983.
3   Essene Odyssey. Hugh Schonfield. Element. 1984.
4   Bloodline of the Holy Grail. Laurence Gardner. Element. 1996.
5   The Dead Sea Scrolls. J.M. Allegro. Pelican. 1956.
6   Taken from 'Names of God', Nathan Stone, Moody and re-translated by P. Gardiner, taking Elohim to mean Shining Ones and replacing was for were.
7   Jesus the Man. Barbara Thiering. 1995.
8   The Fire and the Stones. Nicholas Hagger. Element. 1991.
9   Qumran was occupied by Bedouin (coming from the bedu meaning desert) meaning people of the desert and therefore probably nomadic. Whether there is any age old Shamanistic link between Qumran as being a holy place or not is unknown.
10   The Lost Language of Symbolism. Harold Bayley. Bracken Books. 1996.
11   Hosea says in the Old Testament 'He shall roar like a lion....After two days will he revive us: in the third day ill he raise us up and we shall live in his sight.' In all of this we can now see new translations, not only here, but throughout the whole story which we have thus far believed. The lion or light or Shining One will be risen in 3 days.
         This is prior to the event and is an indication of how this Logos or light of god was going to symbolically install himself into the role. The ramifications of the possibilities are beyond the scope of such a book and you may have to wait for future sources, or even do your own research to find many more.

12   Bloodline of the Holy Grail. Laurence Gardner. Element. 1996.
13   The Lost Language of Symbolism. Harold Bayley. Bracken Books. 1996.
14   The Lost Language of Symbolism. Harold Bayley. Bracken Books. 1996.
15   Ichtheus is very close to the Greek ikkus which means horse or simply 'great light'.
16   Bloodline of the Holy Grail. Laurence Gardner. Element. 1996.
17   Levitation. Steve Richards. Thorsons. 1980.
18   The Lost Language of Symbolism. Harold Bayley. Bracken Books. 1996.
19   Jesus the Man. Barbara Thiering.
20   Jesus the Man. Barbara Thiering.
21   The Holy Blood and the Holy Grail as note 2 and the Bloodline of the Holy Grail see note 4.
22   Polynesian Mythology. Sir George Grey.
23   See the now infamous book by Michael Drosnin, The Bible Code (Weidenfeld and Nicolson) and the follow up by Dr Jeffrey Satinover, The Truth Behind the Bible Code (Sidgwick and Jackson). In the second of these two Dr Satinover points out also that there were a second kind of Jewish sect in existence who Revelation spoke of as 'Jews who are not Jews.' He points out that many of these Jews used symbolism and considered the 'starry host' or stars to be gods.

        This of course was more wide spread than is currently believed and comes from the history of the Shining Ones. Apparently these Samaritan Jews were known as devil worshippers by the mainstream as were the emerging Gnostics. We can see through history that every church has had its dissenters, however it fuels a good competitive edge between them and not only that it allows a church for everybody, all of which would

one way or another come under the auspices of the Shining Ones, who as we have seen simply took on whatever 'front' religion was available (just like the Gnostics) and the secret histories and doctrines of the Shining Ones remained secret. We also see in this book the emergence of a powerful debunking of the codes. Although the book is for the existence of some form of code, for possibly the first time doubts are creeping in.

24   The Dead Sea Scrolls. John Allegro.

25   Things to look for in the other 'messiahs' of the world. (Taken from The Garden of the Golden Flower by Longfield Beatty and abridged by me)

1. Born of a chaste mother.
2. Real father spirit of God.
3. Of Royal descent.
4. Deity in human form.
5. Angels hail virgin.
6. Birth announced by a star.
7. Born in humiliating circumstances.
8. Costly gifts brought by visiting Magi.
9. Preceded by forerunner.
10. Slaughter of innocents.
12. Tempted.
13. Transfigured.
14. Crucified and resurrected.
15. Descended to hell and rose to heaven.
16. Said to return again some day.

This is by far not an all inclusive list and not all the people have been included. Suffice to say the similarities are overwhelming.

Krishna

Born of a chaste mother and father the 'spirit of God. He had royal descent and became a deity in human form.

A star announced his coming and he was born in a cave

or inn or farm. The Magi brought precious jewels and he was preceded by a 'one who would lead the way'. The innocent children were slaughtered.

He was tempted by the devil, performed many miracles, raised the dead, healed lepers, deaf and blind. His beloved disciple was Arjuna or John.

He was crucified on a tree, descended to hell, resurrected, transfigured before disciples and went to heaven. He will return on a white horse when the sun and moon will be darkened.

Buddha

Said to have been born of a virgin by St Jerome. Other similarities have previously been spoken of.

Mithra

Born in a cave on 25th December to a Virgin mother. Travelled, preached and teached, known as the illuminator.

Festivals at winter solstice and spring equinox now known as Christmas and Easter. He had twelve disciples.

Buried in a tomb from which he rose again. Called saviour and lamb.

Followers or soldiers of Mithra wear a mark on their forehead, where the chakra or pineal is.

Osiris

Born 27th December. Great traveller and preacher. Slain and resurrected 'Osiris is risen', Plutarch.

Adonis and Tammuz (see other entries on Tammuz/Thoth/Hermes etc.)

Born to a Virgin called Neith the 'Virgin of the World', killed and was resurrected in spring. His body was said to have been in a hollow tree.

Attis

Shepherd, born of a Virgin, killed and resurrected. His image was fastened to a tree trunk in a ritual of the resurrection. His blood renewed the earth.

Hercules

Great traveller, known as saviour, conceived by his divine father. Died and descended to Hades was resurrected and went to Heaven.

Hertha (Earth)

Goddess of Teutonic peoples said to be a Virgin who was impregnated by the heavenly spirit (Sky God) and the images of her with child are to be found in sacred groves in Germany.

Quetzalcoatl

Saviour God, symbol a cross (see note 26), mother was the Virgin Queen of Heaven. Died, resurrected 3 days later.

Zeus (Classical mythology and head of Gods)

Zeus went to Semele (virgin) and she gave birth to Dionysus the saviour.

Reason for the similarities. The winter was long and people awaited the return of their solar power. This came in December and the winter solstice and spring. The sun had travelled to the other side of the world and symbolically the Shining One went into a cave and came out again enlightened and with new vigour, like the sun does again in spring - with new strength. The sun is literally 'born again' from the other world and just the same Christ was born again from the tomb and the other world of Hades which he visited. New life would then be ours.

The symbolism of this is now lost to us, although we

have had those who have pointed out the essence before. People such as Edward carpenter in his 'The Origins of Pagan and Christian Beliefs.'

26   Cross

The Golden Fleece of classical myth stood for immortality. It was hung on a tree. The gold simply meant glimmering or shining or indeed in Alchemy 'fire' which is the word Alchemists use to skirt around Shining.

Chapter 10
Nurturing

Now that the Essene had played out their role in the passion play of Christ, they were no longer needed as a specific steering group. By the end of the second century AD they had virtually ceased to be. In fact, they had moved on. They had carefully nurtured their newly made religion and taken the roles of Gnostics and Mystics, influencing new developments. Others took over the more scholarly roles as the story had to be laid down in black and white, and all the various parts of the story that had gone wrong, been left out, or were simply last minute additions were securely locked into the Holy Scriptures.

It was part of the plan that variations should emerge. This can be seen by the fact that scrolls, differing in spiritual and dogmatic context have been found in the same place, from the same time and are owned by the same person. In fact, some differing spiritual theologies were actually written by the same person. This variance was to become normal to a large percentage of those who were to move the tide forward. The Gnostics and mystics of the early days were inundated with all manner of ideas. Was Jesus God? Was he a Man? Was he both? Did he have a body at all or was it purely a spiritual body? All this debate played right into the hands of the Shining Ones who encouraged it. They, more than anyone, understood the needs of mankind. They had thousands and thousands of years of learning behind them. Their ancestors, the medicine men of the tribal units, understood how to manipulate men, because quite simply they understood mankind.

The same was true of the Shining Ones in later years. To bring all mankind under your control, you simply cannot give them one religion. This has been proven again and again throughout history. Look at the 'religion' of Communism. This was intended to replace capitalism, religion and all that this entailed. To the annoyance of all communists around the world, it did not work. We are creatures of variety who seldom agree on everything. This itself would be unhealthy, and the strength of the Shining Ones is that they understand this, and they use it. If mankind had been able to agree on all the tenets of Christ, then we would all be Christians now. But someone injected dispute and ideas into the melting pot. Now we have all manner of beliefs, but all from the same original source.

Regardless of whether we agree on the trinity or whether Mary is the Mother of God, Christians are still Christians, and still listen to the Church as if it has ordained power from above. The church leaders still meet up, discuss, implement new ways. Regardless of different dogma and doctrine, they still talk to one another, learn from one another and share the same power of the people. We are all controlled by it. Or at least we were. Now of course we are letting rationality take over and the tide of a new faith must be unleashed; we may see this new wave crash soon. It may be more subtle than a wave, it may seem completely different or it may seem like nothing has occurred. We must wait and see.

The Shining Ones understood human nature. They knew that man needed a variety, a panoply of ideas about the same god. If they could overlay a translucent blueprint of their newly created religion onto the older pagan ideals around the globe, then this would enable them to have their variants without too much trouble. The pagan rituals, dates, holy places and holy people would shine through the veil of Christianity and turn them into new Christian rituals, dates, holy places and holy people. In Britain they spoke to their Druid brethren and developed the mystical Christianity of early Northern Europe. This was helped along with the actual characters from the passion play with living and leading the  people in Europe. Mary is said to have lived in Northern France1 and to have visited England with her three children. The bloodline of this royal family took a strong root in Europe and eventually fed their blood into the veins of the world's royalty. The book by Laurence Gardner does a brilliant job in showing this to be quite possible and highly likely.

Within two or three hundred years the various doctrines of the evolving church were settling down. There were still some major battles on reincarnation, the trinity and the purity of the Mother to be overcome but they were seen through easily with little bloodshed. The people were chosen for their leadership roles within the now organised church and the power was consolidated. We shall see that the Gnostics still held true to the old ways, to the magic and sorcery of the Shaman. On the surface, the church rejected such ways and called these people heretics. They burnt them at the stake and wrote them into history, purposefully, only in later years to hold them up as martyrs and saints. In reality these people were no more heretics than the Pope, who secretly believed in and practised the same ancient ways.

Across Europe the dissenters were crucified as heretics, but they were not real Shining Ones. They were ones who were upsetting the apple cart and were not part of the plan. Their deaths were nothing to do with what they believed and practised. Great Monasteries were erected upon ancient Shining sites around the world, and Abbots, Deans and 'Mothers' were installed as leaders of purity and Light. They met secretly in all manner of places and practised the old ways, subtly including them under the guise of inspiration from the 'Philosophers' and hiding other more secret ways in cipher and code. They would speak the 'Aporrheta', the esoteric instructions revealed to initiates when in the rituals of the Egyptian and Greek mysteries.

From Egypt the influence of the Hermes Trismegistus, the thrice great Hermes, the fabled Egyptian Magi, god of writing and art got under way. This is beyond doubt, one of the most influential Gnostic trips to be taken. The writings date from the third century BC, but probably go back much further. Hermes was the idea of the Greek logos and was, as such, both the Word and the Shining. He was the golden shod emissary and the herald of heaven, and in this was related to Anubis. He was invoked as the 'Eye of Mind' and, as a magical instrument in the form of the caduceus, Hermes the Good Shepherd. In Latin, Hermes the Guide was 'Hermes the Guy de' or Hermes the Shining Sense. (Jesus was the 'Way' and Mercury, another form of Hermes was the god of the 'Way'. Mercury was also the mare (horse) and lizard = light).

The influence is global, both into and out of the Hermes culture The writings go into detail where no other Shining scriptures had done before. The newly found rationalism was a cover for the true magical ways still circulating the world. We have strange cryptic messages of occult lore; the forces in the universe binding it all together, and echoing the 'Christ is all and in all' scenario. It shows us the mind of the Shaman, what he believed in and how he used the forces of nature.

The magic of the practitioner would tell him when it was best to cultivate a plant to guarantee the best fruit, taking into account the strongest position of the planetary alignments. This shows how they understood the interaction between the science of the planets and the gravitational and electromagnetic forces playing on the world around us. It was a fine art, and evidence shows that it had been for a very long time. Hermes is the same god as Mercury, Thoth, Arcas, Agoneus, Camillus, Thaut and Tammuz the gods of Law and Light from cultures across the continents (Thaut was known as Tehuti in Egypt and resolved into 'te Hu ti'; it means 'Shining Hu', the great God of Light. Thaut is also the origin of the modern English 'Thought'. Thah in Mayan means 'worker' or 'creator' and Thau was the supreme deity of the Druids). He was the Light giver who constantly rebirths and gives new life. Hermetic art tells us that the universe is made up of just a few particles, which manifest in different levels and quantities into all manner of things.

This idea, along with many other parts of the Hermetic world was 'current at about the same period in China, India, Greece and Egypt.'2 The core statement of the Hermetic tradition is taken from the Emerald Tablet,5 'That which is above is like that which is below' and we have seen in several places throughout this book that this same philosophy was used across the globe. In Alexandria, the great philosopher and alchemist began his work from this Hermetic footing. Alchemy3 itself was taken from Hermetic thought and developed the symbolism of the 'purifying' process of the idea that everybody could become

Shining Ones, as long as they had eyes to see and ears to hear. Even today the very ideas of Alchemy are misinterpreted by some very famous names in the literary world.

There was no Philosopher's Stone, there was no literal turning of lead into gold. The whole thing was a bluff. Just as Lao-tzu had said, 'He who knows the Tao, tells it not: He who tells it, knows it not.' The very idea of Hermetic and Alchemical writings having the truth at face value level is preposterous. The truth is hidden in the symbolism and you may never know whether you have gained the knowledge or not. That is the idea at the root of the Gnosis, the knowledge is never gained until death. Mystical language hides the fact of endless seeking, the continual yearning after the god who cannot be expressed for everybody, by everybody. The only way to achieve anything like truth was to experience it for yourself.

The idea of Alchemy was a gradual softening of the human, physical self, via much 'heating' in the flames of the Shining god. This would eventually allow the self to become more aware of the basic particles of existence in an almost 'drug induced' manner and eventually 'see' the truth first hand. The circles within circles, the never ending truth seeking was the most perfect solution to a population seeking self-illumination, a nation of people no longer needing a priest in the Holy Temple to talk to god on their behalf. They no longer needed to sell their soul to the Shaman so that he may take it away and bring back answers. The people were demanding to be the 'saints' themselves.

The Bible gave them this in a literal way. We are all saints, said Jesus, all are blessed and all can enter the kingdom of god. It was not necessarily a new movement that inspired the religions; it was a demand from the people, met by the Shining Ones in wonderful game play. They answered the demand with a cross religion sweep of acceptability of the people to seek god direct. There was a catch, however. It was not as easy as merely saying 'I believe'. There was a much bigger price to pay. The road was long and narrow, and many who walked it fell by the wayside. The people could be saved by the great Shining Son of God, but they could not necessarily be enlightened. For this they needed the Spirit of God to come upon them and this took hard work, meditation and prayer. Even today in many 'free' Christian churches the idea of the Holy Spirit affecting a person and bringing the gifts of the 'Shaman' spirit upon them is a badge of Holiness. The ones 'in' the spirit have gifts of tongues, the old ways of interpretation and language skills of the Shaman. They 'fall' in the Toronto blessing style of the spirit, or the trance induced states of the Shaman. Many of those to whom I have spoken who have experienced 'going down in the spirit' have expressed that it was a deep spiritual and enlightening experience.

This was the position that the Shaman was in when he knew he was suddenly the 'Shining One'. When illumination had finally arrived after much meditation, prayer, drugs and probably music and dancing. There is no difference in the Evangelical churches of the world today, where the people are becoming old style Shining Ones. The Shining Ones themselves, however, passed on this 'trick' and moved on to greater depths. These depths are hidden from the ordinary man and woman in Alchemical and Hermetic cipher. They are the same tricks used in the Bible, the Koran and Sanskrit scriptures. Through the ages, many have attempted to interpret these ciphers and codes and have been silenced or have been wrong. A new perspective had to be added to reveal the secrets: the perspective that all things are to be seen through the eyes of the Shining Ones. Read the works of the Alchemists with the knowledge of their kind you now have and see if you can decipher the reality behind the writing. I will give you a clue only, as the truth must await a new book. The secrets are not in the first level of codes or ciphers. They are in the symbolism and then the codes of that symbolism. See the symbolic meaning of turning lead into gold and then decipher that symbolism.

We can all alter ourselves. The way to alteration and the deeper secrets of god is through the 'fire' or 'light'. Phase transition of the soul. There are times and places, powers and secrets which all come into play and all entertain the possibilities of our seeing what the Shining One saw. Alternatively, we could join a Pentecostal church and get ourselves worked up into an ecstatic fervour, 'go down in the spirit' and do a little sobbing while we are down there. I am sure it would be most self gratifying.

Another influence on the religious world came from the 'Pope' of the Shining Ones, Mani (216 - c277 AD). Born in northern Babylonia, he was a deep mystic by all accounts and an inheritor of the title passed from his father. He was a member of the same sect as his father, a Christian sect called the 'almughtasila' or 'those who wash themselves' (self-purification, an allusion to the new way of becoming illuminated by oneself), a hard ascetic order which resembled and continued much from the order of the Essene. The sect was said to be directly descended from Jesus himself. It is said that Mani was visited by a messenger called 'the Twin' who urged him to preach what he had learned. Mani left the sect and went into the world. He preached the idea of a 'constantly returning deliverer' and declared himself to be one of these. He made good headway in the Indian subcontinent, and later wrote a compendium of his teachings called the 'Shahbuhragan'. He converted the brother of King Shahbuhr,

the King Mesene, and power control in that area was once again restored to the Shining Ones.

During his time in the 'service' of the King he sent out messengers and aids to many nations, including Egypt and Iran (later to inspire the thoughts of Islam, almost preparing the way for the ideas to be accepted by Arabia). Mani died a martyr's death under the guidance of the High Priest of Zoroatrianism under the false perception that Manichaeism was a threat to Zoroastrianism. In reality they probably worked together to create a martyr and therefore deify and increase the spiritual impact of Manichaeism upon society. The story of Mani (Manes) shows that as far back as the third century AD the idea that Buddha, Jesus and now Mani were all 'reappeared' interpreters of the truth was a widely held belief, one which Mani himself preached. Mani also preached that Light was the 'way' to salvation and adherence to strict asceticism was part of this struggle for Light.

The Alchemist of later years would also point out in symbolism that the way was hard, was through the Light and would take many years. Mani also taught the age-old, and culturally acceptable, idea of the cycle of rebirths. At the time, Christians, Jews and many other sects were adherents to this view. It was, after all, one of the fundamental beliefs of the Shamans. Just like Jesus, Mani preached the gospel of Gnosis, that the Light can be attained by ignoring the physical plane. Exactly the same belief shared by the Hindus, Buddhists and Zoroatrianists. The followers of Mani could fall into three categories. The Just, those who devoted their lives entirely and led ascetic lives. The Hearers, a sort of halfway house, where the spirit was willing and the flesh weak, and finally the Sinners who were destined for eternal damnation.

One of the early Christian church fathers was St Augustine

(354 - 430 AD) who became Bishop of Hippo in North Africa and wrote extensively (especially and inspirationally about time in a way that betrays his knowledge). He was a Hearer within the Manicaean order. Augustine was simply another vessel between the supposedly different faiths who helped transfer new ideas and evolving ways. If something came up in discussion with a leader in the Manichaean community that would work well in the African Christian market then it was adapted and utilised. Together these religious leaders could maintain control and 'keep an eye' on the world affairs, literally across continents.

Incidentally, the Augustinians, followers of the 'rules' of St Augustine of Hippo, spread out across the world, founding many hospitals (as medicine men), and by 1255 AD they were so large they centralised authority and came under one head.

As if pre-ordained, the concepts of Mani were highly adaptable and spread into the East like a burning fire. All were equal and all capable of attaining enlightenment. The whole world was again coming under the power of essentially 'one way', albeit under many guises. There is, at this point, a small thing about to remember Mani. It was one of his claims that although Christ was a restorer of light, his apostles had written down the story incorrectly and he had come to correct it. There is little evidence that Mani actually said this, but it would make sense.

In Christianity, many superstars were developing, who subtly followed the old ways, invisible but visible. St Bernard of Clairvaux (1090 - 1153 AD) was one of these. Born in Dijon, France, he entered a Cistercian monastery, one of the new teaching arenas and section centres for the old Shining Ones. He moved quickly up the ladder, and became Abbot of the Cistercian monastery at Clairvaux. Stories of great miracles and feats of Shamanistic magic surround him, and his great oratory skill attracted hundreds to the fold. He founded the much maligned and highly publicised Knights Templars (who wore white robes with eight pointed crosses, were responsible only to the Pope and who, after being broken up, formed the Rosicrucians and Freemasonry), who themselves followed Bernard's way and were steeped in magic, Alchemy and dealings with the 'heathen' Muslims. A two-tier system was in order.

On the face of it, Bernard instigated war against Islam and yet beneath he was friendly with their mystical ways.

Bernard held secrets, one of which he released when he confirmed that Mary of Bethany was indeed Mary Magdalene. What else died with him? In 1145 AD he visited Languedoc in France to see the so-called heretics. These heretics, now popularised as the Cathars, were to be wiped out in later years, but Bernard saw no malice in them. He said, 'No sermons are more Christian than theirs.' The friendship between him and the Cathars goes back to the secrets that they held. Bernard knew that the bloodline of Christ had continued, as did the heretics, which is why some said he died on the cross. They also shared the secrets of their past and were all members of the enlightened ones, the Illuminati6 or shining ones. The plots and plans of a developing world were still being carried out, but this time (Pope still meant Father just as the Essene leader was Father) under different titles and in different guises.

The idea of mysticism was breeding. It seemed to be something new to the people. Instead it was the old ways, once kept secret by the medicine man, now open for the people themselves to be involved in. The church, however, did not want the people to have total control, and maintained that many of the mystical ideas were of the Devil, whilst learning and practising them themselves. There were secret Masters, leading disciples into enlightenment. They took them through hard physical training, tough ascetic practices; they contemplated nature, meditated on purity. All the skills of the ancient initiated Shining One. Moses, Abraham, Buddha, Zoroaster, Jain, Jesus, Simon Magus, Zhuangzi, Plotinus, St Paul, were all men with the same skills. There was nothing at all new in the idea of mysticism, the direct relation to god.

Regardless of what is in the text books now, the dates are wrong. We have shown throughout this book that ever since the existence of the tribe there has been a Shaman, willing, eager and insistent on visiting the Great Spirit, the Great Fire or Light to see and attain enlightenment. Nothing new. Just repackaged for a modern age.

In my role as Marketing Director, I advise people of life cycles and new variations for their products when the life cycle is diminishing. There is no difference here. Each new age has nothing new. Maybe a new technological discovery, but never a new spiritual one. Solomon said that there is nothing new under the Sun, and he was right.

This, however, did not prevent the world's leading lights from manipulating mankind; lighting up the pathway with their Shining Light. After all, mysticism is new to those who have never seen it before. The Medieval idea of the Prester John, the ambiguous title given to a supposed ruler of a Christian nation far away, was a man said to have descended from a Magi who had visited Christ's cradle. At the time, there were worries over crusades, concern that Islam was too powerful, so if some ally could be found, it would surely help the case of the power brokers in convincing people to go to war. To add to this, the Mongols were on the warpath with the biggest army the world had ever seen. These 'power brokers' even went to the trouble of sending out false letters to the heads of Europe to convince them of Prester John's existence. He told of his land, of the waters that give immortality (the elixir of life), of the tomb of Thomas (the twin and Crown Prince Philip), and claimed that he had in his possession Magic Stones that controlled the weather. You will be aware by now that all of this was totally symbolic. If I were to put together a publicity campaign, aimed at stirring a frightened nation into war and I had the knowledge that there was no mass communication as such, then I too would have probably dreamed up such a wonderful exercise. The people were even inspired enough to go in search of this fabled character.

The message of the 'self help spiritual guide' was now abroad. It was there in Christianity, new Judaism, Zoroastrianism and now Manichaeism. All cultures were catered for, all tastes satisfied. All except one. There was an area which was like a black void. An area that held all ideas and yet followed none. There were so many beliefs complicating the people that any form of power control was impossible. Every way you looked there was a different god. The Jews were there, but were arguing with the Gnostics and the new Judaism of Christianity. The pagans were all around, still following and worshipping the idols of the old world. There were so many religions and faiths that each Temple, church and synagogue was too small to hold power. Something needed to be done. The rest of the globe was being secured, albeit slowly, and was coming together and falling under the auspices of one or two major religions. The map was looking more orderly from a religious point of view.

Additionally, the way forward had to be planned and it was the job of the mystically inclined Essene, who by now had seeped back into Jewish life and were travelling abroad in Arabia, to find the new or next Mahavira. The Shining Ones were already within the Arabian culture, hidden as priests of the pantheon of pagan gods, just as they had been in Europe and were in Asia. The Arabian Shaman was prophet, soothsayer, medicine man and sorcerer. The Iranian nomadic tribes were of Indo-European descent and the traditions which had followed Zoroastrianism from the 6th century BC had encircled the fundamentals which would later become Islam.

All the old concepts of the Shaman were included: the virgin birth, duality and the trinity, the Light and shining of god. Without doubt, Zoroaster was a priestly Shaman who took the deepest Hindu beliefs with him into a new culture. He communicated the message of god to the people, he drank soma, the trance inducing substance of the Shaman. In one such trance, he saw a messenger from god who led him to the 'All-Highest', the Light in which he saw all the structure of things.

The later Zoroastrians built great 'fire' altars in the wilderness, like massive stone monoliths, a Light in the wilderness for all to see. The Light of Zoroaster was just one of the various pantheons to which Muhammad was accustomed. Among the others were Christianity, Gnosticism, Mysticism, Judaism, Jainism and Hinduism.

Muhammad was born in 570 AD and died in 632. He belonged to the clan of Hashim, part of the Quraysh, who literally dominated Mecca and made up most of its population. The clan Hashim had religious prestige, much akin to that of the family of Jesus. They had similar hereditary rights, especially to offices relating to the Holy 'Kaaba' or 'Hajrat al-aswad', the sacred stone that fell from the sky.

For much of his youth, we are told he travelled as part of a caravan train owned by his uncle. It is said that whilst he was in Syria, Christian and Jewish scholars recognised him as the prophet who would come again. There were miraculous signs and the scene was set. As with the story of Jesus, these little additions go a long way towards solidifying the claim to holiness. Muhammad married a woman trader called Khadija, and while she lived he had no other wife, of course when she did eventually die he had more than just one and a bounty.

Now at this stage we have to remember our Shaman, the caves and the names given to those people called angels. Whilst withdrawing (that's what holy men did and do, and as we know it was part of the ritual of the dying sun to be resurrected again with new life and new wisdom), at the age of approximately 35, Muhammad went to a cave in the wilderness just outside Mecca on Mount Hira. Here he saw Gabriel or Jibril. There was such pressure placed upon Muhammad that he thought he would die. Persuasive arguments of the Shining Ones being symbolically spoken of as 'pressure'. After a short break to contemplate, Muhammad continued to see Gabriel for the rest of his life. From the various symbolic traditions surrounding Muhammad, we can see that other angels visited him, took away his unbelief. He was even taken to heaven (just like all the others). This 'Night Journey' is now part and parcel of the Sufi tradition (mystical side of Islam). Muhammad was the chosen one. The trained holy one who would lead the fulfilment of the final plan.

Once he had taken Medina and then Mecca, Muhammad had delivered the last void in the global family. Now the area could be overlaid with the translucent blueprint of Islam, which differed very little from Judaism and Christianity, due to that being its roots, and as if by magic the world has the variety it needed and the power bases required by the plotters. But how can we be sure that Islam was created by the same traditions, the same background as Judaism, Buddhism, Christianity and Hinduism (not to mention the rest of the globe)? Most scholars will tell you that the traditions of Islam are, without doubt, the same as those of Judaism, Christianity, Zoroastrianism and Manichaeism.

Muhammad had a daughter called Fatima. She is considered to be one of the four perfect women, along with her mother; Mary the mother of Jesus; and Asiyah the wife of Pharaoh who drowned whilst chasing Moses. She was said to be a virgin and yet gave birth to three sons who are recognised as being true heirs of Mohammed's authority by the Shiite Muslims. Her name means 'The Shining One'. Muhammad gave birth to the mystical and beautiful Shining One. He flew, he went to heaven, he went into trance states, he interpreted the scriptures, and was saviour to his people. All the hallmarks of a true Mahavira, a true Shining One.

Within Islamic lore there are the myths surrounding the angels who protected Muhammad. These were real people, just as they were in the story of Christ. It was widely believed in Islamic thought that Muhammad was just another one of many who would and have come to bring us the Light. Moses brought the Torah, Jesus the Gospel and Muhammad the fulfilment. They did not see Jesus as the Son of God, as indeed Jesus himself did not in the literal sense.

Many scholars have suggested that descendants of Judaeo-Christian sects actually brought about the rise of Islam via some strange manipulative planning. They did, they were called the Shining Ones. The blessing, known as 'baraka' is the subtle energy which flows through everything. The purity of the person allows the flow of this energy. The energy is Light. The blessing comes from Allah, like the Holy Spirit of Judaism and Christianity. It is intrinsically linked with the word 'ruh' the spirit of pure light, the Light of Allah (called 'Nur' as in Nuri Muhammad, the Light of Muhammad).

'Jabarut' is the source of divine light, it is the Kingdom of Power, the kingdom of lights; a place between and occupied by those who are pure and full of the Light of Allah. They are 'those that Shine'. The 'Mala'ika are the angels who are made of the light of Allah. 'Ma'rifa' is to witness the divine Light of Allah in the heart. It is the gnosis, the knowledge of Islam. In Islam there is also a tradition called 'Mizan', a balance in life. The remarkable similarity with the yin and yang of Chinese beliefs is obvious. Inward, outward, above, below. It was called the ancient Tao-form of Islam.

Islam allows for the tenets of the virgin, of the second coming and many more familiar creeds. The differences have built over years, and in the early days there was a great deal of discussion between the various peoples. The law of Islam is said to have developed and evolved, to have taken on board the various influences of the known world. The Sufis, the mystical side of Islam, developed its salient features from sources of non-Islamic origin, ascetic and mystical movements.

These were the same people who influenced the mystical Hindus, Christians, Buddhists and all the other faiths. The same mystical enlightenment at the core of each and every faith. The same illumination, the same seeking of divine union, to become a Shining One. With each age, a new Sufi master was to be born, following the age-old tradition. He would be the 'perfect man' ('qutb'). They created a symbolic coding structure to hide their secrets and at times became zealous in their attempts to protect their way.

Part of the Sufis are the 'Marabouts'. They are ascetics and reside in Lodges. They are kept apart, and the word means 'shrine of the holy man', a subtle allusion to the holiness within each one of them, much akin to the spirit residing in the temple of the body. The Sufis main goal is the Light, self-illumination, as we can see in the words of Al-Nuri when he said, 'Once I beheld the Light, and I fixed my gaze upon it until I became the Light.', remarkably similar to the Shaman practice of fixing the divine to gain the illumination.

Many scholars have said that Sufism actually influenced Hinduism and Buddhism. They cite the 'fana' which is the passing away from all objects of desire. Similar, in fact, to the Nirvana, the passing to the place where there is nothing to distract. Nirvana and 'ni-fana' even sound the same. Seeing as Islam came after Hinduism and Buddhism, however, this influence may well have occurred the other way around and come as an influence from the Shining Ones. The Sufis wore white robes and the name Sufi comes from 'Suf' (wool) and means 'one who wears wool'. The cloak of the Sufi is called the Robe of Honour and shows his completeness. 'Tassawauf' or Sufism is the 'ancient way'.

It is a path or 'Shari'ah', and all Sufi mystics engage in seeking after the Light of Allah. It is said the Sufi is 'universal', all over the world. He says 'Allah' until he understands, he is 'Light on Light.' They see a certainty called the 'Yaqin'. This certainty has three ways: knowledge of certainty ('Ilm al-yaqin'), source of certainty ('Ayn al-yaqin') and truth of certainty ('Haqq al-yaqin'). These things must be known before anything is known. In Shiite beliefs, the Imam is the manifestation of Allah ('Ilah' or 'El' means 'Shining much', who was Father of Lights - see Jas 1:17), the Light of the world, he has knowledge and wisdom from the Light and the ability to interpret the scriptures on Allah's behalf. Allah is the Light of the heavens and the earth.

His Light may be compared to a 'niche that enshrines.' In the Koran we find, strangely, that Hermes has been included as 'Idris' and we must be careful how we interpret the Koran with regard to this. Wherever Hermes exists, there is confusion and coding.

There are, without doubt, links between the religions, in history, dogma and doctrine. But more than this. There are underlying similarities of origin, timing, necessity or sheer marketing ability. There are the underlying ancient  practices of the Shining Ones, the massive similarities we have spoken of so many times. Can all this be coincidence? Is the claim that throughout time there has been a constantly watching, monitoring and manipulating priesthood true? That they began as medicine men, tasted power and wanted more? Or is the whole thing simply a confused melting pot of ideas? In my eyes there are too many coincidences. There are too many religious cover ups.

Over the vast period of time, we have never known the real truth. Only now is the true history of Jesus Christ coming out. Only now can we see that he did not die on the cross, that he had children and they became the Kings and Queens of Europe. Only now can we see with our modern technology that the Shroud of Turin is a fake (probably).

Somebody out there knows the truth and has known it for some time. Instead we are given ideas about aliens building Stonehenge and drip feeding us the mathematics for the pyramid. Instead we believe in Atlantis or Lemuria. The government allow stories of little grey men to perpetuate so that we do not ask about the truth. What really was that light in the sky? We would rather believe that it was an alien spaceship than a top secret weapon of the future.

They are happy for us to carry on in our belief, which we eventually end up feeding back to ourselves and self-perpetuating the lie. The same applies to the story of our history. The history of mankind has been 'allowed' to be written down wrongly.

It has been helped along the way by some interfering apostles and monks, but we have swallowed it hook, line and sinker. It is time to consider that not all of our history is about Kings and Queens, wars and battles. It is about human belief too. It is about why we follow that King and Queen and why we fight in that war and that battle. We need to believe that it is worthwhile. God is on 'our' side lads, over the top. The war cry is a little weaker when we have no conviction. How can man be manipulated without a belief system? Ask Marx.

That is the past of mankind. The history. It may not all be true. I have filled in some of the gaps and we are still awaiting new evidence for other parts. Some evidence may be 'created' to dispel my hypothesis. No matter, there will be plenty more. So,  if that is the past of mankind, what is the future? Where are we going? What is the current product under testing? Is it aliens? Are we going to believe in little green men from Mars? In fact this is nothing new. We have had belief in aliens for some time; we called them Angels, and they were ordinary men as well. The fastest growing religion on the planet at the moment is Scientology. The religion of aliens (Xenu) 'created' by a science fiction writer. Sound familiar?

We have left out a great deal. Where did the Shining Ones

disappear to? Did they migrate into the various secret societies of the world? Many myths have arisen, Robin Hood, The Holy Grail, King Arthur. There is truth in these.

The next book will enable us to trace The Shining Ones through the dark ages, through medieval Europe, across the South American cultures and right up to our doorstep. Where are they now? Are there any truths in the conspiracy theories? In the idea of the number of the beast being written on our hands?7 The Christians of the Bible belt think that they are witnessing a grand conspiracy, moving us towards their end times. Nothing new there then. The New Age followers believe the government to be riddled with dark sinister men in black who are out to 'get the earth.' Wake me up when they have finished. What is the truth? What has the most evidence?

The story of The Shining Ones is littered with the paranormal beliefs that they had or at least cultivated. We are only just coming to comprehend the science of these beliefs. The reality of the 'illumination' that the ascetic mystics under their various names attain is something I can only guess at. I have no scientific reason for their experience, which seems to be a universally human experience. It is something that the initiate strives for, meditates over for days, induces trances with drugs and dances and seeks solitude to gain. It is something all mystics, the world over, experience.

Why? What is it that is so appealing? Does it actually happen? It seems from all the discussions that this is God in as close to a physical manner as can be obtained. To see the Light and almost touch it. The feeling is so real that even rational and seemingly level-headed men have believed it to be true (St

Paul). Is this what we are left with after thousands of years of belief? Have people been sent to the lions, given up their lives and died for a dizzy chemical reaction against drugs or exhaustion and fatigue? Have they lived alone without a wife or husband, forfeiting children and a life of luxury for a self induced hypnotic trance? Something that seemed real to the hunter with his lack of knowledge of such science.

Now we no longer need to carry on this belief, we still do. In fact, according to Wade Clark Roof in his book 'A Generation of Seekers', the young of today have no qualms in 'inventing' their own religions. They piece together little bits and pieces of religions until it suits their lifestyle in much the same way that the larger faiths fitted in with the masses. If the Shining Ones are still out there, if their kind has not died out, if they still know who they are and if they care, it seems mankind is ready for your next 'product.' The life cycle on the last one has died. Buddha, be born again. It's time for the second coming. We need a new prophet if we are to ever believe again properly.

I spoke at length with a very senior lecturer from within the

education system in Cambridge, England. He did not wish to be named for the obvious reason that he is in the 'religious' department. After I had told him about some of the things I was going to include in this book he said quite calmly and with a quaint air of old English authority, 'Oh dear, you're going to let the cat out of the bag.'

Emerald Tablet

1   Bloodline of the Holy Grail, Laurence Gardiner. Element.

2   Mysticism, Bruno Berchert. Samuel Weiser. 1994.

3   Alchemy possibly originated its basic concepts in Egypt, China and in the Neo-Platonic schools of Alexandria. The ideas were, as ever, swapped and talked about by the universal Shining One order. They would be the ones constantly developing new products, waiting for the 'life cycle' of the last one to dip before releasing the next, new and improved product upon the unsuspecting population, who thought that they were doing a good job in becoming more enlightened themselves. The word derives from the Egyptian 'khem' or 'chemia' which means 'black earth' and the Arabic 'al' (the) and 'kimia' (Egyptian art). 'The Egyptian Art' is the allusion to the art of the black earth or Egyptian land, the secret art.

The concept of Alchemy has always been portrayed as being the idea of turning base metals into gold, and it was under this cover that for hundreds of years Alchemists enjoyed fame and fortune, power and secrecy within the courts of the Kings.

The secondary concept of Alchemy was to discover the elixir of life. To extend the life of a human. There were many who took up the art and assumed that the teachings were literal. They laboured for years in dirty and hot laboratories trying desperately to turn a lump of metal into gold. Legend has it that the great Hermes Trismegistus founded alchemy, and there is some truth in the fact that Hermetic literature certainly influenced alchemy, although on a purely symbolic and spiritual level.

In 1931 Albertus Magnus (1206 - 1280 AD) was

Canonised. He was a Dominican friar and one of Europe's leading scholars. He was also a magical philosopher and mystic. Albertus used astrology for his magic and took drugs to induce trance states. In these trances he saw the elements of the metals and the various other occult phenomena that were symbolic of the whole Alchemy ideal. That such a friar was allowed to delve into the 'black art' is not surprising, it was practised universally by the clergy and they were patting each other on the back daily, but in secret.

Without doubt, the insurgence of the Muslims in the Dark Ages sped the Hermetic literature and Alchemical art forward. The whole band of Christian monks and priests and Muslim teachers coming together was a regular, if secret, occurrence. Indeed, it is a little known fact that the Knights Templars of the thirteenth century often employed Muslim Assassins and enjoyed the company of those from Islamic background. The Templars are said to have been adept in the 'black art' as well.

Other things to look up if interested in Alchemy are: Alexandria, Empedocles, Diocletian, Geber, Roger Bacon, Sir Isaac Newton, Raymond Lully, St Thomas Aquinas, Philippus Paracelsus, Antione Lavoisier.

4   Thoth, Thaut, Tammuz, Hermes, Mercury. Thaut uses his sword to bring triumph for Osiris and Thor uses his hammer which is the svastika which was the equivalent of the cross of Christ and cross is 'ak ur os' or light of the great Fire.

The Sumerians believed in Tammuz (Dumuzi) the Shepherd God. He was originally a mortal leader and they also believe in the universe being ruled by a pantheon of invisible deities who have human form. The symbolism here is obvious. They do run the universe as we know it, they are in human form, have mortal eyes and prescribe laws. Because they are human. They are hidden not from our eyes but from our 'knowing' and therefore invisible to us as the ones who rule.

5   Emerald Tablet. A legendary object engraved in Phoenician by the fabled Hermes Trismegistus with a secret message only to be 'seen' by the initiated Shining Ones. In circa 1200 AD a Latin version became available, thus preventing the masses from reading it and allowing the clergy (and mostly copied and printed by the clergy, who damned the book) the almost sole rights to its secrets. The main sentence which has been taken from the book is 'That which is above is like that which is bellow' and this has been shortened to 'as above, so below.'

6   Illuminati is the title given to a group of secret societies the dating of which is very difficult but most come from the eighteenth century. Adam Weishaupt (1748 -1830) is probably the most famous of the founders, which itself implies that he was not nearly as secretive as he should have been. The name has been applied to the Hesychasts, the Alombrados, the Guerinists, the Rosicrucians (who may indeed date back to ancient Egypt), the Martinists and the Jeffersonians. Hesychasts - supporters of an ascetic mysticism, Monks of Mount Athos in 14th century. Also known as Palamists from the exponent, Gregory Palamas (1296 - 1350). The aim was to attain the vision of the 'divine light' and gain illumination.

Rosicrucians - secret society following belief in Alchemy and the Qabalah. Developed at later times into Freemasonry in the order known as 'Rose Croix'. 'Ros crux' means 'Dew cross' and may come from the Dhu or Dyu or Hu the Great Fire, god of Light, or it may come from Dew being the solvent of gold. The Cross in alchemy is pure Light.

Qabalah - the Hebrew root 'kbl' meaning to receive, to accept. This is an ancient tradition and was accepted world wide by Alchemists, Magicians and anybody interested in mystical enlightenment. Through the Gematria the Qabalist could 'see' the meaning of the hidden codes. In the same style as the now widely known Bible Code. The classic book of the Qabalist is the Zohar, the Book of Light. Any serious study on the history of mysticism must involve a study on the Qabalah. The symbolism of all the items spoken of in this book are steeped within the Qabalah, the Tree of life, numerology, names, light, astrology, blood. See also the Triangular Lodge at Rushton in Northamptonshire. The most mystical and symbolic building in the UK. Built by Sir Thomas Tresham and based around numerology and the secret number of god (Don't tell anyone but it's seventy two).

7   The idea that we will all have the number of the beast tattooed on our hands or foreheads has been around for a long time and there are many theories from the Christians as to how this will be done. Micro chip implants being one of the latest. The humble bar code has been abused in this area. The universally accepted form of pricing and itemising has come under the watchful eye of our friendly evangelist. The EAN 13 International Bar Code has 13 digits (13 is bad if you're a Christian). The following is an example of how we constantly get 666 out of our bar codes.

Every bar code has three taller bars, one at the start, one in the middle and one at the end. This bar is 6, so all bar codes have 666 on them.

630 nanometers = 630 divided by 6 = 105 = 1+0+5 = 6 = 666.

630 nanometers = 630 = 6+3+0 = 9. 9 divided by 3 = 3

or 3 sixes.

630 nanometers = 6 x 3 = 9 divided by 3 = 3 (add all up = 24 = 2 + 4 = 6.

Each module or bar is equal width. This nominal width is .33mm. There are 7 modules.

= 7 x .33 = 231 = 2 + 3 + 1 = 6

= 3 + 3 x 7 = 42 = 4 + 2 = 6

+ 2 sections of 6 = 666

or 3 x 7 = 21 = 2 + 1 = 3 x 2 sections of 6 = 666

Numerology - the Bibles number system, a second level cipher coding system built up over hundreds of years.

God's Abacus (taken from Proof by P. Gardiner) A remarkable discovery by a man called Dr Ivan Panin more than forty years ago now still remains virtually an untold story. Panin was a Russian, living in America. He was a brilliant mathematician, fluent in Hebrew and Greek, and an was agnostic. The story goes that out of literary interest he decided to read the Old Testament in its original language. The evidence, for the purpose of this book, will be minimal and simplified. Accordingly the reader should realise that there is a wealth of documented evidence to back up all that is told.

To make a start we shall take the Hebrew alphabet. This consists of 22 letters with 5 finals added to make up 3 series of 9 or 27 letters in all. Each letter in the alphabet has a number attributed to it. For example, Aleph = 1 and Samech = 60.

Therefore when a word, sentence, paragraph or chapter is written in Hebrew, it also carries a numerical value.

This numerical value in turn has a spiritual coding and when the passage is broken down different spiritual values are found for each saying, word or name. As a few examples I have chosen the more important numbers in the Bible. Number 1 represents the beginning and unity. Number 3 means completeness or fullness. Number 7 is spiritual holiness. Number 12 is the perfection of the governing body or rulers. So we can see that within the very words of the Bible there can be a more subtle meaning or highlight.

This is not unusual in itself as Latin also has numbers attributed to its letters. Even the English language has a kind of numerology. For example when we take the numbers that are given to the English language and work out the number for the name Jesus Christ we find that we get the number 7. This is then translated to mean 'the mystery'.

What is striking nevertheless is the ridiculous repetition of the number seven or multiples of seven in the original Hebrew script.

Panin found that in the Hebrew Old Testament there were as many as seventy occurrences of this in every passage. Not only that, but in every possible way that the passage could be divided, including grammatical construction. From passage to passage there was an amazing over-arching link of septenary design, which carried on and on throughout the whole of a single book. Also when all the books are put together as one the same remarkable link occurs, as if they were somehow meant to be together. Every passage of every book, and every book of the Old Testament has this design. Nothing seems to upsets its course, not even the long lists of names which sometimes can be laborious.

Getting back to numbers, we find that in each passage there are anything from 12 to 100 features of this design.

To elucidate the impossibility of this occurrence we shall take the possibility of there being only 24 features in one passage, of one book. The stunning mathematical chance is 1 over 191581231380566414000.

This is just the chance of it happening once for a 24 feature passage. Please remember that this occurs throughout the Old Testament, sometimes with 100 features. The chance of this is more than could be written on all the paper in the world.

What about the New Testament of the Christians?

This, the second part of the Bible was written in mainly Greek. The alphabet, correspondingly also has numbers attributed to them. For instance, Alpha = 1 and Upsilon = 400. Therefore, maybe it too has some kind of a design? It does. It is exactly the same as the Old Testament.

But don't take just my word for it, let's look at Mark as an example.

In the last twelve verses alone there are 60 features. A few as follows; 175 words or 25 x 7; 98 words or 2 x 7 x 7; 553 letters or 79 x 7; 133 forms or 19 x 7. This carries on and on throughout the whole of the New Testament unbroken.

It may also be of note that in English there is a strange medieval numerology. This works by writing the numbers 1 to 9 across and the subsequently the English alphabet underneath as follows.

```
1 2 3 4 5 6 7 8 9
A B C D E F G H I
J K L M N O P Q R
S T U V W X Y Z
```

If we write 'Jesus Christ' in numbers, 15131 389912, it equals the total 43, which we then add together to get the final total which is 7. Again, as in the Hebrew and Greek, the English numbers have meanings.

The number 7 means mysterious and austere. Of

course this is just a coincidental analysis, discovered purely whilst investigating numerology and no proof for the Bible is accepted from it. I just thought you might be interested.

Conclusion
The Essence of the
Shining Ones

The story of the Shining Ones and the ancient belief system they employed is complex, and I must apologise for the lengths to which I have had to go to place the scene in your mind.

Egyptian Zodiac
Image of the ancient
Shining Ones

There is good reason for the complexity involved, however. The small-time beginnings of the Shining Ones in the tribal unit, where the medicine man gained control through subtle psychological manipulation and his mysterious skills, gathered over vast periods of time, are humble in origin. The understanding of a deeper truth and of ways foreign to us are now given various names by the scientific community. His apparent control of cycles and electromagnetism gave the Shaman his air of authority and mystery. Using his understanding of the patterns and cycles of the solar and stellar universe and their relationship to mankind gave him an edge, a unique selling point and perspective on man that was his sole ownership. This knowledge kept him in power for centuries. Occasionally, the product he offered needed repackaging. Sometimes it needed research and a new image was created from this research, opening up new fields of exploitation.

When I am selling a product for somebody there is a huge amount of research carried out prior to the launch. Who is buying the product? What is its unique selling point? Where are they going to buy the product? Why? How much will it cost? What is its life cycle? And what do we need to put in place to extend this life cycle? When we have looked into all these questions, and many more, we make a decision on how the image needs to be. Not how we want it to look, but simply how it needs to look to achieve the desired sales. It does not matter whether or not I like the colour green if the people we are hoping will buy the product prefer blue. The early 'faith' marketing men understood all this, and were probably better at it than me.

On many occasions my colleagues and I have joked that setting up a cult with all the right elements would be simple. In reality, this would be more difficult, as the human psyche is very complex. The notion would not be impossible, it would just take an awful lot of effort and time. The resources needed would be huge, depending upon the scale of the operation of course. But somebody got there before us. They have been doing it for a long time. They have employed the minds of the greatest thinkers the world has ever known, and some who have remained anonymous. Add all this to the crucial element of time and we have the makings of a true monopoly. Time is a crucial part of the operation that I do not always have when launching a product. Over vast periods these ancients moved their plans abroad and instigated huge campaigns that would only have been possible with the addition of several decades or centuries of their ideas seeping into the various cultures.

Sometimes the product I am marketing can be sold to almost everybody. In this case we simply package and sell it differently. For instance, everybody needs electricity. The young like to see the wonder and joy that can come from it in their electrical toy gadgetry, young adults like the power it can give them through the Internet and the older still enjoy a nice hot bath, heated by electricity. This is the way we approached selling electricity when I worked for a large electricity company and believe it or not the actual  consumption of the invisible power actually went up.

Our ancient priest understood this element of difference, understood that not all people are the same. The product, with basically the same essential parts, was packaged for all these people. Even within western Christianity we have the lively 'happy clappy' churches and the more traditional solemn churches. The same product, catering for all kinds and packaged in different ways.

The medicine man began and ended with healing. From

physical well being to spiritual dynamics, the process was intertwined like the coiling of the snake. Different words were used for the same practice, and the languages of the separate cultures helped to make the practices 'seem' different. The art of the various civilisations aided the ethnic variance and as if by magic there 'seemed' to be cultural difference. Along the

history of the 'way' these new names and languages opened up, or created, the opportunities for hiding the amazing knowledge of manipulation in myth, and therefore power remained with the initiated. The picture now, thousands of years and millions of words later, is clouded. So much so that the truth itself is a difficult and in fact impossible thing to know.

All we do know is that there is more to the story than we have been led to believe. The standard history books tell the story of the surface. Of what happened, but not always why. Sometimes the history is cultivated to grow in a certain way and at certain speeds, creating the story required. The danger is, that this itself takes away the reality of the story.

It hides, even more than the symbolism, the truth. Behind the standard histories of the nations there is the folklore, myth and legend. Very carefully, the real truths were hidden in these alternative histories. Those with the eyes to see could observe the reality, the truth. The others were content with what they believed to be 'truth'.

Kings, Queens and politicians have been at the forefront of these standard histories. Keeping the masses happy with the natural order and democracy of life. How right was my Muslim friend when he said that we only vote those into power who want power? We should breed our leaders to be what we want them to be. Democracy in that respect is a false democracy. Of course, through history we have bred our leaders, we called them Kings, but even this fell into or was created by the ones who 'wanted' power. Nothing seems to be more corrupt than man.

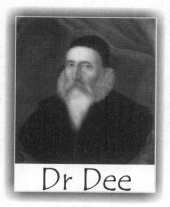

Dr Dee

Behind the scenes of our history, a massive and relatively untold story remains to be told. We have only partly touched upon this story here because there is so much to be told and we needed to lay down the foundations first.

Who now, after two thousand years will believe that Jesus lived after his crucifixion and probably travelled abroad?

Who would believe that he was part of a huge and very clever plot? The essence of the truth has been hidden from us. The story we are force fed has seeped into our minds and over time we have literally come to accept it as fact.

How many people do you know who when asked about god, simply say, I don't really know but I am a Christian or a Muslim or some other 'national' religion? Proof is not the greatest of persuaders, time is.

Faith and time build a strong wall of belief which becomes so great nothing will break it down. Except maybe a constant barrage over time. The belief created was taken on by the faithful who wrote down in the histories which we now believe and without knowing perpetuated the lie which they were now part of. Nobody was or is, impartial. All books, all writings are based upon a bias of some kind. That is one of the first rules of any

Albertus Magnus historian or investigator to understand. When looking back at what was written, understand that somebody wanted to make a point of some kind and it was always their point, not the opposition's. Bias toward a religion, a leader, a war and even a product.

St Nicholas, the great figure of Christmas for so many, was not originally dressed in red. He began his career in white, with a white beard (sound familiar?). Who now, would see a fat man with a beard in a white suit and say that it was Santa Claus? Many years ago Coca Cola took the white image and made history with it, creating the now familiar red garbed, jolly looking Father Christmas. They altered our perception of what this age old Saint actually was. This was just a clever marketing campaign. So too is religion.

It may take another few thousand years for mankind to see things differently, to understand that we have been lied to.

Unless a better marketing campaign emerges from within the

inner sanctum of the Shining Ones to use even this idea to their advantage. Who knows, I might be a Shining One and may very well be the beginning of that marketing campaign to alter man's perceptions.

In Nubia, over three thousand years ago, the King was chosen from within the priesthood (a normal practice all over the globe). When a sacrifice was required to carry away the sins of the nations, it was the King who was that sacrificial offering. With the King, many hundreds of his followers and workers laid down their lives also. Such was the might of the faith. The belief system ruled outright, but only because the people believed in it. The symbolism was carried on forward in time, and was repackaged. The new King of the priesthood was chosen. Christ became the sacrificial lamb, to take away all our sins, once and for all. The symbolism created by this immense plot could now be used every year in the rituals led by the priests. It was so universal that it could be used all over the globe in every culture. The symbolism of death, hell, heaven, resurrection, sun, earth, kings, healing, illumination and much more would easily fit into the existing previously laid down belief systems of the world. In time control would be absolute.

Kings, who were previously chosen by the priesthood would not only remain in their control but as time changed so many things, the king's successors, the politicians, would too. This power is both ancient and terrifying. Never in the history of the world has such a magnificent plan been carried out, with such far sighted goals. Never has there been such a power wielded. When is Christendom going to understand and accept the truth? When will cults stop rearing their ugly heads from the darkness of a lie? When will millions stop issuing forth threats in the name of God and creating dreadful wars over system of control? The answer is simple - when the plan is complete.

I have friends who are Christians. When they had heard just one or two points from this book they were overcome with a fearful disdain. Their 'spirits' were upset. I was speaking for the devil. The truth of Christ, the risen Lord was real, regardless of the evidence. The closed eyes of faith, a dangerous way forward for mankind. This absolute denial of evidence is a problem that time will hopefully sort out. The children may learn and pass on to their children and hopefully eyes will be able to see and ears become open to listen.

One hundred years ago the idea of an ancient priesthood was hinted at by Edward Carpenter in his book 'Pagan and Christian Creeds: Their Origin and Meaning.' He wrote, 'Referring back to the existence of something resembling a great World-religion which has come down through the centuries, continually expanding and branching in the process' The idea was there, the notion that there simply must have been more to all this evidence. Even now we grasp at other reasons for the shocking data.

Take Eric Von Daniken in 'The Return of the Gods' when he says, 'The only way to explain these correspondences is to assume that there must, at the dawn of time, have been a single original teaching...otherwise it would have been mentioned in historical records.' Edward Carpenter was closer than the alien theory, although his ideas were rationalised and simplified too much. The general consensus ever since has been the now familiar independent eruption theory. That all over the globe these beliefs were somehow evolving quite separately. One hundred years ago this idea was accepted quite easily. They were busy trying to come to terms with evolution and the rationality of life in a scientific world. Darwin's ideas were hurriedly fitted in to the basic religions where possible and the decline of Christianity was firmly set. The 'new' faith stirred decades of research which we are now able to put to good use. We have the valuable hindsight that was not open to Edward Carpenter.

Time has served us well in this way and aided our perspective. We no longer need to assimilate religious ideas or tread carefully around touchy Victorian religious intolerance.

Since the ideas of independent eruption or evolution in the realms of belief, we have discovered that world travel was definitely possible. Actual archaeological discoveries are happening constantly, showing that earlier and earlier civilisations did indeed travel long distances in quite sophisticated ways. It may take a little more time for people, and especially historians, to understand and accept that Scandinavians actually discovered America, but the evidence is there for all to see. One day we may discover that the actual discovery was a lot earlier.

A large prehistoric ship was found in fossilised form in the mountain ranges of Ararat in modern Turkey. This ancient vessel has been held aloft by the Jews, Christians and Muslims as being the famous Ark of Noah. There is no reason why there should not be a basis of truth here. Just as there is truth somewhere within the stories of Robin Hood and King Arthur, so too there may be truth in this massive ship and the Noah legend. The Bible tells us the specific dimensions of the Ark, how to build it and from what. Modern ship builders have verified that it would have been sea worthy and would have taken the required amount of animals for the story to be true.

Eliphas Levi

Regardless of whether or not the story is true, it points to one thing: that there may have been vessels built which traversed the globe in ancient times. Note that it is within folklore, myth and legend that the truth of this story was indicated, it is archaeology which is late.

Evidence like this was glossed over or forgotten. Deemed to be irrelevant and dangerously looking back toward the myth in the overtly new rational outlook of the early twentieth century. Writers were almost afraid to appear too factual about myths, and treated them instead like some great classical literature which was there as an art form not history. Nobody wanted to be shot down by science. Unfortunately, attitudes like this can stop the equally creative urges required for good investigative historical research. Now, however, we can read these old myths with the understanding that they do hold truth, just not how we originally perceived. The truth is hidden and needs reading from a different angle.

Cagliostro

Symbolism speaks the truth, not the basic face value. An exciting new way can now be opened up. New interpretations of old and discarded historical material will gradually throw light into our darkened world of truth.

I had often wondered whilst writing this book whether it would ever be published because of what it contains. If there were a group such as the Shining Ones they would still exist in one form or other, surely? They would be hidden deep within some secret society or political club. Their ways more secretive than MI5. Would they still be controlling the minds of men? Would they still hold power? The religions are plunging into the abyss of time. Or are they? New cults are developing and there are many with almost no publicity which are growing at rates beyond comprehension. There are others which have marketing campaigns better than Pepsi.

In the next book we shall investigate this further, but for now I am acutely aware that what I say will come under scrutiny. The press and media is owned by the rich and powerful. Will they take kindly to being exposed? Or will they simply watch my book go by on the river of time and remain unexposed and mocking. If they do still exist then I take my hat off to them and their marvellous ingenuity over the many centuries. I am but one man, in one lifetime. They have been many, over many lifetimes. There is no match.

The Shining Ones. I salute you.

Appendix 1

List of books and manuscripts used in the production of this book.

Where quotations have been used attempts at gaining authority have been sought. Where this authority has not been possible to obtain I would like to apologise to the authors of the quotations for not being able to track you down.

Ancient Egypt, Myth and History, Geddes and Grosset.
Ancient Traces, Michael Baigent, Viking.
Bible Readers Reference Book, McFarlan, Blackie.
Bloodline of the Holy Grail, Laurence Gardner, Element.
Comparative Religion, A.C Bouquet, Pelican (1942)
Dajjal the AntiChrist, Ahmad Thomson, Ta-Ha Publishers Ltd.
Dark Nature, Lyall Watson, Harper Collins.
Dictionary of Beliefs and Religions, Wordsworth.
Dictionary of Phrase and Fable, Wordsworth.
Dictionary of Science and Technology, Wordsworth Edition.
Dictionary of the Bible, Collins.
Dictionary of the Occult, Geddes and Grosset.
Dictionary of World Folklore, Larousse.
Enclyclodepia of the Unexplained, Jenny Randles and Peter Hough, Brockhampton Press.
Encyclopaedia of the Third Reich, Louis L. Snyder, Wordsworth.
Essene Odyssey, Hugh Schonfield, Element.
Exploring the Paranormal, Dr G.K Zollschan, Dr J.F Schumaker and Dr G.F. Walsh, Prism Unity.
Gnosticism, B. Walker, Aquarian Press.
God's Secret Formula, Peter Plichta, Element.
Guide to The Occult and Mysticism, Geddes and Grosset.
Historical Tradition of the Fourth Gospel, C.H. Dodd,

Cambridge.
Hitler, John Toland, Wordsworth.
How We Got our Bible, J. Paterson Smyth, Sampson Low.
Human Antiquity, Feder/Park. Mayfield.
In The Blood, Steve Jones, TSP.
Introduction to Mythology, Lewis Spence, Senate.
Jesus The Man, Barbara Theiring, Transworld.
Jesus, Malcolm Muggeridge, Collins.
Lost Worlds, Damon Wilson, Paragon.
Megalithic Mysteries, Michael Balfour, Parkgate Books.
Mysticism, Bruno Borchert, Weiser.
Mythology, Richard Cavendish, Tiger.
Names of God, Nathan Stone, Moody.
New King James Verision, Bible. Tyndale.
Origins Reconsidered, Richard Leakey and Roger Lewin. TSP.
Perils of a restless Planet, Ernest Zebrowski, Jr. Cambridge.
Primitive Magic, Ernesto De Martino, Prism, Unity.
Proof, Philip Gardiner, Radikal Phase Publishing House Ltd, Nottinghamshire.
Prophecies to Take You Into the Twenty-First Century, Moira Timms, Thorsons.
Religions of the World, Collins.
Sacred Geometry, N. Pennick, Wellingborough.
Sects, Cults and Alternative Religions, David V. Barrett, Blandford.
Signs, Symbols and Ciphers, New Horizons.
Speaking With The Devil, Carl Goldberg, Viking.
Strange But True, Thomas Slemen, Paragon.
The Ancient Earthworks and Temples of the American Indians, Lindsey Brine, Oracle.
The Atlas of Holy Places and Sacred Sites, Colin Wilson, Doring Kindersley.
The Bible Code, Michael Drosnin, Weidenfeld and Nicolson.
The Book of the Hopi, Frank Waters, Ballantine.
The Christians, Bamber Gascoigne, Jonathan Cape.

The Elixir and The Stone, Michael Baigent and Richard Leigh, Viking.
The Fire and the Stones, Nicholas Hagger, Element.
The Garden of the Golden Flower, Longfield Beatty, Senate.
The Gnostic Gospels, E. Pagels. Weidenfeld and Nicolson.
The Golden Bough, Sir James Frazer, Wordsworth.
The Great Pyramid, Peter Lemesurier, Element.
The Handy Bible Dictionary and Concordance, Merril C. Tenney and Alexander Cruden, Lamplighter Books.
The Holy Blood and the Holy Grail, Michael Baigent, Richard Leigh and Henry Lincoln, Corgi.
The Holy Land, J.E Hanauer, Senate.
The Holy Shroud, Tristan Gray Hulse, Weidenfeld and Nicolson.
The Lost Gospel, Burton L. Mack, Element.
The lost Language of Symbolism, Harold Bayley, Bracken Books.
The Meaning of English Place Names, Edward Harrington, The Black Staff Press.
The Mysteries of Mithra, Franz Cumont.
The Mystical Qabalah, Dion Fortune.
The Myth of the Magus, E.M. Butler, CUP.
The Mythology of the Secret Societies, J.M. Roberts, Granada.
The Occult Conspiracy, M. Howard, Hutchinson.
The Origins of Pagan and Christian Belief, Edward Carpenter, Senate.
The Origins of Popular Superstitions and Customs, T. Sharper Knowlson, Senate.
The Orion Mystery, R. Bauval, Heinemann.
The Paranormal, Stuart Gordon, Headline.
The Passover Plot, Hugh Schonfield, Element.
The Return of the Gods, Erich Von Daniken, Element.
The Sacred Chain, Norman F. Cantor, Harper Collins.
The Secret Gospel, M. Smith, Victor Gollancz.
The Tomb of God, Richard Andrews and Paul Schellenberger,

Little, Brown and Co.
The Truth Behind The Bible Code, Dr Jeffrey Satinover, Sidgwick and Jackson.
The World Atlas of Divination, John Matthews, Tiger.
Timelines of World History, Bramley Books.
What is the New Age?, Michael Cole, Jim Graham, Tony Higton, David Lewis, Hodder and Stoughton.
Who Moved the Stone, Frank Morison, Faber and Faber.

Other sources.

The Apocrypha, Talmud, Koran, Bible, Dead Sea Scrolls - Damascus Document, The Community Rule, War of the Sons of Light with the Sons of Darkness, Messianic Rule of the Congregation, Temple Scroll. Writings of Pliny the Younger, Flavius Josephus, Pythagoras, Plato, Hippolytus of Rome, Ephraim the Syrian, Carl Jung, Jeremiah Creedon (Guardian), Foundation for the Study of Cycles, The I Ching (Richard Wilhelm Translation), New Scientist, Nag Hammadi Gospel of Truth, Gospel of Mary, Gospel of the Egyptians, On Baptism. Documents received from the following and used by their permission, Scientologist's, Jehova's Witnesses, Mormons, Jewish Pentecostal Mission, Rosicrucians, Freemasons, Inner Light. Websters Encyclopaedia, Encarta Encyclopaedia, The Unexplained (Focus), Encyclopaedia of history (Dorling Kindersley), Staff at Lichfield Cathedral, New Scientist (21 March 1998 and 11 July 1998), Bible Explorer (Expert Software), Faith in Every Footstep (The Church of Jesus Christ of Latter-Day Saints - press Information CD-Rom).